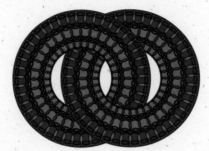

My Mother's Funeral

My Mother's Funeral

Adriana Páramo

A MEMOIR

CavanKerry ◈ Press LTD.

Library of Congress Cataloging-in-Publication Data

Páramo, Adriana, 1966-

My mother's funeral / by Adriana Páramo.

pages cm

ISBN 978-1-933880-39-6 (alk. paper) -- ISBN 1-933880-39-2 (alk. paper)

1. Páramo, Adriana, 1966- 2. Páramo, Adriana, 1966---Family. 3. Colombi-
ans--Biography. 4. Colombian Americans--Colombia--Biography. 5. Mothers
and daughters--Colombia--Biography. 6. Colombia--Biography. I. Title.

F2279.22.P25A3 2013

986.1'36--dc23

[B]

2013007246

Cover photograph © Jorge Royan/http://www.royan.com.ar/CC-BY-SA-3.0

Cover and interior design by Gregory Smith

First Edition 2013, Printed in the United States of America

MEMOIR
CavanKerry ❧ Press

In keeping with our thematic emphasis for all of our
books on *Lives Brought to Life*, CavanKerry Press is
proud to announce the addition of Memoir to
our publishing program.

CavanKerry Press is grateful for the support it receives
from the New Jersey State Council on the Arts.

To my sisters Dalila, Amanda, Ligia and Rocío.

For the sacrifices they made so that I wouldn't suffer.

For carrying me on their shoulders.

Para mis hermanas Dalila, Amanda, Ligia y Rocío.

Por los sacrificios que hicieron para que yo no sufriera.

Por cargarme sobre sus hombros.

Contents

Contents

Part IV

Part V

Introduction

I'm waiting for the day. At some point, I will receive a phone call from Thailand delivering the news of my mother's passing. This is a dark realization, I understand, and the last thing anyone wants to imagine. I also understand that if my mother's life is as long as her ancestors, I may be waiting for quite some time. Still, when the phone rings and the caller ID says the number is from out of the country, I hold my breath until I hear my mother's happy hellohello followed by have you eaten yet? We talk about once a week for about three or four minutes—neither of us is a big conversationalist—but that is enough. Her voice is enough. It signals all is well; it tells me—across oceans and mountains and continents—she's still among the living.

For over twenty-five years my mother had been a few states away, in Illinois, within a day or two drive. There was comfort in that. I could reach her. She worked as a nurse in Chicago before returning to Thailand in 2004. America was never home. Her heart always revolved around the place of her birth. In July 2004, I watched her leave through airport security for the last time and felt a strange distance open. Her sudden absence in my life has made me more aware of my time with her, and as the years pass on, I understand that this time is limited.

But she has prepared me for this. It was part of parental duties. Her death has been a topic of conversation since I was a boy of three or four, a boy who still thought his mother was the prettiest girl in the world. "One day," she would say, "I won't be here."

This line would be followed by words of wisdom: so remember to brush your teeth; so be careful of white girls; so you need to become a doctor and get rich quick. When I got older, I would tell her not to speak of depressing things. I would tell her she was a downer.

"It will happen," she says. "Why fear it?"

Dying, for many of us, is our first fear. It is a recognition that we all have expiration dates. Recall, for example, the first time someone we know dies. Remember how that thought circulates the brain, how we think of them in fragmented memory. They are no longer living chronologically because they have stepped away from our timelines and into an elsewhere. It is this elsewhere that scares us.

Not my mother.

My mother, at least during my time with her, has spoken of her death liberally, with excitement even, at the prospects of her next life. "When I die," she would say, "I hope to come back without my addiction to coffee." "When I die," she would say, "I hope my farts won't stink as bad in the next life." "When I die," she would say, "you will be with me."

And if there is one fear my mother has of death, it's the possibility that I won't.

But what is this talk of death if it isn't coupled with life?

This is the beauty of *My Mother's Funeral* by Adriana Páramo. It is full of life. It is full of love. It is what my mother speaks of when she speaks death. She wants to carry with her thoughts of living; she wants to remember when breath was essential. She wants to remember the story of us.

Introduction

Adriana Páramo is telling the story of us, the living. She is telling her remembered life, her mother's life, her Colombian life. All of it—the hard and the ugly, the joy and the beauty. No distance can take that. Even in America, even after years away from her Colombian roots, even after becoming a mother herself, Páramo, on receiving the news of her mother's death, finds that girl she once was still in her. *My Mother's Funeral* is about a daughter who loves and lives, who desires and dreams. It is a memoir about the moment one receives that phone call from continents away and how the mind spirals, how memory is written and rewritten.

—Ira Sukrungruang

Prologue

My earliest memory of Mom involves a mango. I'm bent over the kitchen sink, kneeling on a wooden bench. Mom is next to me washing two mangos, one for me and one for her. They are yellow and orange with reddish stripes that become brighter at the stem. Mom handles them with extreme care, like they are precious relics made out of thin crystal, pats them dry with a corner of her apron, and puts one under my nose.

"Smell this," she says.

I giggle. I don't know why. Maybe it's because my sisters are gone for the day and right here, right now, Mom is mine, and she is offering *me* a mango.

"Now this is what you do," Mom instructs me. "Roll your sleeves up, like this." She turns the right sleeve of my sweater, fold upon fold, until the wool is all bunched up in my armpit. I roll the left sleeve and wait for instructions.

"Now, take a bite. *Despacito*," Mom says. "*Deje el afán*. Don't chew and don't swallow anything yet. Let the juice fill your mouth first."

She bites into her mango and I into mine. A police car zooms by. Its siren meddles in my ears with the sound of the fruity juice gushing to the back of my throat. Mom lets out a loud *mmm,* eyes shut, her lips closed like a smile. I also say *mmm,* until the juice starts to run down my arm and makes a blob at the elbow. Mom has strict rules about hygiene. I reach out for the tap but she stops me.

"We'll clean up in a second, *Niña.*" She wipes my arm with her apron. "You don't just eat a mango from Mariquita. You experience it."

I'm five years old. I don't know the difference between eating and experiencing anything, let alone a mango, but I understand.

"This is what you do," she says and smiles. This is an important grin. I store it in my heart as the first smile I ever see across my mother's face.

Then she proceeds to lick the length of her arm, from her fingers, still holding the mango, all the way to her elbow. Or at least that's the idea because no matter how far we stretch our tongues out neither of us can reach the elbow.

I don't know how long we stay by the sink, but in my daughter's eye, time melts into a fluid continuum, Mom stands tall next to me, not moving or talking, but being in the moment, and the moment itself has a kind of luscious glitter dust on it.

My last memory of Mom involves a snapper. It's the year 2004. We are at a restaurant on the outskirts of Medellín. Everyone is here, Mom's six children, in-laws, nieces, nephews, girlfriends, my teenage daughter, and Mom. I've been living abroad for more than a decade, and I'm beginning to think that my relatives get louder with each of my visits. They talk over one another. They interrupt and finish each others' sentences. They gossip, carry out simultaneous and unrelated yet coherent conversations over *empanadas* and *chorizos.* Keeping up with everything going on at the table is exhausting. I focus on Mom.

She is at the head of the table, staring vacantly into the white tunnel of light that leads to the kitchen. She seems utterly cast down, like she has given up to the tyranny of Alzheimer's. I have never seen Mom give up. I didn't even know the possibility existed until now that I see her navigate the two worlds blindly: ours with its punctuality and rules, and the other, that timeless realm to where Mom seems to retreat at will. And in this truth about Mom's providence, I recognize the foreboding truth of my own fate: that everything good in my life including my mental faculties can and will change, even be lost, that everything I've built in the past three decades has been drawn, year after year, from Mom's stock of hope and fortitude. Not my own.

I sit next to her. I cup her left hand in mine and ask her, "Ready to order, love?" and she snaps out of it. The mention of food brings her back into our world.

"Yes, I'm starving," she says, but we know that she can't possibly be starving because she had a *tamal* for breakfast and nobody needs food for many hours after eating a *tamal*. Except Mom. My sisters tell me that it's something to do with Alzheimer's messing with Mom's neural center of satiety.

While the waitress takes the orders, I read Mom the menu a few times. As soon as I finish the seafood section Mom wants to know, "Do they have any seafood?" and I start all over. We do this with the poultry and meats sections until Mom settles for a grilled snapper.

"The whole fish or a half portion?" the waitress asks.

"Just a half portion, please," I say, but Mom interrupts me.

"I'll have the whole snapper. Thank you." Mom enunciates each word to the waitress without taking her eyes off me, letting me know that she's still in control. She adjusts her reading glasses. "I can order my own food. I'm not dead yet."

The snapper's crispy head and tail hang over the edges of the oversized plate. Mom's voracious appetite swallows the fish in quick, gluttonous bites. She stores the white meat in one cheek, then the other, and asks me to pass her the tartar sauce as she fishes a bone out of her mouth with greasy fingers. What happened to you, Mom? There is a void between the mother who showed me how to eat a mango more than thirty years ago and the one sitting next to me now, reducing the snapper's body to a mound of crushed bones. And I want to reconcile both mothers into one to love and to honor. But my mind betrays me, and before I know it, I start composing the mother that I would like to have right now at age thirty-eight.

She should eat little and take up yoga, straighten her back, and wear sandals and vintage skirts; learn to play the violin; read poetry out loud; get a female dog with a lustful disposition; mellow her strident whistle and learn birds calls; move back to Mariquita to a cabin by the Gualí River, get into its waters with green waders, and catch fish without bait. I want her to have a farm and grow her own food, be fond of seeds and fruits and give up meat; bathe in natural springs and slowly, in the time it takes to grow an avocado tree, forget about the foolish man she married back in the 1950s and get instead a secret lover who comes to visit her when no one is around.

But that's not my real mother.

My real mother here and now is a seventy-two-year-old woman eyeing my baked potato through the lower half of her bifocals.

My real mother will be dead in less than two years, and her death will teach me a new definition of grief: one that is more than just a hurt heart because the pain is deep and widespread. I will feel her void in my cells, in the follicles of my hair, in the cuticle of my nails, in unsuspected places and at unexpected times.

And although my real mother's story begins way before I was born, my journey with her is a composite of all the women she has been between that first mango and this last snapper.

My Mother's Funeral

PART I

Opal and Topaz #1

In 1992, the year I left Colombia, the six of us lined up by the cala-bash tree outside our home and my brother took our picture. The five daughters struck a beauty pageant pose with skirts pulled up to mid-thigh, our right knees bent forward, pointing in the same direction, right big toes lightly touching the ground, coy smiles across our faces turned sideways toward the lens. I am the one in the middle, standing in front of Mom, her hands on my shoulders. She doesn't hike up her skirt; she holds onto me, her young-est, the one who is about to leave home and country for good.

My father is not in the picture, or in any family album. He wasn't a part of our lives. He was lost without the elixir of constant movement, so he moved away from us. Yet all those years of emo-tional and physical absence were not enough to erase from Mom's heart that lovely beginning—the only part of their story that ever mattered to her.

Against the tyranny of time and at risk of turning an ordinary life into an extraordinary journey or, worse yet, taking quantum leaps of simplicity, I dare to reimagine their lives back then, when

Mom's world didn't extend beyond the Gualí River, when Colombia's violent heart beat to anger and my father's to lust, when Carmen and Mr. B. were all there were. That and the unflinching promise of the unknown.

Early 1950s. Mariquita, State of Tolima, Colombia.

It had been raining in Mariquita for five consecutive days, and the murky waters of the Gualí River carried shoals of fresh fish all the way to *La Plaza Mayor,* where, it was said, tasty *nicuro* could be found flapping their silvery gills right there in the main square. The air, rancid with fish, tomatoes, onions, garlic, and cumin, blew sideways, unbolting doors, unhinging fences, forcing windows wide open. The whole town high on snapper and moisture.

Carmen's parents stood on each side of the door welcoming their guests to their home.

"*Que empiece le fiesta,*" someone shouted. "Let the party begin!" The music started. As was customary, the hosts danced to the first song of the night, a slow *cumbia,* with short, sliding steps. Carmen's father followed his wife across the dance floor, his right hand behind his back, an imaginary hat in the other, courting. Carmen's mother looked over her shoulder, to the right, to the left, tiny gliding steps, stiff torso, flirting.

Carmen sat in one corner of the hall with her sister Gilma. They looked at their parents, at a stranger standing against the wall with arms across his chest, back at their parents.

"He hasn't taken his eyes off of you since he arrived," Gilma whispered in her sister's ear.

"Who?" Carmen asked, pretending not to notice the man smoking a pipe across the room.

He started to walk in their direction. Carmen became flustered.

"Oh my God," Gilma said. "Here he comes."

There he stood. Tall, confident, a flirtatious smile across his dark face. From the back pocket of his white linen pants, he pulled out a red handkerchief, wiped his right hand on it, folded it into four, dabbed at the rivulets of sweat streaming down his neck, and slipped it back into his pocket. Then he walked in Carmen's direction.

"Would the lady care to dance?" he asked and offered her his olive hand.

Carmen took a good look at him. A dark-skinned man with a wrestler's build, dressed in white from head to toe. He was sweating and his *guayabera* stuck to his shoulders, revealing a pair of strong, sun-bronzed arms.

"I don't dance with strangers," she said, looking him in the eye, the way her mother had told her never to look at a man. She switched her gaze to her feet, then his. He wore shiny alligator shoes. She remembered what she'd heard about men with big feet. It was a naughty thought, although she wasn't quite sure what to make of it, for the pleasures of the flesh, she'd also heard, were reserved for married men and she was neither married nor a man.

"Let's not be strangers then." He kissed Carmen's hand, his eyes set on hers. She felt his lips, wet with 29-percent-alcohol-content aniseed *aguardiente* and sweat. Firecrackers exploded in the back of her head, releasing millions of pheromones into the air. She fidgeted with a pleat of her dress as she told him her name.

"Carmen? Like my favorite virgin?" He puckered his lips as he said "virgin." Carmen's nape dampened. It was also the name of his favorite song, "Carmen de Bolívar," which, he said, was one of the 78 RPMs he had brought to the party. And if he played it, would she dance with him? She didn't say a word but knew that she would. No more than ten minutes later she heard the clarinet, then the trombones, the maracas.

7

His hand tapped on her shoulder. Before the clarion voice of Matilde Díaz had finished the first line, "Carmen querida tierra de amores . . . ," Carmen rose from her seat, straightened her knee-length dress, and let him guide her to the dance floor. She felt light-headed and grateful for her diminutive waist and her fleshy hips, which curved under the flowers on her rayon dress. At first, she tried to impress him with a couple of moves she had rehearsed with her sister. He ignored them. Instead, he clasped his hand around hers, up in the air, and placed the other on the center of her back, right between her shoulder plates. The closeness of their bodies made her giddy. When the mambos blared their fiery brass riffs and sax counterpoints, she stepped on his alligator shoes a couple of times.

"I'm not good at this," she apologized. He winked back and said it was nothing.

And when Tito Puente's strident cha-cha-chá played, Carmen kept her gliding steps touching the floor, counting in her head, slow-slow-quick-quick-slow, and turning while executing the steps. Then he added spins and dips, locksteps, turns and sideways moves that she had never seen before. So she stopped trying to impress in favor of following his lead, which was firm, manly, and smelled of hard liquor.

They had playful stare downs until she blushed and looked away; he smiled a cocky grin, and every time he did, somewhere a stallion whinnied. He chugged shots of *aguardiente* and blew smoke hearts in her direction. She sipped freshly squeezed lemonade and tried not to giggle but did anyway. They played this and other innocent games all night long. When they danced, the side of her face brushed his chest, their feet touched, their hands locked up in the air at a respectable distance from each other and, like this, they swayed to *sones, porros,* and *cumbias* until dawn, which was broken with bowls of generous chicken stew, the way any decent party was expected to end in Mariquita.

After the party, her mother, who was an expert in matters of the heart, warned her to stay away from the stranger. "I saw what I saw." Her mother wagged her index finger. "And I don't like it one tiny bit. You keep away from that *negro atrevido*." Her mother said that a man who shows up uninvited to a party and dances all night long with the hosts' daughter is bad news, and she could smell bad news from the other side of the Magdalena River.

"Do not give this *pelagatos* or anyone in Mariquita a reason to question your reputation," Carmen's mother said. "Remember the old adage: *Papaya partida, papaya comida*. Opportunity offered, opportunity seized."

He might have been an outsider to her mother, but he was very popular up and down the river and in the *caserío* on the outskirts of Mariquita. Right there, at the center of the *zona de tolerancia,* the red-light district, sat the big house with the dimmed bulbs where scantily dressed women laughed with abandon and drank hard liquor straight from the bottle, like machos. From him, the ladies of the night received plastic flowers and cheap jewelry; and in exchange for his sexual prowess, the girls gave him flattering names like Stud, Stallion, and Charger. *La Mechicolorada*, the only red-headed whore in the whole state of Tolima, even called him Snake Charmer. Everybody knew why.

He had a ridiculous name that started with the letter *B,* so he went by Mr. B. *Don B.* Very few people knew his full name or his history. Only this was known: he was born into a staunchly liberal family from a very liberal nearby town called Honda. No man surpassed the refined swag of his gait or was more graceful on the dance floor. *La Mechicolorada* started the rumor that his feet didn't touch the floor when he danced. People treated the rumor as if it were fact. He was a suave, silver-tongued man with a legendary ability to guzzle

9

alcohol. And this explosive mixture of liquor and smooth words fueled his powers of seduction. Mr. B. had many lovers across several state lines.

During the 365 days that followed that first party, he came to see Carmen eleven and a half times, once each month—except for that month when, on his way to Mariquita, sleepy, thirsty and hung-over, encouraged by countless shots of *aguardiente* and one too many beers, he stepped into a bar in a secluded conservative enclave upriver to proclaim his political views with every ounce of air in his lungs.

"*Que viva el partido liberal, hijueputa!* Long live the liberal party, God damn it!"

A group of locals, armed with sharp machetes that reeked of human blood, chased him out of the bar and out of town, forcing him back downriver where he had come from.

After eleven clandestine visits during which he wouldn't dare hold her hand, he professed his love in writing, as custom dictated. To write the perfect love letter, Mr. B. needed only two things: a typewriter and a typist. Inspiration and finesse were two things he didn't lack. After traveling hundreds of miles he found what he was looking for: the best typewriter in the whole state of Tolima, a Deluxe Model 5 Remington portable, and the best typist, an educated schoolteacher affected by leprosy, who would have written a wonderful book had it not been for the rinds falling from his hands and face, which kept the keys of his typewriter jammed most of the time.

At first, Carmen kept the trifold letter in the pocket of her dress, then under her apron; and after that, she moved it closer to her heart, propped under her brassiere. At night, while her sister Gilma stood guard, she read the letter that started with "Dear *Señorita.*" She choked up; her eyes welled with tears as she read the first paragraph. It wasn't easy. The words rhymed, took unpredict-

10

able twists and turns, playing games with her head in ways she had never thought words were capable of. If these words come from his heart, she thought, which country is his heart from, and what is its national language? And why is it that whatever he writes or says makes me dizzy, even if I don't understand it?

That night, she fell asleep repeating in her head those written words that would make her heart skip a beat so many times during the next fifty years. *Cuando usted me mira, me siento transportado al cielo de Mahoma enardecido levemente en ópalo y topacio.* Whenever you look at me, I feel transported to Mohammed's heaven, lightly engulfed by opal and topaz. She surrendered, not to the meaning of the words, which she couldn't grasp, but to their finesse, to the conviction that a man capable of writing such a convoluted declaration of love was surely capable of loving a woman with the purest of hearts.

On Tuesday the thirteenth, which Colombians consider to be a much more ill-fated day than Friday the thirteenth, she sneaked out of her house toward a secret ceremony without witnesses. Mr. B. and Carmen were united in holy matrimony at the Church of Our Miraculous Lord of the *Ermita* on August 13, 1951. The local priest, fond of communion wine and of making a little money on the side, agreed to marry them without her parents' consent. In exchange, the holy priest demanded a payment of twenty-five cents, enough to buy him some 32-percent-alcohol-content Cristal *aguardiente*.

Carmen was nineteen, no longer a little girl. She walked home with the poise she thought a nineteen-year-old married woman should show, with a little peacock bounce that made her high heels go click-clack against the hot asphalt. In Mariquita, gossip was a staple, like rice. By the time she arrived home, the news of her marriage had already reached her mother's ears. Small town, big hell.

11

"How could you, Carmen? What have you done?" Her mother's disappointment hung in the air like a stalactite. She stared at Carmen hard the way she would at a grey cloud before a downpour. The silence got so big and so real that it felt as if three people were standing by the door. A shiver of remorse ran down Carmen's spine.

"I'm sorry, Mother."

What else could she say? She was married now and Mr. B., her *husband*, was waiting for her downtown.

Her mother would have liked to kill him, to slap her, to stop them from seeing each other ever again. She knew better. Her youngest had spoken, and they were good Catholic women. Nothing could reverse the promises made before God. She hugged Carmen, kissed her on one cheek, the other, on her forehead; crossed her once, twice. Then she let her go.

Four chubby boys walked behind Carmen, hauling a mahogany chest all the way to the Magdalena Café Bar, where men smoked rolled *Pielrojas* without filter tips, spat wads of foamy phlegm on the floor, and discussed the state of affairs over lukewarm *Aguila* beers. This chest, which had once carried her own mother's belongings in the 1920s, and its contents—clothing, a fan, two hats, one pair of shoes, an embroidered tablecloth, a Bible, and a sex-education book for brides that Carmen's mother had inherited from her own mother—were now all she had.

Mr. B. wasn't too happy to see her arrive with her knee-high chest.

"What's this?" he asked without saying hello.

"My things." Carmen peeked inside the bar. She was aghast at what she saw. *Coperas,* that's what these women were with their fleshy bellies, cleavages, red lipstick, cheap little handbags, and patent leather pumps. They weren't just *meseras,* waitresses. Oh, no.

12

These were *coperas,* their job was to replenish the patrons' cups with *aguardiente.* She'd heard about them; they were known as the ladies of the night. Mr. B.'s voice startled her.

"What if we have to run?" he asked, and the men around him nodded.

Run? she thought. A rush of blood reverberated in her ears. Why would they have to run? She didn't ask questions, and he didn't offer explanations. Afraid as she was, Carmen wondered if Mr. B. liked the sight of a scared woman in need of protection. Was protecting women another checkmark on his endless list of manly attributes?

They would travel east toward the Magdalena River, navigate its waters south for about three hundred miles, and then drive west to their final destination, Armenia, capital of the Quindío state.

"A patch of land where coffee is so abundant—" He paused, then continued, "that the fountain in the main square spews not water but fresh brew."

"Really?" she asked. She was so innocent, so virtuous. She had the qualities of a wonderful wife.

That was when Colombia had lost its national innocence. After Jorge Eliecer Gaitán, a popular leftwing liberal leader, was assassinated in 1948, the country found itself embroiled in a political feud between the two traditional parties, the liberals, known as *cachiporros,* and the conservatives, also known as *godos.* There were riots, vandalism, and pent-up hatred ravished entire villages. Liberals were red, conservatives blue. Red machetes and blue bayonets, blue handguns and red rifles, a dichromatic insurrection and criminality that overtook Colombia during the bloodiest and darkest decade of its young history. Between 1948 and 1964, approximately a quartermillion Colombians died in partisan warfare. This intense period of mass murder will forever be remembered, not as a civil war but as

La Violencia because of the brutality with which the killings were carried out. Crucifixions, beheadings, and hangings were commonplace. Some forms of torture were given names such as *corte de franela,* a cut on the base of the neck, just like a t-shirt collar; *corte de corbata,* when the victim's tongue appeared through a cut in the neck; *corte de florero,* when the victim's arms and legs were placed where the head should be, giving the macabre scene the perverse appearance of a floral arrangement.

Other political and nonpolitical factors contributed to the bloodshed. First, there was Colombia's complex geography. The Andes Mountains, which run through South America from south to north, split into three sections, or *cordilleras,* in Colombia: the Western, Central, and Eastern ranges, which divide the most populated regions into isolated areas. During *La Violencia,* each region developed and fostered not only its own traditions and folklore but also factional rivalries and localized antagonisms. Thanks to a centralized and grossly inefficient government, these internal frontiers belonged to no state in particular and remained lawless for a long time, giving birth to groups of vigilantes, armed bands working for big landowners, peasant organizations, local mafias, and so on, all of which fought each other.

Second, there was the Catholic church, which vehemently opposed the separation of church and state, made alliances with the conservative party, resisted modern ideological trends, and remained staunchly reactionary.

Third, there were archaic political practices. For decades, the Colombian president had had the power to appoint local and state executives to four-year terms in office while local and state legislators were elected for two. The result was an incendiary combination of Bogotá-appointed governors and mayors who were trying to control local and chiefly distrustful legislators.

14

Mix all of those elements, add the fearlessness inherited by Colombians from their Indian, African, and Spanish ancestors, sprinkle with hunger and inequality, garnish with suspicion of the government, the military, the police, the clergy, the rural organizations, one another, and you get *La Violencia*.

Carmen and Mr. B. took a bus and traveled east looking for the Magdalena River. They drove past little villages that Carmen hadn't even known existed. For her, the world's edges were Mariquita's, and beyond that lay nothing but the vastness of the cosmos. When they passed Honda, Mr. B.'s hometown, he told her that one of these days he was going to take her there, for Honda was a real city, not a little backwards village like Mariquita.

"To meet your family?" Carmen asked.

He lit a cigarette. "I ran away from home when I was a little boy. I have no family," he said.

She tried to say something comforting but couldn't find the right words. She watched Honda disappear behind a curtain of dust. They hadn't stopped to eat or rest. They couldn't. In those years of *La Violencia,* whenever night fell, women and children were locked behind doors and the few fearless men still in the streets walked looking over their shoulders, their fingers ready on the trigger, their machetes loose in their sheaths. Daylight was an ally of paramount importance to a staunch liberal like Mr. B.

"I'm thirsty," she said. "I think I'm going to have a *patatús.*"

"Thirsty? *Patatús?*" Mr. B. crossed his arms over his chest. "What do you prefer, passed out and thirsty or dead?" He seemed to have lost some of his initial chivalry. His voice sounded coarse, and she noticed something loutish and common in the way he moved his lips.

Thirst made her dizzy; her eyes filled with tears. "I'm sorry," she whispered and scolded herself for having a *berrinche* in front of her husband.

"Shhh, now, shhh. Damn *godos* can smell fear."

She sensed something similar to foreboding. Maybe it was being so close to the almighty river and so far from home on a dark moonless night; maybe it was the gravel she'd heard in Mr. B.'s voice; maybe all those rumors about the so-called *violencia* were going to her head. Whatever the reason for her pangs, she felt compelled to take a secret vow.

It was at Arrancaplumas, a *caserío* on a bend of the Magdalena River, where Carmen, hungry and with her pasty tongue stuck to her palate from thirst, made a pact with herself: she'd be a perfect wife. She wouldn't worry her husband with the silly nuisances of her life, like being thirsty or hungry or sick. She'd be *acomedida, hacendosa,* the best wife she could be. She would leave behind all her adolescent *remilgos* and be the woman that would make Mr. B. forget there were other women. She'd be his *Virgen del Carmen.*

In Arrancaplumas, Mr. B. hired a barrel-chested paddler and his canoe. He'd be paddling upriver all the way to *La Vega de los Padres,* the Priests' Plain, which the paddler referred to as *La Verga de los Padres,* the Priests' Dicks. Mr. B. didn't find the comment amusing. He shoved the paddler so hard that they almost fell off the canoe.

"Watch your mouth," Mr. B. told him. "This is my wife."

The paddler apologized, sat up on the hull, and wrapped a white cotton poncho around his face. He warned them about certain riverbends where he had seen body parts floating. Carmen shut her eyes tight and covered her ears with both hands. She rested her head on her knees and prayed hard when they reached Calzón de Oro, when they navigated through Ambalema and in and out of Puerto Beltrancito. The river split around an island that was nothing but a dark mound in the vastness of the river. It reeked of rotten fish and something metallic that the paddler was quick to describe as the smell of blood. He worked all night until the night lost its black cloak and the sun peeked through the sky—somewhere between Colombaima and Tavera. Between Tavera and Laguna del Diamante, the paddler pointed at something in the water; it rolled and bounced in the churning waters of a bend, got tangled in some dead branches, then stopped moving. Carmen first saw the teeth, jaws wide open in a silent scream, then the dark eye sockets, then the nose. She gasped, crossed herself more than twice, then began to pray, harder, faster. Farther upriver, they saw a leg, then another. She found herself holding her breath, squeezing her right fist with her left hand, close to her chest, her heaving chest. Her mouth filled with bile, which she forced herself to swallow, for a good wife doesn't bother her husband with silly *melindres*.

They couldn't get off in La Vega de Los Padres as initially planned. No sooner had the paddler docked his canoe in the port's murky waters than someone came running with news. There were *godos* around. Bloodthirsty *godos*. The paddler suggested Ceilán, a piece of something in the middle of nowhere a few miles up the river.

"Why can't we stay here?" Carmen asked.

"Because this town is hot. That's why."

This was true, she agreed. It was already hot with one of those suns that sets wood ablaze, inflames stones, sucks in the water of rivers, strikes you square on your face, and throbs in your head with its monotonous radiance, with its implacable shards of burning light.

Rigor Mortis

People never die in silence. The dying retrace their footprints on their way out of this world. They speak in mysterious tongues before departing. They manifest themselves in trails of light, eerie noises, and apparitions. Their exit can be so boisterous that it sometimes gives the living inexplicable pangs, quirky warnings of the impending loss. Mom taught me that.

I was in central Florida, three thousand miles northwest of Medellín, the night my mother died. I was lying on a couch, dozing off to a ballad playing on television, when I first heard it: a dry thud with no echo and no origin; a single thump so loud and so close that it could have come only from within me. I sat up, short of breath, unnerved, alert, mortified. I turned the TV off and blamed my confusion on the slice of moon lurking somewhere in the sky behind the blinds.

This must have been about the time when my mother's heart lurched and her caved chest heaved in the nurse's arms. Now the thud was replaced with a sharp twinge where I once had had an umbilical cord. I could almost touch the anguish that was settling in the pit of my belly. Mom thought of this type of feeling as telepathic love, although she preferred not to use the word *telepathy;* she'd rather talk of presages, spurts of prescient awareness that some people, especially mothers, experience when their children are in danger. Mothers, according to Mom, could read anything into a situation. A fleeting glance could portend the end or the beginning of something. A butterfly's wing could set off a typhoon. A windmill silhouetted against the moon could mean anything.

The telephone rang. It was 10:30. My sister's voice broke right after I whispered, "*Aló.*"

"Mom just died."

I clutched the receiver with both hands and lowered it to my chest. Something broke under it. The once harmonious world split in half, revealing its cavernous core. The telephone crackled. I heard my sister's voice bouncing off my ribs.

"Are you there?" she asked.

"How?"

"Respiratory arrest."

For a second, I forgot which of my four older sisters I was talking to. I tried to visualize her but couldn't. All I managed to see was a middle-aged woman clearing her throat and trying her best to say "respiratory arrest" without bawling her eyes out.

I collapsed in slow motion. My body trickled down a wall until my chin touched my knees. I thought about Mom's face but couldn't see it. I could see her eyes but not her nose, her lips but not her neck. The rest of her was in bits and pieces. Her winter hands, her velvety ears, her porcelain left knee, her night hair. Mom was fragmented now. She used to be whole.

"Is she—?" I stopped midsentence.

"Sorry, what?" My sister blew her nose, and her voice turned nasal. "I can hardly hear you," she said.

19

"Is she already, you know, cold?" I managed to ask.

"Yes."

"Rigor mortis?"

She took her time to reply. I'll never know whether she was taken aback by the coldness of my question or by the sudden realization that from now on new words would define Mom: deceased, passed, dead, in rigor mortis.

"Yes."

I heard her breathe heavily into the receiver and then sigh.

"I'll be there tomorrow," I said.

"Don't worry. We'll understand if you can't make it. Everybody knows you're far away." My sister's words reminded that I was no longer perceived as a functional part of the family. It was okay if I didn't make it to my own mother's funeral. I had been away from home for twenty years and had slowly become the beloved visitor, someone who came from a faraway place with exotic gifts and then disappeared.

"I'll be there tomorrow," I repeated. Rather, I promised.

One of us hung up.

I remember little things. Our dogs sleeping on their mats, the TV control on the couch, the unfinished glass of Chilean wine, the flickering light of our dated kitchen. I stayed in the same position for a while, on the floor, arms lightly around my knees, chin on my arms. I watched my life happening before my eyes as if it were a movie, unable to act, unable to fully comprehend that my mother's heart had stopped beating and her body was now in rigor mortis.

The words *rigor* and *mortis* echoed in my head. Not long before that night, I had read an article about postmortem procedures. I knew then that Mom's muscles, unable to relax, had caused her joints to become fixed in place. "Rigor mortis," I repeated looking at my hands, my flexing hands, my clasping hands, my throbbing-with-life hands. I wanted to crawl into one corner of the closet and not feel anything.

I made my way to the bathroom, thinking of things that were destined to outlive Mom's body: the smell of the incense she used to burn on Fridays when I was a little girl, the coarseness of her voice even when she was tender, the way she crossed her legs at the ankles, her mysterious sighs that came out like *fados,* her laughter, the pain I caused her when I left Colombia. I crept past the living room that didn't resemble Mom's because I had made sure that my house wouldn't remind me of any of the places I'd grown up in. Past the laundry room that Mom had never had. Past the guest bathroom—the half bathroom—with monogrammed hand towels embroidered with the wrong letters. I'd bought the towels as a joke, but they gave my house a flare of swank that would have left Mom speechless. I stood up at the door and looked up at the incense sticks burning on each side of the sink and the cinnamon-scented candles by the bathtub teasing me with their flickering flames, luring me back in time to the day I had described our new house to Mom.

"What do you mean by two and a half bathrooms?" she asked, chuckling into the receiver. "What's the other half, the kitchen?"

I had been raised in apartment buildings, in improvised additions to greedy landlords' houses, in places with double-bolted doors, creaking floors, and malfunctioning toilets. None of the houses we ever knew as a family had had a half bathroom.

Mom repeated my words, first to herself, then out loud with a lilting question mark dangling at the end, as if ensuring she had heard right. "Two floors and a basement. Two floors and a basement? A master bedroom with *his* and *hers* walk-in closets?" She paused. "Walk-in closets? What are those?"

Every little feature in our home received oohs and aahs of approval from Mom. To us, this was an ordinary middle-class home located in an ordinary middle-class gated community in central Florida a few hours north of Miami. To Mom, it was the icing on

21

the cake, something wonderful at the end of something great, the irrevocable proof that the this country was indeed, as she'd heard, a fantastic parallel universe permanently lit by the glitter of gold where each deserving immigrant is rewarded with wads of banknotes stamped with the faces of highly important men.

"Did you say double garage? Why would you need a double garage, *mija?*"

"To park our cars."

"Cars, plural?"

I pictured her, sitting by the dining table, twirling the telephone cord around her index finger, moving her head up and down with a Colombian nod. The corners of her mouth turned downward, protruding lower jaw, eyebrows raised, maybe even a thumbs-up when she wasn't writing down the details of what she called *una mansión.*

I had been living in the USA for several years before we bought this house, but *the mansion* for some reason was the epitome of my life abroad. Maybe that's why, out of pride—Mom's only excess— never haughtiness, she related the details of our home to anyone willing to listen, making in the process, some fantastic additions of her own creation. So by the time I went down to Colombia to visit Mom, the mansion had twice as many bedrooms, an Olympic-sized swimming pool, and three bathrooms, one of which was so big that it was half bathroom, half kitchen.

When a neighbor asked me if I had seen Enrique Iglesias and would I get his autograph for her daughter, I gave Mom an inquisitive look.

"Didn't you say he lives where you live, right there in Miami *Beesh?*" she asked with a look that said, Oh, let's not let the truth get in the way of a good story.

For a long time I imagined each phone conversation we had would be our last. Once I convinced myself she was dead. I thought I need-ed to be prepared for the inevitable. I went outside, sat under a tree, and spent the afternoon looking at the shadows the branches made on the grass, mourning her. I felt her spirit undulating all around me. She was in the cardinal that flew over my head. The bird sat there looking at me, balancing its legs on the edge of the birdfeeder, not eating, not fluttering its wings the way they do, but watching me steadily. I made peace with the cardinal, with my mother, bowed my head out of love and respect for her and wept. The cardinal wrapped my grief under its scarlet robe, then off it flew. I went back inside my house and called her. I had to hear her voice again.

The only person in my family who died a sudden death was my father's father, Mr. B. Senior, whom I never knew. If Mom were around when the story came up in passing conversation with rela-tives, she would do a dramatic eye roll and scratch one side of her neck the way she always did when she didn't like what she heard. "Death is announced," she would say. "God writes the date of one's departure at birth. What's so sudden about something that God has already decided?"

Mr. B. Senior was tall and couth. He dressed well, walked with a swagger, kept his hair gelled back and his handkerchiefs perfumed, and looked better than any other man in town. He was an irresponsi-ble gambler who drank with abandon and smoked a steady stream of Cuban cigars. He was the best tailor in the whole state of Tolima. And while he wasn't notorious for embroidering *guayaberas* or tailoring men's suits, he was particularly gifted at making women's clothes. That and babies. No woman left his workshop dissatisfied. Not one. He pleasured them all with the same devotion: the married, the vir-gin, the single, the widowed, the young, the old, the desirable as well as the unwanted. Anything with a skirt was fair game.

"That *viejo verde,* dirty old man, chased after anything that moved," my mother told me when I was about ten. "How do you think he ended up with forty-two children?"

I found the idea of having forty-two aunts and uncles and an army of cousins tremendously delightful. The games that we could play, the battles we could wage, the fights we could pick.

"No, no, no," Mom shook her head in disapproval as if she could read my mind. "Those forty-two are not relatives of yours. You hear me? You only have relatives on my side of the family. The good side," she said. *Dios nos ampare.*

Because Mr. B. Senior messed around with married women, it was no surprise that he had an army of bloodthirsty enemies. Up and down the Magdalena River, there were hurt family honors, wounded macho prides, damaged reputations, and lost chastities. And one by one, the threats began to trickle in. The husband of a woman wronged by Mr. B. Senior threatened to cut the tailor's balls off and feed his scrotum to the dogs. Another wanted to slice his throat from side to side and send his severed head downriver. A few settled for a shower of drunken punches that never touched Mr. B. Senior's clean-shaven face but that he managed to return squarely and concisely on his attackers' noses and chins.

One day while he was fishing for snapper in his beloved Magdalena River, a disgruntled husband or father, nobody knew for sure, came down the mountain, hurling insults, wielding a machete, and proclaiming that only one of the two men would live to see the next sunrise. Grandpa never saw the sun again.

"Nothing sudden about that." Mom crossed her arms over her chest. "He died from *problemas de faldas.* Skirts' issues. If you know what I mean."

Mom had painted a clear picture in my head. I knew exactly what she meant. My grandfather wore skirts, and that's why he got killed. He tripped or something. I wondered if he played the bag-pipes and wore funny-looking berets like the Scots in my history book, the only men I had ever seen in skirts. I was so confident about my British ancestry that when, in language class, I was asked to describe my family, I explained it all: My grandfather was a Scot who got killed because he had *problemas con sus faldas.* Problems with his skirts. He tripped during a fight on the banks of the Magdalena River.

The next time Mom and I talked about death was during my freshman year in college, after Grandma died in Mariquita, Mom's beloved hometown. I think Mom cried nonstop for two straight days: first, when we got the news in Medellín, then as we traveled to Mariquita, at Grandma's wake, during her burial. I didn't know she could shed so many tears. I didn't know that underneath the dry surface lay an ocean of salt. I didn't know that behind her hard and unflinching gaze, Mom kept her own aquifer.

After Grandma's burial, relatives and friends went back to my grandparents' house for some food, *aguardiente,* and reassurance. Mostly for the *aguardiente.* My cousins on my mother's side, the good side of the family, sat outside the house on beer crates, rocking chairs, and hammocks. Soon neighbors and well wishers from all over town came to pay their respects, eat, and toast Grandma. Some toasts were made to *la abuelita,* many to Doña Angelina Bermúdez de Pinzón; and those who had never known Grandma but had dropped by anyway for the free *aguardiente,* toasted *a la memoria del muerto,* to the deceased.

Mom was inside, mortified by what she perceived as the little fiesta going on outside, a celebration that got livelier and rowdier with each passing hour, a tradition she would have followed had the deceased been anyone other than Grandma. She refused to come out and instead stayed in the kitchen, chopping strings of pork jerky and cubes of country cheese for the guests. Every time some-one walked into the house to use the restroom, Mom gave them a piece of her mind.

"Do you think this is fair?" she asked waving the knife in the air. "I just buried my mother and all of you are outside *parradiando* while I'm here *mantequiando?*"

Yet she didn't stop toiling in the kitchen until the last guest was gone, or had been dragged out of the house or put into a taxi or escorted to the home of a compassionate neighbor with a spare sofa for a drunk.

That night, she and I lay next to each other on an array of mat-tresses spread on the floor of my grandparents' living room. She was covered from head to toe with a white cotton sheet. Mariquita's nocturnal exhalations billowed the curtains. A timid moon shone through the open windows. Mom looked like a mummy.

I inched my way from my mattress to hers and kissed her on the shoulder.

"What is it?" she asked annoyed. This was a private moment she was having. Could I not see that she was grieving? Could I not see that she needed peace, quiet, and just a moment alone under a yard of ragged cotton?

"Nothing. Are you doing okay, Mom?"

"What do you think? Today I buried my mother."

This was one of those rare occasions on which I looked at Mom and realized that she was more, much more, than a mother. It had, until now, never occurred to me that she and I were daughters. Both had called a woman *Mother*. Both had, most likely, felt comparable amounts of devotion and hostility toward our mothers. Earlier that day, before we left for the cemetery, I walked into the backyard. The sight left me breathless. There Mom stood by the clothesline.

The early afternoon light was behind her, reflecting her silhouette on the white bed sheets drying in the sun. Her body wasn't hour-glass-shaped, but there was something unambiguously triangular contained between her broad shoulders and her narrow waist. Her legs were taut, the skin of her arms firm as she pulled the sheets off the clothesline. I wasn't just watching my mother fold bed sheets. I was looking at a woman.

"What does it feel like?" I asked and regretted my question a second too late.

She lay horizontal, staring at the ceiling fan in silence. It creaked. It screeched. I interpreted its sounds as the only answer I'd ever get.

I turned sideways facing Mom and started to drift away.

"Hard and empty."

Her voice startled me. It was not an angry or a wounded voice, but there was sand in it, a coarse undertone of reluctant resignation.

"You wanted to know what it felt like. Hard and empty. Like a stab."

I didn't say anything. I pulled one foot from under the sheet and rested it on the floor, which was cool and hard under the heel. The pressure of the tile was reassuring, somehow, and made Mom's pain seem more palpable. I rested my head on her shoulder and wondered if somewhere beneath the hard emptiness of loss, there was a sense of flight, of arms spread wide, of mind and heart holding the purest form of love.

Love. Mom never defined the word for me, never spelled it out. But I learned something about love while listening to her prayers. She used to close her eyes and utter words burning with faith. At night, by the sheer power of her recitations, she became soft and even

27

more lovable than during the day, with no rough edges, calm and malleable, like a ball of pink Play-Doh, a supplicant with a long list of requests, none for her own gain. There could nothing so splendid as the sight of Mom—Jesus in His feminine form—on her knees, looking at her wooden crucifix, imploring the celestial son to intercede with the heavenly father in terms so endearing that they made me close my eyes and long to be the fifth corner of this otherworldly geometrical kingdom: the Father, the Son, the Holy Spirit, Mom and me.

"*Jesús*. Chucho. Chuchito. Please protect my girls." I liked the sound of this request, so I imitated Mom.

"*Jesús*. Chucho. Chuchito. Please protect *mi mamita*."

"Don't you dare say that again," she scolded me, both of us still knelt by the cross.

"Why not?"

"Look, what's the pharmacist's name? *Jesús*, right? And what do we call him? *Chucho*. What's your math teacher's name? *Jesús, si o no?* And what do we call him? *Chucho*. Now do you think you can call God's son *Chucho?* Like he is your little friend?"

"But you do."

"Oh, that's a horse of a different feather." And I believed for the longest time that, whenever Mom couldn't explain something to me, it was because of certain issues with a white Pegasus.

I loved the softness of her knees, the silkiness of her elbows. Mom loved Nivea. The aromatic ointment inside the white and blue circular tin of Nivea skin cream was Mom's weapon against the coarseness of life and time.

"I want to have skin this soft," I said to Mom, my tiny hand cupping one of her knees.

"And *I* want to have skin this soft without having to smear myself with Nivea." Mom stroked my cheek with an open hand. Her fingers were rough from chopping and peeling food using her own hands as a cutting board; her knuckles were calloused from years of scrubbing our clothes, bedspreads, and curtains on the cement ridges of the washing board. The coarseness of her hands made the knees and the elbows all the more appealing, like pieces of candy waiting to be unwrapped, like lotus lilies floating in a swamp.

"Promise me," she pleaded, "promise me you'll forever be my little girl."

"I promise," I said with one hand flat on my five-year-old heart.

Then Mom cupped my face in her hands and made a long litany of confessions I did not understand. She told me she was tired and felt she could not go on. She leaned in and whispered more in my ear, told me more about why she needed me to be her little girl forever. She gave it all to me, in my cheek, in my ear, her despair so spiky and her need so big that they got tangled up in my hair, her words so hushed I thought I was dreaming. I don't remember all the words she said, but the Nivea smell, the warm closeness to her face, the tinge of pain, her lips on my neck: I'll never forget.

She was named after the *Virgen del Carmen* because she was born on the same day as the virgin, the sixteenth of July. That made Mom a little bit like a virgin.

"Is that what you think?" she asked me. I wasn't sure how to answer that. I was six, maybe seven, and all I wanted to do was to compliment Mom, make her feel special.

"Yes, you even look like sisters," I said looking at a black and white painting of the virgin. Mom looked at it for a few seconds as if considering the similarities.

"That's sacrilegious," she scolded.

"What's that mean?"

29

"It's like a sin, like comparing San Antonio to Antonio the plumber." Mom tilted her head as if trying to collect all the right words in a single spot. "The virgin is sacred. Me? I'm nothing. Just *un burro de carga*. A beast of burden."

I had seen a *burro* before and Mom didn't look at all like it. But every time she said it, there was gravel in her voice, a grit made of bitterness and discontent, something that told me that a beast of burden was not the woman a little girl should aspire to becoming. *Un burro de carga* was Mom's manifest:

4:00 A.M.: Wake up. Cook the maize. Put the grinder together. Grind. Prepare dough. Make the *arepas* and *café con leche* for breakfast. Send three girls and one boy to school. Give the boy a bag of homemade sweets. He'd better sell them all.

5:00 A.M.: Hand-scrape the wooden floors with Bon Bril scouring pads. Sweep the dust. Apply the red wax by hand, on all fours. Slip the sleeves of an old sweater up to your ankles and shine the floor. You never know when your husband might show up.

7:00 A.M.: Take a shower. The water is freezing cold. Ignore it. You have more important issues to worry about.

7:30 A.M.: Take the washing off the clothesline. Fold it. Put aside what needs to be mended. You have only black and white thread. That'll have to do.

8:30 A.M.: Wake up your youngest one. Make her one boiled egg and a small *arepa*. She is too small for coffee. Comb her hair into tight braids. Teach her the ABCs so she doesn't grow up to be *un burro de carga,* like you.

9:30 A.M.: Start the washing while the little one scribbles her first words. Scrub those trousers on the cement washing board. Wring those uniforms with all your might. You've got knuckles as tough as elephant ears.

11:00 A.M.: Get the little one ready. It's cold outside. Bundle up and walk ten blocks to the butcher's shop. Ask for a pound of bones with some meat on them, if possible. Haggle if they charge you extra. Forget it. Get the damn bones without any meat on them. Avoid the bakery on your way home. You don't want your little girl to ask for things you can't afford.

11:30 A.M.: The wind is picking up, and it's beginning to rain. Another winter morning in Bogotá. Take your *ruana* off and give it to your child. You really don't need a sick kid. Stop by the little farmers' market. You want potatoes, plantains, cilantro, onions, and fruit. Count your money. You have enough for only potatoes and cilantro.

Noon: Walk back home. Take a detour and look for rentals. It'll have to be something smaller, darker, colder. Something more affordable. When you get home, change your clothes before you catch a cold.

2:00 P.M.: Look at the pound of bones, now look under the sink where you keep your groceries. Throw into the pot everything you deem to be edible. You've cooked bone soup six days in a row. Be creative.

3:00 P.M.: Your girls arrive home from school. Give each of them a bowl of soup and an overripe banana. Tell them off if you catch them making faces at your soup. Tell them they are *desagradecidas* and swallow hard as you say it. They'll know you mean it. Ask them to clean the table and put the dirty *trastos* in the sink. They'd better hang up their uniforms and start studying if they don't want to do the dishes.

3:30 P.M.: Your boy comes home. He did sell the sweets. He lost the money. Spank him hard. How else will he learn to be a man? Serve him lunch: bone soup and an overripe banana.

4:00 P.M.: Clean the kitchen. With a scouring pad scrape the pot you

31

used to make the soup. Notice how the aluminum of the pot comes off and leaves your fingers black. Do not stop until the kitchen is spotless. Your husband may or may not be back today.

4:30 P.M.: Start mending. Mend those socks. Mend the uniform blazer. Sew in that loose button. Cut that yard of cotton into little rectangles. Your eldest just had her first period. She needs more cotton pads.

5:00 P.M.: Get the ingredients ready to make more sweets. Your son will sell them tomorrow at his school. It humiliates him, but a man's got to do what a man's got to do. Cook the maize for tomorrow morning.

6:00 P.M.: Pack the sweets. Make sure that everyone is studying, including the little one.

7:00 P.M.: Start ironing: everyone's uniforms, bedsheets, underwear, tablecloths, aprons, sanitary pads. There is dignity in clean, well-ironed clothes. Teach your children that.

9:00 P.M.: Realize that your husband is not coming back today. Count your money. You have enough for another week. Two if you tighten your belt. Pretend that your back doesn't hurt.

9:30 P.M.: Lock the kids in the house. Bundle up and go around the corner to the telephone booth. Call that lady that offered you a job washing clothes for her. Tell her yes and ask her if you can bring a little one along.

10:00 P.M.: Make sure everyone is ready to go to sleep. Prepare their lunches: one overripe banana and one orange each. Make sure their shoes are shiny and their uniforms impeccable. You are poor, not filthy.

The next day, get up and do it all over again. That's your destiny. That's what happens when a woman doesn't go to school. She ends up being *un burro de carga*. And when your husband comes back,

32

lie with him and get pregnant. Have another baby girl. Name her Adriana and hope that she is the last one and that she doesn't become a beast of burden.

The article on postmortem procedures also said that maximum rigor mortis is reached twelve to twenty-four hours after death. By the time I arrived at Miami International Airport, Mom had been dead for eight hours, and all I could think of was the article I had read: the rigor affects the facial muscles first, then spreads to the rest of the body. The joints are stiff for one to three days; then the tissue starts to decay, the muscles relax, and digestive enzymes start to leak.

I had a feeling that if I truly understood and accepted the decay process that Mom's body had started, I could, somehow, be close to her. Closer than anyone already physically present. I figured, for a fleeting second, that this was all it took to make the pain more bearable: a quick process of understanding followed by acceptance. But then I remembered that the article had also said that the enzymes moisten the dead organism and that meat is generally considered to be tenderer if it is eaten after rigor mortis has passed. And then the feeling was gone and the void left behind made me start having crazy thoughts. Like maybe I'll buy a ticket to Perú or Kenya and stay there indefinitely. Maybe I won't ever go back to Florida after this is all over. I could rent a tiny house in the countryside and write one book after another.

"Final destination?" the airline ticketer behind the counter asked.

"Medellín," I said. "The other side of living," I added, but she was busy checking my passport.

I looked at her: fresh brown eyes that had just woken up to a new sunny Floridian day, manicured hands with peaceful-looking fingernails, impeccable makeup, hair glowing with hope. The grace with which she moved told me someone had made her *arepas* and hot chocolate with *campesino* cheese for breakfast. She looked like she had been blessed before leaving her home, like a woman's hand had made the sign of the cross before her eyes and kissed her on the cheek. She looked whole. She didn't look the orphan type.

On my flight from Miami to Medellín, I stared not out but into the window next to me. In my reflection I saw my mother. I tried to imagine what it must have been like for her to die asphyxiated, and before I knew it, I was holding my breath. Six seconds. Twelve. I worked my lungs to full capacity. Nineteen. Twenty-five seconds. I held my breath until my head felt like a pressure cooker without a valve. I saw glittery stars under my closed eyelids. Twenty-nine. I scrunched my face into a knot. "Mom," I heard myself whimper as I exhaled. Then I allowed myself to crumble. I asked the flight attendant for a pillow and a blanket, turned myself into a cocoon of fleece, and didn't come out for the duration of the flight. All was quiet inside my chrysalis, my thoughts, my sobs. In my pupa were just me, grief, and the occasional appearance of an ember of light.

I was on my way home to bury my mother.

Skeletons

1971. Bogotá, Colombia.

Our landlord must have conceived the second floor—our home—in a drunken stupor. It was not quite a house but more like a collection of afterthoughts, a box that, for reasons of greed or need or both, the landlord decided to build atop his old house in less than a week. The project was simple: Get together a group of cousins and friends. Entice them with free beer and *aguardiente*. Don't let them down; they tend to leave with ease when cheated. Get a truckload of cement, a truckload of red bricks, nails, wood, PVC, electrical wires, the works. Expertise is not required. Men know these things intuitively. Build an apartment or something barely habitable. After the tenants move in and the rent money starts flowing, build a third floor. There isn't much to see outside, so forget about windows. It's cheaper that way. Assume that the next tenants are responsible parents, so don't fence the terrace or install handrails on the staircase. Leave everything unfinished. Don't care. The next tenants are six girls. They'll fix everything. Women know these things instinctively.

Our small terrace, nothing more than a slab of cement, protruded over the second floor, threatening to collapse and bring the
building down with it, an architectural feature that kept Mom in
constant state of paranoia. Yet she was adamant that we were middle class—not bottom-line middle class but upper middle class, a
family on the verge of making it big, of taking that leap forward
from nowhere to somewhere, from the periphery of the society to
its upper level. Mom was extremely status-conscious; and awareness of our class membership was an important aspect of our family life because it regulated the reach and size of our aspirations, it
modeled how we behaved.

Two things were clear. First, Colombian society was divided
into four classes: the upper class, the middle class, the lower class,
and *el pueblo,* the masses. Second, we were neither upper class
nor *el pueblo*. We weren't upper class because we owned no land,
had no wealth, had nothing to do with government, church, or the
military, and lacked *abolengo,* which is to say we didn't have distin-
guished lineage or a respected family name. Páramo, a Spanish last
name that supposedly we inherited from a priest who had arrived
hundreds of years ago with the conquistadors and had broken his
vow of chastity, was uncommon. We weren't upper class because
we didn't belong to any *rosca,* those capricious elite systems that
linked influential individuals with institutions and made any process difficult for those not included in it. We weren't upper class
because we had no *compadrazgo,* that ritual kinship of godfathers
and non-blood-related allies who had each other's backs.

On the other hand, we weren't *pueblo* because we were not il-
literate like the masses were. We lived in proper housing, not in
cambuches or *ranchitos,* as the very poor did; and no matter how
bad our finances were, we always had *los tres golpes diarios,* three
daily meals, and we never had *pan calao con agüepanela,* round

36

toast with sugarcane drink, for supper. Also, we were neither Indian nor black and, because of this, Mom said we were white, despite our dark skin. Carmen's daughters were middle-class white girls on their way to the upper class, if they got good grades and kept their virginity intact until marriage. And no one, no one, could tell her otherwise.

The problem was that Mom didn't understand the intricacies of Colombian social stratification. She didn't know that, to be considered middle class, the family breadwinner needed to have a regular job with a steady income. This was something that my father, whose skills were confined to maneuvering heavy machinery, had never had. Mom overlooked the fact that we lacked the financial ability to maintain a middle-class lifestyle. By virtue of my father's unstable jobs and unpredictable salaries, we had slipped into the upper lower class, at best.

Then again, Mom was too busy raising six children, and I was too young, to know any of this.

Maybe it was the precarious architecture of our house, or the bitter cold of Bogotá, or the fact that my nineteen-year-old brother had knocked up his fifteen-year-old girlfriend, or all of the above, but Mom had been in a foul mood all week. She accused his girlfriend of entrapment, of using "you know what" to keep my brother from becoming someone. He, who was supposed to finish his engineering degree, get a job at a respectable firm, and be the family breadwinner, was about to start a family of his own.

"With the butcher's daughter. The butcher's daughter, of all girls." Mom's eyes looked as if they were about to pop out of their sockets. "All skin and bones." She rolled her eyes. "Well, skin, bones, and you know what."

He must have asked Mom for advice the evening I eavesdropped

37

on them. He sat at the dining table, his eyes cast down. Mom adopted a peripatetic attitude, orbiting around him, corralling the young bull into a pen.

"What do you want me to say? Huh?" Mom yelled at him first from behind his chair, then again while facing him. "You really did it this time." She shot an angry look at him; it was the kind of look that could put out candles at the other end of the table. "Be a man. Go fix what you screwed up." Mom pursed her lips and shook her head. "You weren't supposed to be like your father. You were supposed to be the man of the house, to look after your five sisters. Now what? Tell me, genius. Now what?"

I smiled at the sound of the word *genius*. Mom slapped the table twice with open hands. The noise made me jolt, and I braced myself for my brother's explosion. I anticipated an outburst; an I'm-not-a-little-boy-anymore type of thing. My eyes ran from Mom to my brother, to the table, to a grain of rice on the floor, to Mom, to my brother. But he said nothing. My big brother, ashamed, sat still.

"Go and be a man. Go," she said. "I hope your girlfriend is happy. I hope that—" She paused as if searching for the worst possible insult. "I hope that butcher's daughter is satisfied now that she screwed up your life for good."

"Connie, Mom," my brother said. "Her name is Connie."

A couple of weeks later, it was official. My brother, who had worked at two jobs to pay for college, was moving out. He put his guitar into a beat-up leather case, packed his things in a little duffle bag, and left without saying goodbye.

Cows' brains. That's what Mom cooked the day my brother left. Whenever she was in a foul mood, we all paid. She cooked angry food, which is to say, we ate angry food in tense silence. The brains kept slipping off Mom's fingers as she tried to wash them in the sink. They looked like a conglomerate of cauliflower heads covered by a thin membrane that made them appear wet. Red blood vessels traversed the yellowish matter.

After the veins and the membrane were removed, Mom dropped the brains into boiling water. She added bouillon cubes if she was splurging or plain salt if she wasn't. The day my brother left, she used salt. As the brains cooked and their surface became tender and malleable, their smell also changed. It went from gamey to homey; it morphed from alien and backwards to something familiar, something that made our bellies twitch.

On the kitchen counter Mom chopped garlic, onions, and tomatoes, although it looked as if she were doing much more than just chopping. She was murdering the white bulbs of the onions and, with them, she was killing something else. She swung the hollow green ends into the garbage like she was trying to fling them out of the kitchen. What a wild chef Mom was that day.

"My biology teacher says that the green end is the most flavorful part of the onion," my oldest sister Dalila said, looking at the scallions in the can.

Mom shot her a narrow-eyed, watch-it look. "Who's cooking, me or the biology teacher?"

We knew better than to take the issue any further and watched in silence as Mom sautéed the onions and the tomatoes in reheated pork lard. When the mixture was ready, she jumbled it up with the garlic bits, the cows' brains, and three eggs. She beat the concoction with fury. The fork's prongs rose and fell, breaking the gelatinous texture of the brains, the viscosity of the eggs, and in a moment she had created something very similar to scrambled eggs, filled with protein and maybe unsuspected diseases.

"I have a project for my biology class," my oldest sister said. She was the only one talking. My other three sisters and I knew that Mom was not in a talking mood. We didn't scrape or clatter our cutlery against the plates. It was a quiet meal.

"I could get an *A+* and extra points if I complete the whole thing," Dalila said. I looked at her and couldn't help noticing how perfectly shaped her nose was, how much lighter her skin was than mine, how, when she smiled, her teeth shone even and white like marble sculptures.

"About time you bring home good grades," Mom said. "What is it you have to do?"

"An anatomy project," my sister said. "We need to assemble a skeleton."

My mother, who had never been known as squeamish, had no qualms about this. If her daughter needed a skeleton to do well in her class, a skeleton she would get. Or two, as it turned out.

Back then, graves in Colombia were not final resting places. They were a liminal phase of the disposal of human remains. The bodies were buried in graves leased for five years. At the end of the term the remains were disinterred and the surviving relatives given two options: to increase the term of the lease or to rebury the body in perpetuity. In either case the caskets—if still in good form—were reused and the graves leased again. Disturbing the dead used to be a good business. When the bodies went unclaimed, they were placed in plastic bags and thrown into common graves, which were later incinerated or buried for good, depending on the resources of the cemetery—the final touch of social stratification. Yet accidental disinterment sometimes happened. Twenty years later, my grandfather's grave would be mistaken for somebody else's whose lease had expired, and his remains would be disinterred. Mom would go to the cemetery in Mariquita to leave flowers on his grave and find the place desecrated. She would spot his remains in a burlap bag among the undertaker's tools, other burlap bags containing unclaimed bones, and an army of worms creeping

40

out of a skull. She would cry, humiliated and indignant, lamenting that this would not have happened had her family been upper class.

A week later, my oldest sister didn't come straight home after class as she usually did. By the time she walked in, it was already dark and everyone had gathered around our most precious possession, a burgundy RCA Victor tabletop tube radio.

"Well? Did you get it?" Mom asked. She was looking for a radio station, moving the needle east and west, tapping the dial, sighing, trying again.

"Yes, ma'am," my sister said as she kissed each of us on the cheek. Her school shoes were muddy and the blazer of her uniform was splotched with what looked like dry clay.

"We'll talk about it later," Mom said.

My sisters and I watched Mom in silence as she worked the knob to the right, to the left, the needle reverberating above 92.5, the sports radio station.

I don't know where Mom got her quirks and tastes. She was uneducated, never had a job outside the house, and made friends with no one. We were her life. The kitchen and the washing board were her home. Whatever she knew about the world, she learned either from radio programs or from my father. She referred to the sports she liked as *deportes pa' machos,* sports for machos, but she never said if the machos were the players or the fans. She liked soccer, boxing, bullfighting, and cycling. Our Colombian cycling team, known as *Los Escarabajos,* the Beatles, set Mom's heart ablaze with patriotism. Because we were not allowed to socialize outside of school, I had no notion of what other mothers were like. So I assumed that my classmates, like me, prayed that Pepe Cáceres, Mom's favorite bullfighter, had a good kill; for favorable boxing knockouts; for spectacular kicks and frenzy-inducing goals.

41

Tonight Muhammad Ali and Joe Frazier were meeting in "The Fight of the Century" in Madison Square Garden. Mom had been following the careers of the three Titans from America—Ali, Frazier, and George Foreman—who were making history one brutal punch at a time. They were all members of Mom's Boxing Hall of Fame, along with two local heroes of the ring: Antonio Cervantes, known as "Kid Pambelé," our very own WBA junior welterweight world champion, as well as Rocky Valdez, the youngest addition to her boxing altar.

"What's going on?" I asked. Mom and my sisters were glued to the radio. Mom sat still, the rosary wrapped around her wrist, her right ear touching the radio speaker, her nose breathing on the dial knob. My sisters bit their knuckles and played with each other's hair, gasping with Mom in perfect sync like a claque of old widows.

"It's a boxing match," she said looking at the radio.

"What's that?" I asked not expecting an answer.

Her explanation was fragmented. "Two men. Fight. Muhammad Ali and *José* Frazier. A square like this," she said, drawing a box on the back of my hand.

I remember a white handkerchief on her lap, a wooden crucifix perched on the wall above the radio, her eyes closed and twitching as if she were watching a movie underneath her eyelids. Her shoulders jerked inward, dodging punches, delivering invisible upper cuts. Mom looked like she was having her own fight against the air in front of her and was winning big.

The commentator said that Ali was calling Frazier "Uncle Tom." This took Mom by surprise. She turned the volume down. "*Tío* Tom? *Tío* Tom?" she asked.

One of my sisters volunteered an explanation "It's a book," she said, but that didn't make sense to anyone.

"Imagine that. A young man fighting his own blood in the ring."

The early rounds belonged to Frazier. Ali gave away points by leaning on the ropes. Round after round Mom shouted lame insults at him into the radio grille: "What are you doing, *bobo?* Get off the ropes, you donkey, you lazy beast, you sloth!"

The fight swung back and forth: Ali jolted Frazier; Frazier almost dropped Ali. Neither boxer yielded, but in the end there was only one winner: Uncle Tom, much to Mom's chagrin.

By the next day Mom had added Ali's loss to a long list of ongoing grievances. It wasn't simply concern about his boxing career. Rather, she had rooted for Ali, she had prayed with fervor for him, and he had lost. His loss symbolized one more thing that Mom had put her faith into that had given her nothing in return. If God would not make such an impersonal wish come true, what were her chances of getting a more meaningful wish granted?

We hadn't heard from my father in weeks, my brother had moved out, Mom was running out of food, utilities were about to be shut off, she had caught my sister French kissing my cousin Fernando, and now Muhammad Ali had lost. She toiled all day long. I followed her around as she cooked, swept, and mopped; washed clothes and dishes; dusted the house and cleaned the windows; ironed and mended our socks. The simple act of being in her presence was exhausting.

Then the doorbell rang. My sister was back from school. She walked in with a grin on her face that Mom understood well.

"Where is it?" Mom asked.

"*It* is in a plastic bag. I put *it* outside in the patio," she said, looking at me, then looking at Mom as if asking for permission to talk about "it" in front of me, her five-year-old sister.

Just like that, my sister had brought a corpse home after school, as if arriving with a dead body in tow were an everyday thing.

The day took on a festive mood. Mom turned the radio on full blast so that she could hear music on the patio. I trailed behind the two of them, wishing to be invisible so that I could witness this moment that promised to be a big grown-up deal.

"What is it?" Mom asked as she tied her apron around her waist.

"A girl," my sister said, rubbing her hands together, anticipation lingering in the air.

"How do you know?"

"I packed her with my own hands. It's definitely a girl."

"How did you get it?"

"The nuns from school know a snatcher."

"A body snatcher?"

"Yes, ma'am."

"Oh well. If the nuns know him that means he is a good man, and who could blame a good Catholic man for making a little money on the side."

The body snatcher had refused to touch the girl's tiny body, or what was left of it, by virtue of her age and by the fact that she could have still been in purgatory, which was not a place he wanted to deal with during his lifetime. So my sister had rolled up the white sleeves of her uniform shirt, knelt on the moist ground by the common grave, and proceeded to transfer the little girl from the white casket into a plastic garbage bag. It was a girl, my sister knew that much. She had a few cascading curls and a pink sock on one of her feet, which my sister slipped off and sent flying into the common grave.

There were no ceremonies, no rituals, no Hail Mary's, no *rest in peace* chants. There was an *A+* at stake, and that's all my mother cared about. Nothing would stand in the way of her children's education.

"No girl of mine will grow up to be *una ignorante* like me."

44

That's what she used to say on good days. On bad days, when any of my sisters brought home anything less than a *B,* Mom's tone became spiteful. "It's all right not to be smart. Corín Tellado has more trashy romance novels in store for you to read," she would hiss. "Lots of things to do for *mujeres ignorantes,* there are always kitchens to be cleaned, pots to be scrubbed, floors to be waxed—" She would go on like this until the rest of us went to bed, leaving only the sister with the bad grades to listen.

While my sister took the body out of the bag and placed it on the terrace's cement floor, my mother organized a bonfire in a corner behind oxidized tin barrels and pieces of broken lattice. Both made several trips in and out of the house until they had gathered enough cooking utensils, detergent, bleach, an assortment of scouring products, and several steel-wool pads of varying grades. Over the fire Mom placed the colossal pot she used every Christmas to prepare tamales from scratch. They sat on Coca-Cola crates next to the boiling pot.

My mother tended the fire with a twisted yet ladylike pose, knees and ankles tucked together away from the heat, eyes locked on the girl's dead body, an aura of childish curiosity surrounding her. And my sister? Maybe it was the fire, maybe the excitement of having a dead body a few meters away from me, but that day I confirmed how stunningly beautiful she was. Nothing could have been as spectacular as the sight of Dalila's face shimmering in the dying sun. She looked womanly as she stirred the cauldron, with her unbuttoned uniform shirt exposing the tops of her generous breasts. Her nascent smile revealed her teeth and the impish dimple on her right cheek. I understood why our cousin Fernando, on a visit from the country, had wrapped his arms around her one afternoon when they thought nobody was watching. They had locked lips, done a little dance with their heads, and he had caressed her face with the

45

backs of his fingers. Watching them made me want all of that for me. I wanted to know what being a woman felt like.

Now, beside the fire, my sister had hiked up her skirt to mid-thigh and tucked its pleats between her shapely legs. They were pale and silky, but her knees were hairy and blotchy as if they were not part of the same body. She'd been shaving behind my mother's back and must have cut her knees with the blade. I held my breath and prayed that Mom didn't notice. But Mom had a winsome disposition that evening and whistled to the music as my sister scraped the skin off the little girl's bones. The shrill of scouring sounds filled the large patio and reached all the way to the back wall of the kitchen where I stood, tiny and awkward. The only other kid in the house was the little girl my sister was cooking on the terrace; the only other little girl I was allowed to be close to was being dismembered behind oxidized tin barrels and pieces of broken lattice that would never make a fence.

A familiar smell, like tentacles, reached every corner of our small house. It was the aroma of bone soup, which Mom cooked at least twice a week. After a trip to the butcher, she'd bring home a big bone, preferably with some meat still on it, and then add water, salt, green onions, rice, a few beans if they were available, and a sprinkle of cilantro. It made the house smell like the kitchen of a mom-and-pop restaurant.

But a few hours later, the fanfare was over. The sun had sunk behind the mountains, and the house was throbbing with the noises of the night—sirens, screeching cars, the barking of all the stray dogs in the world—and the city, a jungle of asphalt and criminals, glimmered through our kitchen window as a series of intermittent flashes of sad, low-wattage yellow lights.

My mother came into the kitchen and turned the radio off. She let out an exasperated sigh. My sister followed in silence. She'd

46

been crying. Something had happened on the terrace. I was dying to know what it was, but I knew the drill too well. Whenever I dared to interrupt an adult conversation or ask inopportune questions, I got a familiar *al baile de las gallinas no van las cucarachas.* In a hen's party, cockroaches are not welcome. Grownups were the hens. I was the cockroach.

"Either you put in too much caustic soda or too much bleach," Mom said to Dalila, after she came out of the bathroom wearing pajamas, her uniform in her arms, ready to be washed by hand.

"The *monjas* didn't tell me how much stuff I needed."

"Something disintegrated the bones. Ask the nuns at school tomorrow."

The *A+* seemed unattainable now, and Dalila was crying. But Mom was undeterred. "Can you get another one?" she asked my sister, who now held me on her lap.

"I'll have to check with the guy at the—" she paused, covering my ears so that she could say the word *cemetery* . . . as if I knew what a cemetery was.

The night my sister melted the little girl in Mom's pot, we were sent to bed earlier than usual. I woke up in the middle of the night. Mom wasn't in bed. I tiptoed my way out of the bedroom we shared and went looking. She was outside on the terrace, sitting low on a Coca-Cola crate, wrapped in a wool *ruana,* smoking a long, skinny cigarette. Plumes of white steam and smoke rose from her mouth. A blast of icy wind did something with her hair; it made it rise in patches, as if the strands were wild stalagmites caught up in the moment. Then she extinguished the cigarette and buried her face under the *ruana.* Her back seemed to swell, and her shoulders rolled up and down like choppy waves. I had never seen Mom cry and wondered if that was what she was doing. Maybe she wasn't

47

crying but shivering. Maybe she was doing both. She must have had gone outside to get away from the terrible sounds of the leaky faucet in the kitchen and the paint flaking off the walls, the malfunctioning toilet, the bed fleas doing their strident summersaults with whirring wings and steely fangs—all those unbearable noises of the night.

The little girl's skeleton did not make us more or less aware of our own mortality. Mom's mind did not work like that. She had allowed my sister to bring a skeleton home so that her daughter could get a good grade, not so that she could teach us a lesson on the transient nature of our existence. Accordingly, a few days later, my sister arrived from school with another corpse. This time it was an old man's. Surely his bones would endure my sister's scraping and acid-bleach concoctions better than the little girl's had.

After the bones were scraped, boiled, and bleached, the painstaking task of putting them together for Dalila's class began. The terrace was littered with white pieces of paper. On them, with brown marker, my sister had written *F* for femur, *T* for tibia, *C* for clavicle, *U* for ulna, and so on. After labeling the parts, my sister gathered them into groups—right hand, left foot, upper torso— while my mother, drill in hand, readied herself to assemble the parts of a man who had once been a whole.

"I got this *cosiánfiro* at a junkyard," Mom said, brandishing a spool of old twisted wire. *Cosiánfiro* and *cosianfirulo* are made-up words, Colombianisms that don't exist in any dictionary but offer such versatility that every Colombian knows their meaning. Any object whose name she had forgotten was a *cosianfirulo;* anything whose name she didn't know was a *cosiánfiro.* Or vice versa. Mom unraveled the wire, straightening the tangled bits, and then cut them into lengths with a pair of oxidized pliers that I'm sure she'd bargained for at the same junkyard. When Mom wasn't cutting wire or drilling holes into the old man's bones, she was looking over my sister's shoulder at a rectangular poster of the skeletal system, which Dalila had borrowed from the nuns.

"This looks like it goes here," Mom said, pointing first at a mound of bones and then at the diagram. Her guesses went both unchallenged and unheeded. My sister understood that every one of Mom's uneducated outbursts were mere attempts, clumsy yet loving, to be part of a school life that had never been offered to her.

That Sunday, all the bones were lacquered and assembled in place on a shiny oak structure. My sister revealed it first to Mom, "Ta-da!," and Mom showed it the rest of us, "Ta-da!" We hugged, did silly celebratory hip dances, and drank hot cocoa with more milk than water, just for the occasion.

"Should we give him a name?" Dalila asked.

"Carlos Santana, like the guitarist, please, Mom, please," another sister pleaded.

"If we are going to name him after a singer, it has got to be José Feliciano," my middle sister suggested.

"José Feliciano? The blind guy?" Mom asked. "Isn't it enough that the man is already dead? Let's call him Mammy Blue, like the song your bother used to sing to me before he got in the sack with the butcher's daughter."

"Mammy Blue? That's not a real name," Dalila said.

"Well, then, the old man shall remain unnamed. Everyone to bed," Mom said, clapping her hands. "Case closed."

The old man was a hit at the school—so much so that, after giving my sister a well-deserved *A+* and the promised extra points, the nuns asked that she donate the skeleton to the science department. "We'll think about it," Mom said, claiming ownership.

Her initial objection was mainly moral: she had heard rumors of certain sexual liaisons taking place at the convent in charge of my sisters' school. What bothered her was not the idea that the nuns had broken their chastity vows. "One thing is a nun and a priest, a nun and the milk guy, but this nun-on-nun business?" Mom said, as she played patty-cake, patty-cake with her hands as if she were making *arepas*. "I think not." She shook her head and wagged her right index in the air. No.

Mom was not short of euphemisms for homosexuals, nor was she shy to use them in front of us. Instead of using *marica* or *maricón*, both profanities, to describe a homosexual man, she would call him *mariposa*, butterfly. Some of her other terms were *maniquebrado*, limp-wristed; *aliquebrado*, limp-winged; *dañado*, rotten; *volteado*, turnover; *roscón*, doughnut; *loca*, flamboyant woman; *floripondio*, flower bouquet; *torcido*, bent; *delicado*, effeminate; and *del otro equipo*, batting for the other team. So when the nun-on-nun business came up, she made it clear that there was a playful way to refer to two women who do things to each other. "One woman is called Lesbi and the other one Ana, then you put them together. See what you get?" Another term, uttered under her breath, was *machorra*, butch. But the most colorful euphemism had to do with our corn tortillas, which, according to Mom, looked like women's genitalia. It was borderline vulgar, and only Mom was allowed to use it: *areperas*, a term that alluded to women who handle *arepas*, hence her patty-cake, patty-cake hand gesture.

During the days that followed the skeleton project, we all grew fond of the man-skeleton, and the idea of donating it to the nuns seemed to fade further away with each passing day. Mom hung it in various places, and the shotgun layout of our house made it impossible to escape its presence. Not that we would have wanted to: he was now a part of the family; and whether we were eating, doing homework, or cooking, the old man was always in plain sight. For a while he hung above the oxidized frame of a window overlooking the patio. His whole body fell against the opaque glass; when the sun reached a specific angle, the skeleton projected its shadow along our dining table and its eight mismatched chairs. The light peeked through his ribs leaving little white arches on a set of crocheted coasters. Mom used to stare at him as she did her chores—as she swept, as she cooked, as she prepared the starch for the shirts of my sisters' uniforms, a thick mixture of flour and water in which she dipped collars and cuffs before ironing them.

But the man-skeleton never lasted long in the same position. Because it was blocking the only source of sunlight in the house, she decided to pin it against the wall by the dining table, with his arms stretched out like Jesus'. Mom thought this position was very nice, very Christian, but he had to be moved again because the weight of his body was stretching the nylon that was keeping his bones together. In time, the man-skeleton ended up hanging from the ceiling right in front of the bathroom door. We either had to move his legs to one side so that the door could be opened or spread his legs apart and make our way in and out of the bathroom by ducking our heads beneath his crotch.

These days the landlord was knocking at our door twice a day, sometimes three times. Mom went from being apologetic, to humiliated, to outright desperate. From opening the door and offering him *café con leche*, she took to hiding, teaching us to shut the curtains, turn off the radio, and tiptoe around the house so that the second-floor tenants would not tell the landlord that she was home.

A cloud of tension moved in with us. Mom said very little. My sisters brought home good grades and did chores in silence, while I made myself invisible, light, undemanding. I watched Mom take pictures down, empty drawers, throw things into plastic bags. Dalila took the skeleton down, kissed him on the teeth when Mom wasn't looking so that we could have a laugh, and put him into a box. My sisters and Mom had a few emergency family meetings behind closed doors, which Mom got to calling women's councils. I was not allowed in. The meetings were for *gallinas*. I was a *cucaracha*.

The good news was that Mom had brought home a pair of school shoes. The bad news was that one of my sisters would have to wear them. They were Grullas, a brand that made one's feet stink with offensive *pecueca* of the acidic type and looked like something a foot soldier would wear on his first day of service: plain, black, rough-edged, and round tipped, with cheap-looking laces and soles so thick they lasted forever, which was why Mom liked them.

"Which of you was complaining about old school shoes?" Mom asked my sisters, all of whom did their best to look busy. Nobody wanted to go to school with a new pair of Grullas.

"Was it you? Or you?" Mom asked as she undid the laces and shined the shoes with a piece of cloth.

They all responded, "I'm good," or "Not me. Thanks, Mom."

"Is that so?" Mom asked. Cocking her head, she gave each of my sisters an inquisitive look before slamming one shoe, then the other, on the table. "Do you think I'm a bank? Do you think money grows on trees? Do you think I have a stash of money under the mattress? Huh?" She jerked her head forward with each question. "All of you bring your school shoes right here. I'll decide who needs a new pair."

While my sisters scrambled for their shoes, Mom mumbled, "Are we rich now? Too high class for Grullas? How many children would kill for a pair of new shoes? *Desagradecidas. Ingratas.*"

The four girls lined up with their school shoes in their hands, and Mom took a good look at each pair—the soles, the insides, the

52

seams around the edges. She decided that the shoes best suited the youngest of the four, who was eleven. "You're about to start middle school. You can get a few years out of these," Mom said, and by "a few years" she meant that my sister would graduate from high school in this very pair of Grullas.

My sister looked devastated by the gift.

"What? You don't like them?" Mom asked.

"They're too big for me. I'm a size 5. The shoes are size 7," my sister said.

"I know. That's the point," Mom explained. "You will grow into them. You'll walk funny in the beginning, like this," Mom walked around the room with her toes pointing sideways. "But I'll stuff the tip with old socks, and by the time you finish high school, you'll fill the tips with your own toes."

"You'll walk like a duck," Dalila whispered, while Mom went looking for a rag to fill the shoes.

"More like a clown," my second-oldest sister said.

"Like one of those little soldiers in *The Nutcracker*," my other sister said. "Join the club." And the three sisters marched out of the room walking like a duck and a clown and a wooden soldier. The eleven-year-old followed in silence.

Mom dabbed rubbing alcohol on an old rag and stuffed my sister's new shoes with it. "They'll be size 5 tomorrow," she said and winked at me. Then she sat me on the kitchen counter. I felt old and wise now that we were the same height.

"Soon all of us are going to play a game," Mom said in a mischievous voice, but the corners of her mouth betrayed her; they pulled downward the way they did when she was sad. Our game, she explained, would teach the landlord, that jokester, a lesson. "We'll stay up all night until it's really, really dark outside. Then we'll sneak downstairs very quietly," she whispered.

"Like mice?" I asked.

"Exactly. Like mice."

My sisters and Mom packed everything they could in cardboard boxes. Every day of the week, one box disappeared. When there were only two boxes left, Mom said to Dalila, "Take the damn skeleton to school tomorrow." Mom looked around as if taking stock of the empty house. "The nuns can have José Feliciano or Mammy Blue or whatever the hell his name is. They win." She threw her arms in the air in surrender.

The next day, we had our last angry meal in that house. It was dark inside. Either there had been a power cut or the utilities had finally been shut off. By the light of a kerosene lamp, Mom cooked bone soup on a kerosene stove, and the food tasted of smoke and fuel. Nobody complained. We ate, thanking God for providing us with the food and Mom for cooking it. *Gracias madre, que dios se lo pague y le de la salud.*

Then we stayed up all night and waited in silence until it was really, really dark outside.

PART II

Opal and Topaz #2

Here in Florida, now in a bitter January freeze, I look at the six of us in the picture once more. My sisters wink at the camera. My mother's brown eyes squint in the sun. I notice that she hasn't changed; she has a small face, a regal nose, short eyelashes that never curled, sparse eyebrows, dark lips, and a head of short wavy hair that has been grey since I was a little girl. I don't remember a younger version of Mom; she's always been old.

I'm twenty-six in this picture; Mom is sixty and she is short, shorter than me, which strikes me as odd because I always thought that Mom, at 5 feet, 7 inches, was the tallest woman I had ever known. Or so it seemed.

My sisters and I have wide smiles for the camera. Mom does too, but twenty years after the photograph was taken, her timid smile looks less like a grin and more like the prelude to a cry, like she is about to cave in and break stridently.

The town of Ceilán was also too hot. The paddler took Carmen and Mr. B. downriver to a little village whose name had been forgotten. When they arrived, the dust that had been simmering in the daytime heat had already started its whirling dance. The swirls of yellow grime grew in intensity, spinning and sweeping across the derelict village, lifting clouds of garbage, whipping their faces with hot wind that reeked of animal carcass.

The pair walked toward the small motel where Mr. B. had reserved a room for their first night together. It was a dim two-story building whose sign was missing a few letters. The floor creaked when they stepped in. A cloud of cigarette smoke led them to a dark lobby, where all the furnishings seemed to be varying hues of red: an old loveseat, a wall-to-wall velvet curtain, a carpet in desperate need of sweeping, a broken piano with missing keys. A dim bulb flickered behind the desk. Down the hall someone was singing a tango, and laughing.

"Hey, stranger." A sleepy woman greeted Mr. B. at the desk. She wore cherry lipstick that didn't stop at the corners of her mouth, and her face, caked with white powder, was framed by a single bushy eyebrow that hung above her honey eyes. She clasped a long thin pipe between her teeth; it dangled as she spoke.

"Is that the wife?" the woman asked Mr. B., running her eyes over Carmen from head to toe. Not waiting for an answer, she winked at Mr. B. and led the pair down a dark, damp corridor with closed doors on each side. The newlyweds followed in silence. Mr. B. seemed embarrassed. He walked looking down at his pointed alligator shoes, kicking cigarette butts across the floor. Carmen watched the woman's generous hips, which swayed and bounced with each long, unhurried step. She wondered if Mr. B. would like her to walk like this madam.

The woman shook a key ring from the pocket of her black nightgown and opened a tiny room at the end of the hall. As she held the door open for the couple, her eyes locked on Mr. B.'s. Wordless, she waved them in with her free hand. Carmen walked in first. Mr. B.

hung back for a few seconds; and when Carmen turned around to say thank you, she saw the woman whispering something into his ear, which must have been funny because Mr. B. flinched a bit as if something had pinched his rear. Behind them, two *mulatos* hauled Carmen's chest, now covered in dust.

She sat down on one corner of the bed. The sheets had brown stains—maybe coffee, maybe blood, maybe both. On the torn mosquito netting above the bed she saw cigarette burns and traces of dried snot. The ceiling fan wobbled and squeaked. Carmen began to cry. The harder she tried to contain her tears, the more violently they flowed. She sobbed and sobbed, trembling so hard that the bed rattled.

"I'll make it up to you. I promise," he said, one knee on the floor, his hands cupping hers. "I have a job in Armenia. This," he said pointing at the grim room, "is only until we get there. I promise."

But the more promises he made, the harder she cried. His promises became more colorful and more outrageous. They morphed into plans: what they were going to do now, what they would do in twenty years. By midnight, he had bought them a house in suburban Armenia and was driving a brand-new Jeep Willys like the ones that army officers and rich coffee growers drove.

His words were soporific, and eventually her tears dried up. "That'd be nice," she said. "That'd be so nice."

A light sleep came over her like a wave brushing her face. The wobbly fan and the stained mosquito netting disappeared into shards and fragments of life rearranged in a gratifying cocktail of dreams. Then the sorcery of the night closed in, dark, silent, peaceful, but after a while she woke up to a medley of noises that she could not identify. A distant tiptoe turned into a quick shuffle. Someone was rushing along the corridor.

"What's going on?" she asked.

Mr. B. lifted his head and tried to guess what the commotion was. "Don't know. Maybe someone gave Rita *conejo* again," he chuckled. "I bet some low-life is cheating *Rita la tuerta* out of her money." He explained that one-eyed Rita was the most affordable girl in the house. Perhaps a cheap john was sneaking out of her room before she could count the money with her good eye.

Whoever was running along the hall had now stopped in front of their small room. One, two, three open-handed bangs on their door were followed by a frenzied shower of punches. He got up, strode around their bed, banged his shin on Carmen's chest, invisible in the dark, and finally opened the door.

The madam stood there, disheveled. She hadn't had time to close her robe all the way up. He could see one fleshy shoulder and the edge of a flaccid, shivering breast.

"You've got to go. They're coming for you. And your wife," she whispered, out of breath.

"They who?"

She stammered, "One of the *mulatos*. He knows you. He chased you down the river, I don't know when, but couldn't catch you. He was drunk. Today he is sober. And his cousins. All *godos*. The hatred in his eyes. Sweet Jesus. They're coming. They'll kill you first and then all of us. Not good for business. Please leave. Oh, God, your wife. The poor thing. They'll fill her belly with a *godo* baby. That's what they said. Go now, Mr. B. One horse outside your window. Go."

He shut the door, extinguished his cigarette, and pulled Carmen out of bed. "We need to go now," he said. He gave her shoulders a hard squeeze and a push, and she winced at the thought of a life of such squeezes and shoves. Groggy and trembling, she followed him to the window. Never had she felt more vulnerable, never had she missed her sisters and her parents so much as she walked behind her husband toward the unknown. He slid the window open and quietly stuck his head out, looking down and around the dark

60

streets with a quick reconnaissance glance. He pulled himself onto the ledge, where he sat for a moment, and then jumped. Carmen heard herself whimpering like a wounded calf.

"Jump. Quick," he commanded.

She leaned out over the ledge. There he was, mounted on a saddleless horse. He looked as regal as he had on the dance floor. He held out his arms. Flustered, she shook her head, taking a couple of steps back. She didn't know how to ride a horse.

"Damn *godos* will kill us both if we stay. Now jump." His voice was coarse, like it carried pebbles with jagged edges in it. She took a deep breath and looked down. He had bad skin. She hadn't noticed this until now, as a sliver of the starry night shone over half of his face, exposing small craters that resembled the surface of some remote planet. His face looked as if it had been battered in a succession of fistfights. He was ugly-handsome with mischievous almond-shaped eyes aslant in his dark face. On his right cheek beneath the corner of his eye was a crescent scar that caught the moonlight. Even under such dire conditions, Mr. B. carried himself with impressive military bearing. And this splendid composure created an opening, an isthmus between clouds. How could she not love him?

She sat on the window ledge, swung her legs over it, crossed herself, and jumped with eyes closed. Mr. B. helped her to get onto the horse the only way she would mount it: like a lady, with legs tightly crossed over one side of the horse, her breasts away from Mr. B.'s back. She fastened her arms around his waist. His hands looped the reins. "Ready?" he asked. She nodded. Tears of terror streamed down her face. Mr. B. pressed his calves against the horse's flanks. He clicked his tongue, and the animal broke into a gallop, out of town and into the night.

Carmen heard a loud bang in the distance. "What was that?" she shouted over the horse's panting. He didn't answer.

Hot air whipped their faces. Carmen's body shook with quick

convulsions of horror and her throat felt dry, her tongue pasty, her mouth filled with dust and bugs. She heard the bang again.

"Did you hear that?" she shouted between stifled sobs.

"Fireworks," he shouted back. "It's the Assumption of the Blessed Virgin Mary." Naturally, she believed him.

Three days later, the couple arrived in Armenia, a small city of little white houses with red roofs. It was as beautiful as he'd promised: clean, quiet, simple. The air carried a whiff of coffee from the surrounding mountains. The fountain in the main square spewed crystalline water, not coffee, but she wasn't disappointed. His comment had been a joke, she now understood. A funny, funny joke. She needed to sharpen her sense of humor, for she was learning that men liked to play tricks on women.

In Armenia they finally consummated their marriage. Face to face on their pillow, he opened his heart and confessed that three nights earlier, as they had lain in bed fully clothed, she had looked more innocent, and therefore more desirable, than ever before, with her mouth half-open, her hands folded over her generous chest, her svelte legs crossed at the ankles. He told her he had used all the restraint he could muster to not lay a finger on her; puffing smoke rings to distract his mind, to keep his hands from following his hungry eyes as they had traveled up and down her unconscious body, was the hardest thing he'd ever done. "'Get a hold of yourself, big guy,' I kept telling myself," he told her. Although his trousers had bulged and throbbed with contained passion, he was determined to wait. A virgin is always worth waiting for.

"Had push come to shove," he whispered in her ear, "two doors down the hall was *Rosa la peligrosa,* a thick woman of insatiable sexual appetite capable of bringing a dead man back to life in less than five minutes."

"Really?" she asked.

"So I've heard," he smirked. "Also, farther down the hall was *Ana la aspiradora.*"

"The vacuum cleaner?" she asked.

He explained. Ana lived up to her nom de guerre by pleasing her clients with a munificent mouth and a tongue so long it could wrap itself around a client's perineum for a few extra pennies. "In other words, she can suck a man dry."

"Oh," she said, a little embarrassed, a little indignant, a little flattered that such a stud had not succumbed to the powers of a human vacuum cleaner.

"Or I could have gone to the lobby and chugged some *aguardientes* and maybe dance a tango or two with Irene," a busty young woman with white baby skin and a crimson mouth, who spoke with a foreign accent and could change her nationality as swiftly as she could dance. She'd claimed to come from so many different countries, even countries that nobody had ever heard of, that her true provenance was no longer of interest to anyone. She was Irene from somewhere else, the tango dancer, that's all there was to know.

After this hushed, heartfelt confession—the first he'd ever made to a woman— his lips met hers. Under the sheets, in his arms, Carmen had crazy thoughts. It occurred to her that his hungry mouth tasted of champagne, even though she hadn't tasted any alcohol before. Then she remembered the joke about men with big feet. It was true after all; who would have thought? Her body eased under his weight and the age-old ritual possessed them. They rose and fell, rose and fell into an unknown wilderness of goose bumps and moans.

Afterward, groggy and content, she suddenly realized that she had made it to the other side: she had crossed the threshold that a woman passes through only once in her lifetime. She relished the memories of those minutes—his body rigid, strong; hers quivering, malleable. How he had seemed to know her body like a poem learned by heart; how utterly lost to flesh both of their spirits had been; how she, wet and open, had given herself so willingly, so passionately, and how she had emerged from the momentary death shining with lust she'd found in the twirls of his tongue.

"I could die now," she said, breathless.

"Don't you dare," he joked sleepily. "More where that came from." He turned on his side.

"I would walk over burning coals if you were at the other end waiting for me," Carmen whispered in his ear. "Would you do the same for me?" He didn't reply. He was fast asleep.

Carmen fell asleep thinking that she still didn't know the meaning of opal or topaz. Such nice words. That night she dreamed of walking on burning coals. Charred flesh. Open wounds.

The Wake

Like a fairytale character waking up from a trance, I find myself in Medellín, city of eternal spring, city of flowers. Its more than 3 million residents call themselves *paisas,* as if they were citizens of a different *país,* some tiny, storybook country independent from Colombia. Standing by the iron gates of Campos de Paz, the Fields of Peace Cemetery, I wake to everything around me, like a Sufi contemplative, surrendering completely to a sensorial homecoming party. I listen to the *paisa* accent, a cadence that is both familiar and familial, and ask myself why I ever left this place. I hear their *seseo*—the distinctive stress that turns ordinary *s* sounds into soft *sh*—I drift in an ocean of *sh, sh, sh* waves crashing against these luscious mountains and wonder if the people will still accept me as local even though I have lost my *paisa* accent. Here I am, in a perfect place with the perfect temperature: 25 degrees Celsius, 77 degrees Fahrenheit, under a soft breeze that is neither cold nor hot but playful, messing up everyone's hair, laughing as it swirls and bounces off the mountains encircling the Valley of Aburrá. I had forgotten how much I love this city.

Campos de Paz hasn't changed. The entrance still sounds and feels like a flea market. Fruit and flower stalls compete for every inch of space near the gates. A newsstand blares *vallenato* music; and behind an improvised magazine rack, a haggard man blasts salsa songs from his boom box. Vendors crowd the taxi as the driver slows down to let me out.

"*Eavemaría*," he shouts when a tawny girl with leathery skin and big bright eyes shoves a bouquet of red roses into his face. "Get this shit away from me." He pushes the flowers away, sneezing and cursing.

"Orchids, gladiolas, fresh roses. Buy from me, my friend," the little girl chants, looking the driver in the eye, unafraid and determined to make a sale whether he likes it or not. I open the door of the cab to let myself out; but before I can react, a man pushes me back in with a tray holding four *salpicones*. One of the plastic spoons brushes past my nose. Sunny bright mangoes, crimson strawberries, porcupine pineapples, sunset papayas, devilish mangosteens, carmine melons. Chop them all in cubes. Toss them into a glass of chilled apple-flavored soda. Add condensed milk. Top generously with whipped cream. Stick in a cigar-shaped waffle. Eat with abandon, for there is no place in Medellín where one can find a more delicious *salpicón* than here at the cemetery. That's why we call it *salpicón de muerto,* dead man's cocktail.

Afflicted with a severe case of Medellín melancholia, I start to climb up the slope that leads to where the dead lie. Mom is somewhere up there, atop a hill flanked by luscious gardens and manicured lawns. Her body is in one of the eight viewing halls arranged in sets of twin bungalows that look like summer chalets. I walk slowly. I'm embarrassed by my own sluggishness. I should sprint up the hill and burst through the door pretending I am ready to be helpful. I should deliver something vital, something unique, a cloud of made-in-the-USA oxygen for Mom, a novel time machine that reverses its course so that we could go back to yesterday and take turns at offering her our breaths as she gasped for air. Mouth to mouth. Breathing each other's air as if we were Inuit throat singers. I have nothing like that to offer.

Medellín sits five thousand feet above sea level. My lungs take notice as I climb the hill, lightheaded and dazed. I hear rustling coming from behind the bushes. Something heavy is creeping and crawling behind a row of hedges on my left. I hear or think I hear the same noise moving along with me, climbing the hill by my side. The noise dissipates somewhere behind Mom's bungalow, swiftly overtaken by earthier sounds. The viewing next door features a rowdy crowd of mourners wearing flashy sneakers with untied laces, low-slung pants that expose their checkered boxer shorts, and long belts that slap their thighs and get between their legs as they walk. The mourners amble slowly, as if they own Campos de Paz, their shoulders swaying, hips swinging, exuding gangster swag. A refurbished school bus rests idle in the parking lot across the bungalow. I'm sure they arrived in it.

Mom would not have liked the sight of these people. They are from the *comunas,* the lawless barrios up in the hills where poverty and hopelessness fuel a culture of drug trafficking, extortion, and murder-for-hire. They are as tough as they look; so when I greet a couple of them on my way to Mom's hall, I don't expect a reply.

When I arrive at the funeral parlor, I am immediately mobbed by everyone in the room. My four sisters rush to greet me at the door, their eyes red, their breath quick and ragged. We embrace and cry for a few minutes—they in loud moans, me in stifled sobs. I'm afraid that if I break down, if I let go, I'll never be able to piece myself together again. My sisters all wear dark outfits that match the gloom on their faces. They would make a perfect black-and-white funeral portrait, the sort one might see on a Greek island or in a little village in the heart of Italy. From the sobriety of their hairdos to the paleness of their mouths, my sisters' appearance makes sense: quiet shoes, dark tailored suits, blouses that don't crumple after a dozen hugs, lapels that don't get stained by others people's lipstick. I, on the other hand, look like a long-lost friend from abroad who has been nice enough to fly into town on short notice to be with them in a time of need. I'm wearing torn, faded jeans, a pair of cheap cowboy mules, and a white gipsy blouse that is too translucent for my sisters' taste. I can see them thinking, You've been in the USA too long.

There is an underlying sense of urgency in the air as my sisters, friends, and relatives rush to hug me; but I'm not in a hurry to get through these moments of crying, touching, gasping, sobbing. I want to stop time. I want to hold each of them in my arms, smell them, take note of the scars that time has imprinted on their faces. They, however, have no time for any of this. For them, this is an emergency. For me, the emergency was yesterday before I got the news, when changing from torn jeans into something more appropriate didn't cross my mind.

As if leading a procession, my sisters hold me by my elbows and show me the way to the casket. My knees shake. I need to stop for a second and breathe. I tell them that I'm fine, that I need a couple of seconds, that I'm tired because I haven't slept in thirty-six hours. What I don't tell them is that I'm numb: that my upper lip has gone stiff, that I can't feel my toes, and that I find comfort in my numbness because this deadness makes me feel closer to Mom. I wipe my hands on my thighs and feel the skin peeking through the holes in my jeans. I haven't shaved my legs in days and this insignificant detail makes me sob a little.

"Are you coming?" one of my sisters asks as she squeezes my hand. We are both trembling, reeling, as we hold hands.

"In a second," I mumble. I can't stand the thought of looking at my mother. She's dead, and death transforms everything. It alters a face, a smell, an aura; it reduces us all to a pile of bones, skulls, teeth, and hair. Does Mom smell like some say dead people do? Has her mouth taken on a feral quality, lips pulled back, half-open in a suspended *O* like a silent scream? Are her eyelids completely closed or can people see the white of her eyes? Is she discolored, like a painting left out in the sun?

I escape my sister's grip and grab a cup of tea that I don't drink but that gives me an excuse to drag myself from one corner of the room to the other. I smile; at least I think I do. Faces and more faces present themselves to me like unwanted gifts. I don't know most of them. They are neighbors, friends of my sisters, old folks from Mom's seniors' group, strangers with coffee breath, pearl necklaces, and dark stockings, all of whom take me in their arms with hurried squeezes as if I were their own prodigal child. They say things like "Oh, you're the one from the USA." I try to correct them, "No, I'm from here, don't you remember me?" but they don't hear me, possibly because I'm not saying anything. Maybe I'm standing against a wall, one foot resting atop the other, pretending that one foot touching the floor means that half of me is free and only half is really here, clutching the strap of my backpack, silent, still, like an old photo.

"Give me a second," I say to whoever is steering my shoulders. I want everyone to leave me alone with my mother. My chest is tight; my eyes itch. A rush of self-pity invades me. I want to hear Mom's voice. I want to hold her face in my hands. I want Mom back. I want *mi mamita*.

The gloom of the funeral parlor—the marble tiles, the metal chairs, the flower stands, the cold air—makes the hair on the back of my neck rise. At one end of the room, underneath a wooden crucifix, lies Mom, inside a grey casket that looks too long for her short frame. At the foot of the coffin rests a pink and white cloud of magnolias. Orchids and roses flank the sides of the casket. Birds of paradise stand proud on a pedestal inches away from Mom's head; they are orange and blue with hues of bruised-apple red and look like an angry chaos of feathers. I have never seen so many wreaths in so many sizes, so many Corinthian stands or so many resin crucifixes. The scene is ugly. Although there may be beauty in imagined funerals, in heartfelt eulogies and spiritual rituals and last-minute displays of love, this is my mother's real funeral; it is swift and unexpected, devoid of beauty, painful and grotesque. Mom's body is decaying in front of everyone; it is releasing enzymes and juices that tenderize her flesh.

A delivery boy arrives with more "flowers for the missus." I hear oohs and aahs as he places a magnificent bouquet of white roses on a table. I dig my fingernails into the palms of my hands. I think, Someone, somewhere, please stop the damn flowers from coming this way; make a wall, redirect them, deliver them where they are needed: playgrounds, birthing rooms, hotel suites, rehab centers. My Mom's body is decomposing. Please, go away, flower boy. This is not a celebration. Think of her flesh, my God, her flesh is rotting. Soon it will stink, and there won't be enough flowers on the planet to mask the stench. Someone, somewhere, please turn these flowers into something quieter, more respectful, less exuberant, less colorful. A stalagmite would be nice, white handkerchiefs, balls of crumpled paper. Anything but flowers.

I don't know what is stirring inside me, but I think it's anger. I want to punch the delivery boy square in the face, the little bastard, to go on a flower rampage and thrash them all. I feel like breaking things and putting fists through walls. So I walk up to the table with the white roses and crush a handful of pearly buds in my fist. The sticky sap oozes out of the crumpled roses. I rub the mess on my wrists and behind my ears. I lick the juice off my index finger and wipe the rest on my jeans. A quivery heat lifts from my skin. I hope someone smells it, feels it, sees it, quenches it.

I walk outside, figuring that I can keep my distance from reality as long as I don't have the casket in sight. My brother is leaning on the veranda rails. He seems lost in the green vastness of the cemetery grounds. I never know what he is thinking. The shape of a leaf excites him as much as the blueprint of a building does. He is a quiet man who doesn't say much but sees everything. Sometimes when we tease him about being so quiet, he retorts that that's what happens when a man grows up surrounded by women. They emasculate him. They never give him a chance to talk. This is probably true, at least in my family.

"Hey, little sister," he says, as if we had seen each other yesterday, though we've really been apart for several years. The truth is I have seen my brother only a few times since the day he moved out to marry his pregnant girlfriend. He was nineteen; I was five. As soon as Mom found out that he was going to be a dad, she declared his girlfriend persona non grata. She wasn't welcome at home, and my brother, understandably, took his girlfriend's side. It's fair to say that when he started his own family, we lost any chance of having him in ours. It's also fair to say that his attachment to our family was never umbilical and that moving in with his girlfriend must have seemed much more appealing than growing up sandwiched between five girls and an overpowering mother. We adjusted well to his absence. Weeks could turn into months without our seeing each other. We didn't miss him, and I'm sure he didn't miss us either.

I say, "Hey," back to him and let him hold me in his arms. He is darker and thicker around the waist than he was when I last saw him. The dimple on his chin still softens his face when he smiles, giving him an impish look.

"How come you're not inside?" he asks, his thumb pointing back at the viewing hall.

"I don't know. Cowardice, I suppose." I gather my frizzy hair in an improvised, crooked braid on the back of my head.

My brother says something, but I'm distracted by the sight of the hearse that has come to transport the body next door to the chapel. A few seconds of commotion ensue. We hear hushed voices, shuffling, the ring of a metal chair against a tiled floor.

"What's going on next door?" I ask.

"Medellín. That's what's going on," he says. "Remember twenty years ago, when only the wealthy got buried here? Well, that's changed."

"That's social mobility, I guess," I say.

"Social mobility *à la Colombiana*." He scratches his head, and I notice that he does it exactly the same way Dad used to, with a quick finger gallop across his scalp. "The rich moved to bigger and better cemeteries, and this 'middle class' took over."

The crowd next door intimidates me. It's the kind to avoid in dark alleys, at convenience stores, in bars. It's the type of crowd you don't want to cross. "Are we in danger?" I ask him.

He turns on his heels and leans against an upright beam that separates the contiguous vigil rooms. He nudges me and invites me to also turn. Now we both face the room and Mom's grieving crowd. "That's where the danger is," he says, looking in. "These guys next door are nowhere near as dangerous as an army of wailing women." He swats a mosquito on his forearm. "What you consider dangerous and unstable is not. Trust me, out-of-control grief is."

"Aren't you grieving?"

"With all my heart, but my grief is private," he says. He clears his voice and asks without taking his eyes off of Mom's casket, "Are you going to see her? I mean, to look at her?"

72

"I don't know yet. You?"

"Nope," he says, "No way."

He clears his throat. I fidget with something in the pocket of my jeans.

He looks at his watch, taps it with one finger, puts it to his ear. "Any idea what time it is?"

"Can't even remember the last time I owned a watch," I say. "I'm going to give you a digital one for your birthday. About time you switch."

"I'm old-fashioned," he jokes.

I look at his wristwatch. It must have stopped working at some-time during the morning hours. "Mom would have fixed that piece of junk with her supernatural powers," I say.

"With her what?"

"You know, like Uri Geller."

"Uri Geller the mentalist? The spoon bender?"

I nod.

My brother scratches his neck, his chin, his head, and says, "Okay, I've got to hear this one."

And so I tell him that Mom was convinced that the clairvoyant from Israel had roused in her what she liked to call a "dormant tal-ent." I tell him how I used to stand by Mom, spoon in hand, eyes shut, mind focused on Uri Geller's soothing commands as they trickled out of our black-and-white TV, willing my mind to control the matter held between my thumb and my index fingers, talking in my head to the spoon, repeating Uri's instructions along with Mom.

"Bend, spoon. Bend, spoon. Bend. Bend," I say, rubbing an imaginary spoon between my fingers.

My brother shakes his head and smiles. "That's hilarious," he says.

I tell him that, a week after the spoon-bending exercise, we did

73

it all over again, this time with old watches that had stopped working a long time ago.

"Work again, watch. Work again, watch. Work. Work," I say now with a little squint.

He scratches his neck, smiles, and looks at the mountains in the distance. "Did you ladies get anything fixed?" he asks, trying not to laugh.

"Nope," I say. "But it wasn't for lack of trying. We also tried to fix an iron and an old blender and even to erase a scratch on one of her old 78s using our mind-over-matter mantra."

"And?"

"Nothing. Apparently I was too young to generate enough positive energy. But Mom? She fixed all sorts of stuff with the sheer power of her mind. When nobody was watching, that is."

He purses his lips trying not to laugh but does anyway and snorts, which makes me laugh as well. Then we fall silent and mourn again. A light wind traverses the valley. The trees sway, their leaves rustle; a yellow butterfly dances on the banister, and in this moment of levity, I'm truly happy. I close my eyes and offer my face to the sun with mouth slightly open. I want to bite into Medellín.

"That's a great story," my brother says. "Fantastic."

"Want to hear another one?"

Putting his arm around my shoulders, he gently moves me away from the rowdy *aguardiente*-chugging crowd chatting next door. "Sure."

"Did you know that Mom always wanted to slip a foot under a car?"

"Are you telling me that Mom wanted to commit suicide?"

"No, I said, *a foot*. She wanted to have the courage to do it. She used to tell me how grand it would be to have one foot run over by a sixteen-wheeler."

"A sixteen-wheeler? What the hell. Why not a lighter car, like a Renault 4?"

"Funny you should ask that because I asked her the same thing. You know what she said every time?" I begin imitating Mom's coarse voice: "A Renault 4 doesn't count. It's too light. If I ever do it, my foot will have to go *bing* and *bang*. You don't even get a peep from an R-4, the tiny things."

"What?" he asks, half-amused, half-incredulous. "Are you making this up?" He cocks his head as if waiting for me to tell him I'm kidding. When I don't, he says, "That doesn't sound like her. Not a bit."

"Don't you have any did-you-know story for me?" I ask.

He sucks his teeth and pinches his throat. He swallows something hard and dry. "Mom changed a lot over the years," he says with a frown. "In other words, the mother I had in the fifties and sixties is not the same mother you had in the eighties."

My sisters have told me stories about that mother, about the beatings, about her out-of-control rages. They talk about them without resentment. My brother who, according to the stories, got most of the beatings, never talks about them. He is matter of fact, as he was on the day he took me to the top of a mountain when I was a teenager. He wanted me to see the village that the hydroelectric plant he had built would flood on the following day. The people had been relocated, and the village was doomed to disappear under the water. "Sometimes, in order to create, you have to destroy," he had told me.

Now he says, "I've got a good one. Picture this: I'm five, maybe six, and Dalila is four, maybe five. I'm sitting on the toilet taking a dump. My shorts are around my ankles, and Dalila is sitting on the floor playing with my shoelaces. I'm dying to teach my sister all the cool words I know. So I go, 'Repeat after me, *Pendejo, pendejo.*

75

Carajo, carajo. Maldita, maldita. Marica, marica. Puta, puta,' and so on."

I hide a chuckle.

"Then I look up, and I see Mom's feet under the bathroom door. You know what I did? I wiped my ass and asked Dalila to repeat the words I had just taught her and when she finished I told her off loud enough for Mom to hear. 'You bad girl. You shouldn't say those words. If I ever hear you again saying those filthy things, I'm going to tell on you.' I washed my hands and left the bathroom, pretending that I was scandalized."

"And Mom?" I ask.

"She was gone. Years and years later, she told me that she had heard the whole thing but had been too amused to say anything."

We laugh some more, and I look over my shoulder to make sure that my sisters can't see us laughing. I catch sight of my reflection in a window: a disheveled middle-aged woman looking like a weary hippie stares right back at me. Inside are my sisters. They huddle together as if they are cold. A primeval instinct still lingering in our collective minds. Herds of animals huddle in a circle when in danger. It is a beautiful sight. My sisters wipe each other's tears with fistfuls of Kleenex and gaze at each other with wounded eyes. Then they notice me standing outside, and by noticing my presence outside their circle, they recognize my absence within. I think they have been angry at me ever since I left Colombia. I have removed myself from them—not completely but enough to have become an outcast. I want to pull them close to me and tell them what I'm feeling, but in the years since I left the country, I seem to have lost the ability to do that. More than anything, I want to apologize for leaving Colombia for Alaska, as if I were deliberately looking for the farthest possible corner of the United States, for taking my daughter with me, for forfeiting my Colombian engineering degree in favor of an American one in anthropology, for not flying home when my father died, for speaking a foreign language, for being in Hawaii while one sister had a hysterectomy and in India when she got married and in Kenya when another sister had a nervous breakdown and in Sri Lanka while our favorite aunt bled to death in Mariquita and in Kuwait where I fell in love with a foreigner and in Turkey when Mom was diagnosed with Alzheimer's and in sunny Florida when she died. I want to run to my sisters and surrender to this powerful surge of love I feel for every one of them. And then I want to apologize some more.

My sisters look at me from inside the parlor and wave me in. My brother pats me on the back and tells me that only I know, only I can decide when and whether I'm ready to go back inside. People stare at me as I walk toward my sisters, and with each stare, the holes in my jeans grow bigger and slowly I become painfully aware of my nakedness.

By the time I reach the middle of the room, I start sobbing and have to take a detour. I seek refuge behind the first door I find. It's a small tiled room with empty buckets and wet mops that smell of lavender. I'm breaking down in the maintenance room, alone, away from all those hands and arms that grab and tug and pull and squeeze. I'm breaking down here, surrounded by brooms and dirty sponges. I look at myself in a broken mirror above the sink. I tell the face in the mirror, You're still Adriana, with a tawny face and black curly hair. I have earrings on, cheap African figurines that hang from wires. I'm still me. But I can't get my mind to work right. It is still operating on yesterday's facts; today hasn't sunk in yet. Then someone knocks on the door.

"What are you doing?" the youngest of my sisters asks when I open the door.

The weight of trying not to say, "Falling apart, why?" causes me to say, "It's nice in here."

I'm moving, methodically, through grieving stages. This is how I go from to the stage of despair to the stage of reorganization. I start talking about mundane things, things that have a pulse, tangible things. Like this guy who won a pile of money in Jeopardy, what's his name? About a friend of mine who has a selective olfactory system: she can smell cinnamon but not rotten eggs. Isn't that interesting? About going to see Rod Stewart in concert and almost catching one of the soccer balls he kicked to the audience.

"That's enough," my sister says with a voice that tells me she knows how I feel. She is six years older than I am, but our souls have always been in sync. I'm the youngest one, still known to my sisters as *la niña,* as if I have never grown old.

"Come say good-bye," she whispers and starts walking towards the coffin, looking back over her shoulder the way mothers do with a stubborn child who refuses to come out of hiding. She goes to stand by the coffin, assuming a watchful position like she is guarding an ancient treasure. Then she bends over, and suddenly I fear that she'll start writhing like an octopus on top of the coffin. She kisses the glass that separates my mother's face from hers. I wish she wouldn't. I don't want Mom to be seen. This is not a spectacle, I think to myself. There is nothing to see here.

But there is something to see. There is a dead woman, and I wonder what my sister is experiencing right now. I wonder if, instead of the cold glass surface, she closes her eyes and feels my mother's dark skin touching hers, hears her breathe, cool as the kiss of a ghost. My sister looks up at me, waiting. I look down at my cowboy mules and fake interest in something on the floor. My throat begins to swell. I think I'm going to pass out. I turn away and walk back outside.

"I'm exhausted." It's all I can muster to say to my brother as I cross the veranda. I have passed two mornings and afternoons awake, and somehow this consciousness without respite has shredded my mind and body to fatigue.

"Still want to know what's going on next door?" he asks. I nod. He tells me there has been a raid. The dead man was a gun-for-hire wanted by the police; a few of the henchmen attending his wake were also on a wanted list. A SWAT team hidden in the hearse had gone in, taken prisoners, and disappeared without firing a single shot. "Maybe we have our own Colombian Rambos," he says so matter-of-factly that I start to sob, softly at first and then so hard that my words become unintelligible, elongated. I am filled with shame.

"Why are we having our mother's funeral next door to a *sicario's*? Not a thief, an extortionist, an embezzler, but a *sicario?* A hitman? Of all criminals, Mom's body had to be next door to an assassin's?"

My brother doesn't hug me; instead he pats my hand resting on the wooden rail. "She doesn't know," he says, and for the first time, his voice quivers. "Mom is dead."

Mariquita

It's about four A.M. The six of us—five girls and Mom—are woken by loud banging on the door. The first bang shakes the house. The second bang loosens the nails that hold down the planks of our wooden floor. The third bang, the most dramatic of the three, makes the nails spring out of place, clinking and clanking as they roll across the planks. My sister, the one closest in age to me, clutches my wrist under the covers as if she is drowning and then bolts out of bed and into the oak armoire. I hear her whimper. Then there is silence. Urine trickles from beneath the door.

Hurried noises slither from Mom's bedroom—a shuffle of feet as she searches for her old slippers, a hand scanning the wall for the light switch, the swish of her beige shawl as she tosses it over her shoulders, the tap of her hand on her breastbone as she commands herself to remain calm. She walks downstairs toward the door that is beginning to burst at the hinges. But before Mom reaches the door, a drunken kick unbolts it. She steps out of the way, out of drunken Dad's way, and lets him pass her by as if she is a pocket of air.

The next day, as soon as Dad disappears behind the bathroom

door and Mom goes downstairs to fix him breakfast, I jump into their bed. His side smells of nicotine, cologne, farts, and stale coffee. I look for Dad-free spots where my body can't catch his cooties. Slithering over to Mom's side, away from his scent, I bury my head in her pillow and breathe her love into me. As I dig my scrawny seven-year-old toes between the mattress and the headboard, I hear a rustle underneath Dad's side. I lift one corner of the spring mattress and discover a stash of magazines with pictures of women who don't look at all like Mom. Mom is dark and homely with darker circles under her eyes and silver streaks in her hair. But boy, these women! One is blonde, naked, sitting on the edge of a bed, and staring right at me. Her tongue sticks out like she is trying to catch a fly; her spread legs expose a body part that resembles a fresh wound. I compare it to mine and find no similarities. I flip the pages. The things that men and women do to each other in this magazine give me an empty, throbbing sensation in the pit of my stomach. It reminds me of the time I looked out the window of the sixth-floor doctor's office where Mom takes our stool samples to have them checked for parasites. Or the time Dalila took me to ride the roller coaster at the amusement park where she was selling ice cream. That same feeling of vertigo rises up and down my throat, teasing, frightening, inviting, making my mouth dry and sticky. I wonder if Mom knows Dad keeps pictures of wounded women under his side of the bed.

Dad eats his breakfast in silence, sulking, rattling his fingers on the table as if planning a battle, flexing the hand without a fork as if readying it for a fencing match. Mom serves him so much food that it spills over the sides of the plate. He gulps his eggs without looking at us or our empty plates. He has seconds. We are looking down, staring at our empty plates, elbows off the table the way Mom has instructed us. But I can't fight the need to sneak a peek at him. I raise my eyebrows first, then my head, until I see Dad's face gleaming in the morning sun. The corners of his lips shine with streaks of our last piece of butter as he chews with his mouth open, the way Mom says decent people shouldn't eat. Finally he pushes away the half-empty plate and leaves the table without saying a word.

An hour later a yellow taxi arrives, blowing its horn twice like a signal. Dad runs upstairs, drags a suitcase to the end of the corridor, and hurries downstairs again, passing me without seeing me. Mom follows, asking, "What am I going to do, huh?" He makes two more trips up and downstairs. Mom and I follow him. Each wooden step, with the passage of years and the weight of our lives, worn to concavity. Mom looks just as worn.

"What about the girls? Huh? You're abandoning five girls?" she asks, shaking her right hand with outstretched fingers. I want to ask him about the naked women under his side of the mattress, but the air in our tenement is tense and heavy like the sky above us is about to crack open.

But Dad isn't listening. He is peeling himself away from our lives; he has shut his heart to us like an unpaid utility. Panic settles on Mom's face; and just when I'm sure she is about to scream or collapse, she grabs me by the hand and draws me close to her as we stand by the door. Her apron smells of onions.

Dad leaves in the yellow taxi. By the time the cab has reached the end of the block, Mom's fingernails are buried in my right shoulder. It hurts, but I don't move because I know she is hurting more than I am. She covers my eyes, but I can see everything. The taxi rounds a corner and disappears into the sun. Mom looks old and wasted. I fear that the burden of the last twenty years will crush her at the shoulders. I'm thinking that I won't be able to catch her if she collapses, but she presses my head against her side and lets out a small moan. "Good riddance," she says under her breath, but I know she doesn't mean it. I glance over her hands and look for crossed fingers, the unmistakable sign that she doesn't mean what she says. Her fingers are not crossed. "Let's get back inside," she murmurs. "It looks like it's going to rain." She presses my head closer against her side.

Outside the sun is shining brightly.

Once Mom releases me, I think of the list of things she has taught me about Dad, about men. I think about this list often, for it gives me comfort and turns our world and its chaos into a crystal box where what you see is what you get. Everything makes sense whenever I add an item to my list.

A real man is the absolute head of the household; he has a commanding presence and doesn't waste time on subtleties like *thank you, please,* or *I'm sorry.*

Your Dad ran away from home when he was your age. That's why he is a lonely man who is always looking for his mother without realizing it.

Men are always busy with important thoughts, even when they look idle. A good Catholic wife doesn't burden her husband with silly little things like *your children need shoes* or *X is failing math* or *Y has chickenpox.*

Women can go without food for long periods of time. God made them strong like that. But men need a lot of food to survive. God made them eating machines.

Some men claim to be bohemians, but only a few, like your Dad, are the real deal. Free-spirited men like that are not made for family life. They don't walk; they fly.

Men are like ships lost at sea. Women are seaports, their anchors buried into deep sand for life.

Two weeks later, the six of us sit down at the table for supper: bone soup, a banana, and a glass of weak fruit juice. The radio is on. "The Night Chicago Died" by Paper Lace is number one on the Billboard Hot 100 chart. After dinner, Mom announces that we are going away for a while to forget and forgive. I suppose she means to forget about Dad and to forgive Al Capone for all the people he killed in the song.

So we go to Mariquita, my mother's hometown, the only place where she ever feels whole. She always says that Mariquita is hot and damp, like a woman's heart, and that's why it's located a little to the left of the center of Colombia. She also says that this place is as savage and stubborn as a man's head, especially during the rainy season, when the rivers spill their waters and gallop fearlessly across the fields, filling the air with the musky scent of trout.

Mom's sister Gilma and my grandparents have always lived in Mariquita, in houses so old that nobody remembers when they were built—houses with little wooden doors for windows and tiled floors, with outside bathrooms and cement washboards, with dark kitchens and mosquito nets, with low ceilings and stucco walls, with backyards bursting with trees and mysteries. Time doesn't seem to touch these houses; they, like the town itself, retain somewhere within aromas of times past: camphor, laurel, turpentine, and wet earth.

Soon after we arrive, we hear that the *chupacabras,* or goatsucker, has been at work in the neighborhood, terrorizing animals on a nearby farm, where a calf was found with its blood drained and two peculiar puncture marks on the neck. Nobody knows what a *chupacabras* looks like. Some say that the creature is a vampire, half-man, half-beast, who roams the countryside looking for animal blood. Others say that it looks like a kangaroo or an alien or a panther with a forked tongue, that it leaves a stench of sulfur in its wake.

Down the road, there are stables with *paso fino* horses whose manes and tails have been neatly plaited. That's the work of the

84

goatsucker, Auntie Gilma tells us, the unequivocal signature of *el chupacabras.*

"You know the *chupacabras* doesn't attack humans," she says, looking at Mom, who is already shaking her head. "But it's best not to tempt fate and stay indoors at night. Just in case."

Mom, however, doesn't believe in monsters. She says that the only thing we need to be afraid of is people, especially men. She crosses herself and sighs dramatically.

"If God wanted to suck the blood of a cow, he would do that himself without any *requeñeque.* In any case, do you think that God has nothing better to do than to play with a horse's tail? *No faltaba mas!"*

All I have to do to experience the mysteries of Mariquita is to venture into the stretch that connects my grandparents' and my aunt's backyards, a mile of trees, bushes, wildflowers, and birds. During the day, I climb the mango trees, whose fruit is not a mango but a *manga*, with a feminine *a* that makes the fruit juicier, plumper, and a thousand times sweeter than a masculine mango could ever be. I play at spotting the fruits that will soon fall off the tamarind, papaya, orange, and mandarin trees. A guava tree leans on the fence that separates the two houses, exuding a syrupy pitch that sticks to my clothes whenever I walk by it. Near the well stands a *mamey sapote* tree, whose fruit, Auntie Gilma jokes, turns men into rods and keeps them charging like crazy bulls, though I don't understand the benefit of having a charging bull inside the house, let alone a man who is stiff and cold like a rod. Mom's favorite tree is the avocado that stands in one corner of my auntie's little forest. It bears fruits so greasy that oil oozes like melted butter out of the cut green flesh.

This playground by day becomes a purgatory by night. Full-moon nights are the worst. Pale light glimmers through the tree limbs, transforming everything into a maze of moving monsters that stalk little girls who are late for supper. Shapes, smells, and sounds interweave into a canopy of suspended leaves and branches above my head. I imagine hungry fingers clutching my ankles, bloodcurdling screams, chants being whispered in unknown tongues. The mythological beings that Aunt Gilma talks about crystallize in the dark. On some nights, I see *La Llorona* crouched under the avocado tree, weeping, asking God to bring her back the children she killed herself. On some other nights, I can feel *La Madremonte* breathing mouthfuls of soggy air on my neck. Mother Mountain rules the winds, the rains, and all the vegetation on earth. She protects nature fiercely and punishes those who invade her territory by making them get lost. I'm certain it's only a matter of time before this mossy ghost with leafy fingers catches hold of my braids and whisks me up into the air, banishing me into a cloud of equatorial rain.

Luz and Juan, two neighborhood children, are also here. They always are. Their mother, who works all night and sleeps all day, has never been married but has many boyfriends. We are not allowed to talk to her. Auntie Gilma says that children have no business talking to a woman who drinks a lot, throws lots of parties, and wears tight blouses and short skirts.

Auntie Gilma looks after Luz and Juan, feeds them, teaches them right from wrong, and lets them call her *Auntie*. I heard her complain to Mom. Apparently the priest had told her that her good deeds were a waste of time because bastard children go to hell no matter how hard you try to save them.

Like me, Luz is eight years old, but she never gets to play outside in the sunshine because she has asthma and is always battling mysterious allergies that make her sniffle and constantly blow her nose. Juan is different. He is in the eighth grade and knows everything worth knowing, revealing the mysterious world of adults to me without reservation, using grown-up words we are not allowed to utter. When I ask him where he gets all this information, he says he is like a refurbished antique car: he may look new and shiny on the outside, but he has very high mileage under the hood.

Mom says that Juan is bad news and has instructed me to stay away from him. My aunt Gilma calls him Juan *el Malo*; and I heard her telling Mom that if she ever catches him playing with himself again and molesting her poor hens, she's going to take him to the church of *La Ermita* and have the priest exorcise his dick.

"And do you know why *el chupacabras* doesn't touch the horse's forelock?" Juan asks me. We are hiding under a bed, one of the few places where we can spend time together because he is not allowed to be alone with any girl. "Because the forelock looks like the hair on a woman's crotch, and *el chu-chu-chupa-pacabras* doesn't like pussy."

I nod and laugh. Juan *el Malo* laughs too, thinking that I get the joke, but I'm really laughing because he is beginning to stutter. Sometimes to avoid this unpredictable stutter, he strings together long breathless sentences, talking until his face turns purple, his words become gurgles, and his tongue sticks to the roof of his mouth.

The rules of the big city don't apply here in Mariquita, where we are as free as we'll ever be. We don't have to lock any doubled-bolted doors at night or lie to the landlord when he comes looking for the rent. We don't have to queue up around the corner to wait for the "unofficial" propane truck to bring us gas cylinders with malfunctioning valves that shouldn't be sold because they leak but that Mom buys anyway because they are cheaper than the good ones. She says they are easy to patch with old socks stuffed with mushy soap.

None of that happens here. In Mariquita, we obey the rules of the land. And rule number one is to leave Margarita alone. Margarita lives with her father next door to Auntie Gilma. Both of them are crazy and violent. He keeps her in a cage in their backyard and hoses her down twice a month. Nobody hoses *him* down, though; and if you pass him in the street, the stench makes you jerk your head back. Margarita seems immortal, like a wild angel, and has lived in this cage for as long as I can remember. Her father wheels the cage out of the house at first light and back inside at sunset. She wears dirty rags, her matted hair harbors an army of lice, and her skin is covered with oozing sores and infected mosquito bites inhabited by mites. She doesn't speak but grunts like an angry ogre; and when she soils herself, she retreats into a corner of the cage sucking her thumb while her dad throws buckets of water at her and shouts the kind of dirty words that only adults are allowed to say.

Juan *el Malo* and I spy from our side of the fence made from *guadua* bamboo and begin to throw things at Margarita. The aim of the game is to hit her on the head. We throw pebbles and banana peels; we shoot spitballs. Whenever we hit our target, we high-five each other and take turns calling her names and taunting her with riddles.

"Do you want to know why she is crazy?" my cousin asks as we widen the space between two bamboo culms. "Because she got knocked up when she was like fourteen."

This makes sense to me. A blow to the head can make anyone crazy. But he corrects me. "No, not that kind knock, you *boba* little girl. The other kind. But don't feel too sorry for her because by the time she got knocked up she had already lost her three vi-vi-virginities. Yes. Didn't you know a woman has three of them? The mouth, the butthole, and the other one."

I give the three virginities some thought but conclude that this stupid fake cousin of mine means the Trinity: the Father, the Son and the Holy Spirit.

"That's why at night we can hear her cries," he adds and then tells me, "She is *La Madremonte*. Her soul leaves the cage at night and she wanders around looking for little girls." His hands find their way under my hair and his fingers trot across my nape. "Haven't you felt her p-p-p-pulling your hair at night when you walk outside in the yard? *No*? How about blowing hot air on your n-n-n-neck? Yes? And when you turn around you don't see anything?"

Yes. I have felt every single thing. "You too?" I ask, my arms breaking out in goose bumps.

"No, *boba,* she only goes after little girls, and I'm a man, can't you see?" he says grabbing and squeezing his crotch with both hands. "Here, touch down here, so you know for sure that I'm a man." He grabs my wrist and guides my hand towards his crotch, looking over his shoulder, making sure nobody sees us.

I am considering the offer, trying to decide whether or not it's a good idea to touch Juan down there, when we hear Mom's voice: "Juan? Where are you, *plaga*?" She calls him the plague, but he doesn't mind because Auntie Gilma calls him worse names. He presses a finger against his lips and commands me to be quiet as he crawls away, walking backward, keeping an eye in Mom's direction. The earth trembles under my feet with each of Mom's urgent steps, and I wonder if she ever does anything leisurely. With her, everything is important, everything terminal, everything full of twists and knots, like my hair on Sundays before she braids it with brisk yanks of her broken comb.

Mom walks toward the cage, unafraid. I hold my breath. How can she be this bold? Doesn't she know how dangerous Margarita is? Stealthily, I climb the mango tree, wrap my legs and arms around one of its branches, steady my body, and peer down at Mom. She leans on the *guadua* fence, looking toward the cage, and something within her seems to break loose. I think she is weeping, and I want to ask why, but then I hear her say, "Poor thing." She opens the gate and walks toward the cage. I expect Margarita to flail at Mom through the bars, to grunt and throw a couple of fiery punches into the air, but she doesn't. Something within her seems to melt.

Mom kneels on the ground, takes hold of the bars with both hands, and begins to whisper to Margarita. I think I hear her singing something slow and sweet, like a lullaby, and then she says, "You can't see it, but I also live in a cage." The two women interlace their fingers. I imagine that they're making a quilt. One brings patches from the drawers of her insanity, whimsical patterns splashed with stolen colors; the other brings patches from hand-me-down clothes, mended socks, and sleepless nights. They look at each other and the rough edges of their faces disappear. They become smooth and fluid like the pebbles of the Gualí River.

Yet I'm concerned about Mom's remark. I can't stand the thought of her being caged. I slip down from the tree and run back to the houses, searching behind doors in one, underneath heavy furniture in the other, frantically looking for a cage. Wherever it is, I'll set Mom free. I'll bring down the bars, I'll destroy the lock, I'll burn the pad, until all that was hard and restraining around her is turned into ashes—soft, powdery, light.

Rule number two is to stay away from the shower stall behind the chicken coop. It's a dingy, roofless room with four unfinished concrete walls. This room has a name: the iguana stall. It's not much to look at, and Auntie Gilma is the only person allowed there. When she goes to the iguana stall to take showers, she comes out dry, like she hasn't even dipped a toe into the water. She says this is because the iguana stall is for dry showers, whatever they are.

"Bullshit," Juan *el Malo* tells me. "Don't you know what's in the iguana room or why it's called iguana?"

90

I shake my head.

"Auntie Gilma keeps mar-iguana in there. It's a happy plant with leaves like this." Juan draws a star in the air with his finger. We are playing dominoes in the middle of the living room, where people come and go and Mom can keep an eye on us.

"Let me see your hands at all times, *plaga*," she shouts from the corner where she and my two aunties are playing a game of Parcheesi. "*Zángano!*"

"She is dying of ca-ca-cancer. You know what cancer is?" he asks covering his mouth so that the three women can't tell what he is saying. "It's a thing that turns Auntie Gilma's insides black, little by little, like a flesh-eating ma-ma-maggot, unless, of course, she has her mar-iguana fix. Oh, man, so-so-some people have all the luck."

I grab my belly with both hands, instinctively.

"What? You don't believe me, little cousin?" He glances around, and when he thinks Mom is more interested in defending her yellow pawns than in monitoring us, he invites me to go outside with him and sit on his lap under the mango tree. He winks at me, slowly, flirtatiously, and I giggle nervously.

"Don't call me *primita,*" I say.

"Why not?" he asks.

"Because we're not really cousins. That's why."

"What did I say about the hands?" Mom says. "Show me the hands." Her eyes widen, her neck jerks forward, her eyebrows lift. "Don't make me tell you again."

Juan shows her his hands and whispers to me, "Want to see? I'll show you the plant if you want me to."

I can't help myself. I want to see the plant that makes Auntie Gilma happy. Maybe I can get some for Mom, and she can be mar-iguana happy when she is in the cage, which by now I'm convinced

91

is somewhere back home. Mom could use some mar-iguana, I'm sure. I have seen her sitting in the dark smoking a long white Parliament, then setting down the cigarette and dropping her head into her hands. Her shoulders jolt like she is crying, although I have never seen her tears.

Juan excuses himself from the living room. In a few minutes, I ask permission to go over to grandma's house. We meet by the iguana shower. Juan *el Malo* is squatting by the door, his nose flattened against the opening between the cement floor and the door, sniffing the mar-iguana odor that emanates from the stall. He says that he is giving himself a head start. Then he shifts to a more solid kneeling position and locks his hands together. "Get up on my hands, quick," he orders. He wants me to climb over the wall and unlock the door from the inside. "I won't look up your dress. I p-p-p-promise."

When I finally manage to unbolt the door, Juan slips in and closes it behind us. The interior of the stall is disappointingly plain: a makeshift table, two lamps, some pots and plants under the light, and, in a wooden box under the table, a few hand-rolled cigarettes that Juan moves back and forth under his nose like as if he's playing a harmonica. "Oh man," he says, "I'm getting hard just s-s-s-smelling these." He puts one under my nose, but I don't smell anything and I don't get hard either, whatever that means. Each cigarette has a letter on it, which Juan says represents the day of the week so that Auntie Gilma won't get high twice in one day.

"High?" I ask.

"Yes, *trabada.*"

As Juan tries to decide which joint to steal, we hear Auntie's voice. "Juan? Where are you, you devilish thing? Don't let me catch you flogging the frog again. Juan? I swear, I'll tell the priest if you are doing a loner with your boner."

We drop into silence and stare at each other, unsure of what to do next. I notice how ugly he is, dark and chubby with a shiny flat nose and the straightest hair I've ever seen, like he's wearing a porcupine on his head. His face is covered in acne, and the two especially impressive pimples framing his forehead resemble horns. Maybe Auntie Gilma is right, maybe Juan *el Malo* is the devil himself. But what he lacks in looks he possesses in charm. I'm drawn to him like *el chupacabras* is drawn to a horse's mane, not the forelock.

"I catch you milking the snake once more, and I'll send you packing," Auntie Gilma says.

"What's she talking about?" I ask, climbing onto Juan's hands again. He says that the frog and the snake are pets that no one is allowed to see, no one, but if I'm a good *primita,* one of these days, he'll introduce me to his one-eyed friend Boner.

It's Sunday morning. Soft wind meanders into my auntie's house, making the mosquito nets over our beds flap into our faces. Through the open windows, street vendors cry, *"Morcilla caliente, lleve la morcilla!"* A few minutes later they add, *"Gelatina e' pata, gelatina e' pata."* In Mariquita, even the street vendors seem to know exactly what I like: black pudding and calves' foot jelly. I wish we could stay here forever, but Mom says that's impossible. We have to go back to the big city so my sisters and I can finish school and become doctors and lawyers, not brutish mules like her.

I don't like it when she talks like this, but that's what she calls herself: *una mula bruta.* Sometimes she says donkey, sometimes mule. I wish she would choose a different animal, one that better represents what she does—perhaps a honeybee or one of those spiders that spend their lives working on their webs. But my fourteen-year-old sister says that Mom is guilt-tripping us; that every time she describes herself as a beast of burden she is blaming us for her poverty, her ignorance, her backaches, and every other calamity in her life. My sister plans to be a psychologist someday and says she will give us all free therapy because a family with an absent father and an overpowering mother is a recipe for disaster. She believes that Mom is emasculating us; and when I tell my sister that I don't know that word, she says that *to emasculate* is the same as *to castrate*—figuratively, that is, because we don't have testicles. My sister goes on and on about a guy named Freud and something called psychoanalysis, but honestly, I just want her to shut up and help me choose a beautiful animal to describe Mom.

Luz is sick again. She is running a high fever and had an asthma attack this morning that left her with a throbbing headache. Now she is wheezing and gasping for air like a dying snapper, and Auntie Gilma has applied generous amounts of *vicpaporú,* Vicks VapoRub, to her chest. Mom and Auntie Gilma treat *vicpaporú* like a magic potion, one that can cure everything from common colds to cramps to pneumonia. I'm sure Auntie Gilma uses *vicpaporú* on her tummy along with a mar-iguana jar labeled "r" for rubbing.

While Luz's mom sleeps through another hangover, Mom chops green onions—to bring the fever down—and slices potatoes—to soothe the headache. Auntie Gilma continues working the chest rub. Luz will spend the morning lying on the couch with slices of potatoes on her forehead, chest covered in green *vicpaporú,* and her feet wrapped in newspaper bundles of scallions soaked in warm ethylic alcohol.

We are raucous today. A neighbor's dog wanders in through the back door carrying an old shoe in his mouth. I play tug-of-war and the dog growls. My sisters find "The Night Chicago Died" on Auntie Gilma's transistor radio and sing along in dubious English that doesn't sound at all like the song. A neighbor's daughter who is the same age as I am walks in with her cousins, twin girls from the city, with sunburned skin and mischievous freckles on their noses.

But Mom has a low tolerance for chaos, even more so now that my dad is gone. She barges into the room. "Enough with the noise," she thunders. The dog drops the shoe and cowers under the table. "Tomorrow, all of you get purged. Parasite-free. Let's get rid of those worms and those amoebas and see who's laughing at the end of the day."

When Mom is not looking, we sigh, gag, roll our eyes, blame each other for provoking her. But it's too late. Mom has spoken, and whatever she says, goes. No questions asked. Mom is assertive, stubborn, controlling, smart, capable, gutsy. Nobody questions Mom. *Nobody*. The neighbor pushes her freckled cousins out of the door. "Let's get out of here before Doña Carmen makes *purgante* for the whole neighborhood."

The next day, as promised, Mom prepares the laxative, a thick and revolting concoction of bitter herbs and warm cod-liver oil. We gag as Mom forces the mixture down our throats. Within minutes, we are tripping over each other on our way to either the indoor bathroom or the outdoor latrine. But Juan *el Malo* has decided to smear his shit around the edges of the hole so that we are too disgusted to use it and it becomes exclusively his. He spends a couple of hours in there, during which Auntie Gilma makes several rounds of whispered threats. "Are you milking the monkey? Slap the salami again, and you'll see. I'm talking to you. If I tell your mother that the other day I caught you petting the dog, she'll kill you. You hear me?" We don't hear a peep out of him. I giggle at the thought of him squatting over the stinky latrine with a monkey on his head and the dog licking his shit.

By noon, our intestines are empty and our backsides sore. One of us passed a roundworm which made me think about the butthole virginity issue. Our bellies rumble with pangs of hunger and thirst, all of us are empty except for Luz. She hasn't made a single trip to the bathroom. Mom pours another cupful of the dreaded concoction down Luz's throat and waits. Nothing. Worry zigzags across Auntie Gilma's face. She believes that, out of all of us, Luz is the one who most needs parasite-purging. Auntie is convinced that stomach bugs, probably flukes, are causing her asthma attacks.

"That and being a bastard girl."

"Well," Mom says with a tilt of the head and an eyebrow rise. "Do you want me to finish her off?"

Auntie Gilma nods slightly, helpless.

Mom's solution is one of her infamous homemade enemas. Buy potassium-rich soap—generally the cheapest in the market— let it froth in lukewarm water, pour suds into the enema bag, connect one end of a hose to the bag and insert the other end into the patient's rectum, empty the bag's contents into the body, wait a few seconds, watch the patient make desperate runs to the toilet. Repeat every six months.

By the time Luz emerges from the bathroom for the last time, a foul odor slithers behind her, impregnating the house. We all go outside to avoid the stench. Pale and weak, she sits with Juan and me under the avocado tree. "Auntie Carmen almost killed me," she says, tears streaming down her bony face.

"But she made you feel better," I counter.

"I guess." Luz shrugs without strength.

I tell her that she is lucky she is a big girl. Had she been a few years younger, Mom would have made her go by sticking a thick green onion soaked in oil up her ass.

Juan laughs. "That would've been funny as hell."

He thinks I'm joking.

The night before we leave, Auntie Gilma treats Mom to a private cupping session. I've seen my sisters do the cupping therapy to relieve Mom's back aches, which she says are caused by *vientos malos,* bad winds that percolate through the skin. Now Mom will be naked from the waist up, and nobody is allowed in the room, which is dumb because when she gets the cupping done at home, she lies on her chest and we can't see anything. What I think is that nobody is allowed in because Mom and Auntie Gilma are like little girls when they get together. They giggle, gossip, and tell each other off-color jokes.

They've decided to lock themselves into Auntie Gilma's room. I spy through the keyhole. Mom lies facedown on her sister's bed, a white towel covering her lower half. My aunt rubs baby oil on Mom's back, then lights a candle over the oily skin and holds a cup inverted over the flame. Once the air within the cup heats up, Auntie Gilma presses the cup against Mom's back, where it forms a vacuum, and then starts sliding it around. The idea is to preserve the suction seal as the cup glides and thus suck out all of the bad winds that are hurting her.

Mom turns her head and is now facing the door. I wonder if she can see me though the keyhole. She closes her eyes, slowly, like she is falling under a spell, and lets out a sigh of relief through her half-open lips. Auntie Gilma moves the cup around a five-inch-long scar on the right side of Mom's lower back. She shakes her head at the sight of it. Her face reveals a mixture of pity, respect, and reluctance. She bites her lower lip, tilts her head to the right and then to the left, and finally blurts, "You all right living with only one kidney?"

"Don't start, please. I've told you before, I have two of those."

"So you think I believe that one of your kidneys just *fell* and the doctor *lifted* it into place? I've never heard stories of kidneys moving around."

97

There is some kind of secret involving Mom's kidney. A few weeks back, I caught my oldest sister crying, saying to Mom that, had she known, she would have given her heart. But even I know that people can't live without a heart. I must have misheard. What I know is what Mom is now telling my aunt: her right kidney was lower than the left, so the doctor moved it up into place.

Auntie Gilma moves around the bed, and I can't hear everything she says, only the repeated words *money, organs,* and *black market*. She moves back and her voice comes in more clearly. "So either the doctor tricked you and stole it from you, or you sold it to feed the girls." She lifts the cup with a pop.

"Stop that nonsense right now, won't you? Don't be *malita* and give me another *ventosa*."

"Suit yourself," Auntie Gilma replies, lighting another candle.

She repeats the cupping process several times until I can tell all the bad winds have left Mom's body. Her transformation is clear. Thanks to the suction cups and Auntie Gilma's magic, she has traveled back in time to when none of us existed, when she lived under this very roof and the summers were clammy, the afternoons sluggish, and life as simple as the white towel around her waist.

"I have a joke for you," Auntie Gilma says, tucking two strands of her thinning hair behind her ears. I notice how little hair is left on her scalp, how mangled the veins of her arms are. She rubs her hands together in anticipation of her joke, and at this instant, years seem to fall from her face. She is no longer the auntie battling cancer; she is a teenager about to say something so naughty that only another teen would understand. Mom giggles, even before Auntie Gilma starts talking. "A guy picks up a prostitute and spends a couple of hours with her at a seedy motel. A few days later, he finds he has caught crabs. He chases down the prostitute and says, 'Hey, hey, you gave me crabs.' She replies, 'What'd you expect for five bucks? Lobster?'"

Mom laughs so hard that the cup on her back bounces off onto the tiled floor, letting out a fart noise that makes her laugh even harder. Neither of them makes any attempt to pick it up. Auntie Gilma has tears running down her face. She massages her ample brown chest with one hand and fans her face with the other. Looking up at the ceiling fan, she says, "*Que Dios me perdone*, may God forgive me." But her repentance is short-lived. As she helps Mom with her dress, Auntie Gilma remembers another joke. I can't hear the whole thing, and I'm mortified by the blank spaces left in between the fragments that tell a story about the town whore treating the town idiot to a freebie, a sixty-nine. Then more whispers, more stifled chortles; Auntie Gilma is speaking and laughing at the same time, but somehow Mom understands every word because she laughs too.

I crane to listen. The whore (I know what whores are; Mom calls them the ladies of the night) and the idiot go to a seedy hotel. I'll ask Juan where the Seedy Hotel is. It must be a very famous place because everything funny happens there. Maybe it's a circus. Then comes a punch line that I can't hear but that makes the two women laugh so hard they don't notice I have accidentally pushed the door open. I close it stealthily and continue to watch through the keyhole.

I've never seen Mom laugh like this. She is sitting on the edge of the bed, slapping her thigh with one hand, stamping one foot, her body rocking back and forth in wild joy. Her face glistens with sweat, which my mind imagines as glitter because it makes her look prettier and happier. I want to stop time. I want Mom to be this lively when we get back home. I close my eyes and pray to God that when we get back to the city Mom finds someone to tell her jokes about numbers, especially sixty-nine; sea creatures, especially crabs and lobsters; and the Seedy Hotel. Already I am picturing a red neon arrow pointing at a sign that reads, "Welcome to Hotel Seedy, Home away from Home." Or something like that.

We are leaving Mariquita. Juan is supposed to help us carry our suitcases to the bus terminal, but he is nowhere to be found. I know where he is, but I don't say anything. He is spying on the twins across the street. He climbs the calabash tree in their backyard and stares at them while they sunbathe in their matching hammocks. He says he's studying them for a science project, to see if Mariquita's sun produces freckles. I know he's lying, and I don't really care. Mom says that we can carry our own stuff, that we don't need a little boy to help us with anything, let alone *un atembado,* a silly one. I want to tell her that actually he is the smartest kid I know. But I know better. I don't want to cross her.

The five of us walk ahead of Mom. We carry three suitcases and two cardboard boxes full of fruit, *aliñado* bread, and a *yunta* of salted *bocachico* fish that Mom bought cheap because it is the end of the *subienda,* which means the *bocachico* season is about to end and the merchants are trying to get rid of it. When we arrive at the bus station, Mom does the same thing she's done ever since I can remember: she straightens her back and takes long elegant steps toward the ticket booth for the Rápido Tolima. Then she says, "Six one-way tickets to Bogotá, please," loudly enough for anyone around to hear the word "Bogotá." She says it's important that the passengers know that these six women are going to the country's capital, the big city, not some insignificant village along the way.

The Rápido Tolima's fleet of old buses offer the cheapest and also the most uncomfortable ride in and out of Mariquita. The six of us sit on three double seats, one behind the other. Mom and I sit together on the third row. She gets up every few minutes to check on my sisters, strains her neck and looks around to scan for malicious men with malicious looks who might be having malicious thoughts about her girls. Nothing escapes her gaze: the live chickens a passenger has hidden in a burlap bag, the pig another passenger has stuffed into a suitcase. She realizes that there is something wrong with the bus. She doesn't drive and knows nothing about cars, but she understands what a bus in mint condition should sound like, and this one in particular doesn't. She knows that in forty-five minutes the bus will make its first rest stop in Honda, where we won't be allowed to use the bathroom because she says we can catch diseases down there from sitting on filthy toilets. She knows we won't complain, even if our bladders hurt.

"Can I rest my head on your lap?" I ask Mom.

"No."

I don't ask why. I'm not supposed to question Mom's decisions. And the moment the bus starts moving, I'm grateful that she didn't let me rest on her lap. She gets up to check on my sisters so often that she looks as if she is walking home rather than riding the bus. Somewhere in the back, a kid throws up; and the smell of vomit, animals, and human sweat curdles into a thick, simmering vapor under the midday sun. A whiff of salted fish slithers out from beneath our seat.

"I'm going to pass out," I tell Mom.

"This is really not a good time to be a baby. Nobody is having a *patatús* here, you hear me?"

I do hear her and I don't pass out.

When the passengers start complaining about the heat and the locked windows, the driver shouts insults back at them. "What, what? Are we all high class now that it's hot and sticky?" he demands, glaring at us through the broken rearview mirror. "If you're so delicate, why don't you go on Rápido Ochoa?" He tosses his head at the air-conditioned coach parked next to us at the rest stop.

From our bench with broken springs, I look into the coach. Its seats have high leather headrests and look plush and inviting. Even the people who ride the Rápido Ochoa coach look different from us. They are sunburned tourists, dressed in cutoffs, miniskirts, and spaghetti straps, wearing straw hats and baseball caps printed with words in English, words that might as well be screaming, "We've been to the United States and you haven't." They drink cold Coca-Colas and munch on bags of Lays potato chips bought from the street vendors who rush to their windows, which roll up and down effortlessly. These Rápido Ochoa people look happy. Children call their dads *papi* and their moms *mami,* and that's why we call rich kids *hijos de papi y mami.* My sisters and I? No, we are not *hijas de papi y mami.* We are Mom's girls. Carmen's girls. And we're poor and are not allowed to wear shorts or spaghetti straps, or call Mom *mami,* or drink Coca-Cola because it's bad for our teeth, or waste Mom's money on silly hats, or munch on chips because we eat real food like the fish we have tucked under our seat, which Mom will cook in a cast-iron skillet, and when each fish is perfectly browned we will pop the whole thing—tail, scales, eyes, and all—right into our mouths.

As we cross the bridge over the Magdalena River and start our painful ascent to the mountains, the bus begins to splutter and struggle. Mom mumbles, "*Se lo dije,* I knew it,*"* just before it breaks down. A fleet of shiny Rápido Ochoa coaches passes us by, their curtains drawn, protecting their passengers' faces and arms from the scorching sun.

Our driver turns the radio on and plays romantic boleros to placate his passengers' ire. Some protest ensues: not all the passengers like boleros; the ones in the back with the chickens and the pig are from the coast, and they want some *vallenato* music.

"Want *vallenatos*?" the driver asks, wiping the sweat off his face with a red rag stained with car oil. "Give your damn pig a damn ac-cordion. What? You think I don't know you have a pig there? What? You think I'm a *hijueputa* retard?"

They shout obscenities at each other, the passengers from the coast and the irate driver, but Mom is singing to the boleros on the radio and shielding my ears from the exchange. Through her fingers, I can hear the driver calling one passenger, *gonorrhea*. I chuckle at the sound of the word. I think it's funny that men use diseases to insult each other. Mom is right: men are dummies with a limited vocabulary.

Neither the static crackle of the radio nor the obscenities hurled back and forth in the air rattle her. She gets up, checks on my sisters, and sits down, singing to herself, "*Sin ti / no podré vivir jamás,* without you / I will never be able to live." She is unmovable. I look at her as she leans back on what's left of our headrest and think, Who is this woman? A jack of all trades, she'd say if anyone dared to ask her. She is a plumber, she repairs home appliances; she is a cook, a physician, a philosopher, a Samaritan, a ruthless dictator, a shrewd bargain hunter who eats very little, sleeps a few hours, and works all day long. Who is this woman singing boleros amid chaos, breathing with ease air so thick that not even street vendors venture inside our bus? What kind of woman is Mom? *Sin ti / es inútil vivir / como inútil será / el quererte olvidar.* . . . I fall asleep and dream of empty cages and birds of paradise perched on a tree branch hanging above Margarita's backyard.

Radios

Three years after the fight of the century, we gathered once more around our beloved tube radio, this time for "Rumble in the Jungle," a fight for the World Heavyweight Championship between Muhammad Ali and George Foreman, known to Mom as *Jorge* Foreman. Things had changed around our home. Father was gone; so was my brother. My three oldest sisters had dropped out of school and found jobs in Bogotá. For them, high school had to wait. The well-being of our family was in their hands.

"This is going to be good," Mom said wrapping the rosary around her fingers. "Ali'd better get off the ropes this time. He's what, thirty something? He can't compete with this kid Jorge."

Ali started the fight with a ferocious attack, and the audience went wild. We could hear the spectators in Zaire chant, *"Ali boma ye! Ali boma ye!"* an African mantra that put my two sisters, Mom, and me into a trance and seduced us with its foreign cadence. We didn't know what it meant and didn't care. We were high on Ali and chanted along with our invisible African friends: *"Ali boma ye! Ali boma ye!"*

Mom thumped the table with her palm. Grains of salt reverberated on the wood. She kept the pounding, on and on, until she fell into a steady five-beat rhythm; her pounding melted into the noises from Zaire, and soon my sisters and I started smacking our own palms against the table. *"Ali boma ye! Ali boma ye!"* and it felt like we were building something big, something important, a tribe of angry, thump-crazy, sweaty, women warriors.

All of a sudden, Ali went to the ropes and allowed Foreman to hit him. Mom cried, "No, no, Chucho, Chuchito, help him! God, get him off the ropes, please, Heavenly Father!"

But Ali had different plans. He spent round after round leaning on the ropes, staying loyal to his "rope-a-dope tactic," absorbing Foreman's punches, taunting him with "Is that all you got, George?" or "My grandma punches harder than you do," which made Mom snort.

Toward the end of the fight, Ali sprang from the ropes and delivered a sequence of flawless blows that sent Foreman to the canvas. The fight was over in round 8; Ali had reclaimed the WBA/WBC heavyweight titles. We jumped up from the table and hugged each other as if Ali's victory were our own.

When the fight was over, the commentator translated the spectators' feverish chant: *Ali boma ye!* meant "Ali, kill him!" Mom, being a God-fearing woman, started counting beads. She faced the radio as if directing her repentance towards Zaire and whispered an apology to Jorge Foreman for wishing him dead. "We don't speak African, Lord. Forgive my girls and this old sinner. We'll never chant anything we don't understand. And please, heal poor Jorge's eyes; Ali really did a number on that guy. Amén."

She switched the radio off and let her fingers linger over its burgundy surface as if saying good night. Then she moved it back against the wall and covered it with a white crocheted coaster. She looked at it before leaving the kitchen, again before switching the light off, and once more when she went back to rearrange the coaster so that it fell loosely over the grill. The radio looked like a deformed giant's face, with the speaker grille forming a high forehead, the knobs serving as eyes, and the bank of lower buttons resembling a toothy mouth. Those ivory teeth remained a mystery to all of us. Mom knew that one button was for something called short wave and another for long wave. The other buttons, whose function nobody knew, went unused and eventually became clotted with food debris and kitchen grease.

On either side of the radio was one big knob. The one on the right was the AM/FM tuner, while the left hand knob had two functions: its inner part controlled on/off switch and the volume, while the outer part moved a red cable inside a transparent cabinet for best reception. Finding a radio station required patience and determination, both of which Mom had in abundance. That radio was the center of her life, bringing her news from around Bogotá and from countries beyond Colombia. It was as if we children were holding her hostage in this dimly lit kitchen, and her only ties to the world beyond the confines of the stove were the waves of information crackling through the radio.

The year I turned eight, Mom introduced me to *Aquí Resolvemos su Caso*, "Here We Solve your Problems," a thirty-minute-long radio show dedicated to heartbroken and jaded women. Dejected writers sent letters to the host, whom they treated as advisor, friend, and confidant. In return, she offered her best advice and, as a token of respect for their privacy, addressed them by a descriptive nickname, sometimes a single word, sometimes a combination of words that best described the brokenhearted correspondent. Thus, if the advice seeker wrote about being pressured to have sex, the host's answer opened with "Dear Harassed." If the correspondent wondered whether she should forgive the man who had deserted her, the answer started with "Dear Abandoned." If the writer was in love but not ready for marriage, the host began with "Dear in Love but Hesitant."

At 4:30, right after school, Mom would tune into Radio Todelar. The show's host, a motherly-sounding woman, gave her female listeners a warm welcome: *"Bienvenida, amiga."* The letters were mainly from *mantecas*, maids, who were literate enough to write and mail a letter but marginalized enough to seek a stranger's opinion and believe in it. One, for instance, told of a husband who had walked out on her and their ten children. The landlord, a man with a great heart, had offered her to take care of the lot in exchange for her "company." She was broke and desperate. What should she do?

Mom sneered as she ironed our bed sheets. "A landlord with a great heart? Huh? And he would like her *company?* I know what *company* means. Even *I* know."

Another correspondent explained that the man of the house had been sneaking into the maid's quarters while the lady of the house slept. The maid was now pregnant, and her employers wanted nothing to do with her. Mom held the iron in the air and turned to face the radio. "Dear Pregnant," she said, imitating the host. "If you didn't want to end up with your belly full of bones, you should have kept your legs crossed. Next letter."

A young man threatened to leave his girlfriend unless she gave him *la prueba de amor, a* proof of her love. Mom rolled her eyes. "That's the oldest tale there is," she said, folding the bed sheet in half. "Dear *atembada,* let him go." Mom sprinkled the sheet with water and ran the hot iron over the fabric back and forth in a perfectly straight line. "Good riddance! *La prueba de amor? La prueba de amor?* Who falls for that one nowadays?" She shook her head and folded the bed sheet again and again until it looked as if she had just picked it up off a store shelf. "The only true love is a mother's love.

107

Everything else is a lie," she said, eyeing me across the dining table she was using as an ironing board.

She licked her index finger and tested the bottom of the iron. The dampness made a *pss, pss,* and a plume of steam rose. "Listen and learn, Adrianita," she said, solemnly looking at me, looking through me. "All men are the same. They have this one thing in mind and want only this thing from women." She wouldn't say what the thing was. But whenever she talked disdainfully about men, I thought about my father and wondered that he had done, what kind of pain he had inflicted on her to make her resent men she didn't even know, like these men mentioned in *Aquí Resolvemos Su Caso.*

I didn't miss my father. Yet sometimes I caught myself imagining that I had a father who was longing to be with me. Once in a while, walking home from school, I would pick a man in a suit coming toward me, his facial features blurred by distance and traffic, and I would ready myself to be recognized by him, to leap into the bear hug of a father who couldn't wait any longer to hold me in his arms.

My mother never stopped referring to my father as Mr. B.; and although she rarely mentioned his name after he walked out on us, occasionally she would impugn him for being wealthy, for living *una buena vida* while we lived in *la inopia,* for having nothing to do with us. His absence turned him into a highly malleable character. I could imagine him any way I wanted, any way I needed. I could give him attributes he didn't have and come up with good reasons for why he had abandoned a woman with six children, why he had never visited us, why he seemed to have forgotten we existed.

Our RCA Victor radio was Mom's life, everything that pulsated beyond the confines of our home. It brought to our day-to-day more than boxing scores and "Dear Jaded" letters. There were also the news, bullfights, soccer results, the schedule of the power cuts, soaps, and music, especially boleros. Mom said that through music, I could learn everything there was to know about love. Music could be sweet like a bolero or bitter like a tango. Because tangos were for men, Mom favored boleros. Their slow Cuban beat had made its way to kitchens and ballrooms everywhere in Latin America, where it fused with more local rhythms. Mom loved all of these variations: the bolero-son, the bolero cha-cha-chá, the bolero danzón, the bo-lero mambo. A bolero was, to my mother, a sort of stethoscope for hearing one's own heartbeat. It could be sung, hummed, and danced to. A lover could drink himself senseless listening to a bolero—even kill to one, if the bolero carried a rage swift and mindless enough.

When Mom listened to the Los Panchos trio on the radio, the air stood still and the pendulum of time stopped midsway. Her eyes became smaller, like a little girl's, and the veins on her neck swelled with emotion, bulging like contained dams. She knew the singers' names and nationalities: Alfredo Gil and Chucho Navarro were Mexi-cans, while Hernando Avilés was from Puerto Rico. She knew that Alfredo Gil had invented the *requinto* guitar, which was smaller and tuned to a higher pitch than a standard guitar was and gave their boleros a distinct sound. Rivaling the Los Panchos trio was the San Juan trio. Mom loved them both; yet when Johnny Albino left the San Juan trio to join Los Panchos, she was delighted. Together, Johnny Albino and Chucho Navarro were magic to Mom's ears.

When one of my sisters brought home the Beatles' rendition of *"Bésame Mucho,"* Mom was indignant. She didn't appreciate a group of stinky-looking *mechudos* singing her stuff in English. But one day, as Mom was scanning the radio stations, she stopped at the sound of *"Solamente Una Vez,"* only to realize that it was an English version of her bolero; it was Bing Crosby singing "You Belong to My Heart." She shook her head but didn't change the radio station, which was playing a show about the impact and popularity of the bolero outside Latin America. When the host played "*Somos Novios*," a sweet bolero by Armando Manzanero, interpreted by Perry Como under the name "It's Impossible," Mom pursed her lips and clicked her lips but left the radio on.

Doris Day came on with "Perhaps, Perhaps, Perhaps." "Is that how you say '*Quizás, Quizás, Quizás*'?" Mom asked no one in particular. "That's it. Those gringos managed to ruin what was already perfect."

Then Connie Francis sang "*La Paloma*" in Spanish. "She's all right," Mom nodded. "Not bad for a *gringa*." The corners of her dark lips turned down, her lower jaw protruded, and her eyebrows rose in approval.

Next came Nat King Cole singing "*Tres Palabras*" in the most atrocious Spanish Mom had ever heard. "No, no, no," she said, shaking her hand in the air. "*Aquí es donde la puerca tuerce el rabo*, this is where the pig wags its tail." Boleros in English were one thing, but boleros in botched Spanish she would not listen to. "Do you know who the hell this guy is?" she asked, glaring at the radio. We were alone in the room, so I assumed she was asking me.

"No, ma'am," I said.

"Of course you don't. You're a kid," she said, pinching my cheeks playfully with one hand while she looked for a different radio station with the other. It was 6:30 on a Friday evening, time for the program *Boleros en Su Ruta*. Hugo Romani opened the show with Mom's favorite bolero, "*Verdad Amarga*," or "Bitter Truth," one of those songs that made Mom morph into a woman. She sang the two first verses in duet with him. The verses spoke of a heartbroken lover faced with a bitter truth: the lovers can't be together. It's their fate.

110

Her voice came out like a lament, as if that specific bolero told the exact story of her life. Her hands opened from her chest in semicircular offerings as if she were delivering a speech. In the kitchen's dim yellow light, her face softened and deep sadness hovered around the yellowish sixty-watt bulb illuminating the kitchen. She listened to Romani with a passion that I, her child, hadn't known she could store in her heart. To me, she wasn't a woman; she was a mother, a very different thing. A mother was self-sufficient, tireless, requiring very little to stay alive. A woman, on the other hand, had needs, secret needs. I knew this from listening to radio soap operas. A woman's heart was a labyrinth, a complicated maze surrounded by mine fields that no man could walk in or out of without setting off.

By the third verse of the bolero, Mom's face had contorted, as if Romani were tugging at strings beneath her skin. Her voice quivered as she sang in an angry undertone. Then came the fourth verse and Mom's surrender. She delivered the words in a broken whisper while Romani, in the background, carried on with the song. *"Tal vez mañana puedas comprender / Que siempre fui sincera / Tal vez por alguien llegues a saber / Que todavía te quiero.* Maybe later you might understand / That I was always sincere / Perhaps someone will help you see / That I still love you."

By the time the guitars had quieted and the host had taken his audience to commercials, Mom looked old and spent. Her short grey hair took on a wild air; her lips were pressed together tightly to hold back tears; her frown was deeper. Her pain, mysterious and intricate, had somehow also become my pain, the ache of a loveless marriage burdened by a heavy chain of children. By the end the show, I had promised myself that I would never leave her side, never get married, never go anywhere without her. I would always be around to kiss her tears away. I was there now, a tiny, pony-tailed woman in the making.

111

Meanwhile, as Mom sighed over her boleros and while she jeered and sneered at the brokenhearted women of *Aqui Resolvemos Su Caso,* I kept imagining the ever-growing number of people who lived inside the radio. Muhammad Ali, Jorge Foreman, José Frazier, the singers, the bullfight narrators and *toreros,* those scorned women, even the woman with the monotonous voice on Radio Sutatenza, a PBS station—all of them crammed into a twenty-inch-long tube radio. I made it my mission to look after them.

Sitting behind the radio, I peeked through the holes in the back panel. I saw lights and tubes but not people. Yet they must be there, I thought, and they must be hungry. So when Mom was busy in her bedroom, I pushed a few grains of cooked rice through the holes. I didn't understand how sweet Mom, good-hearted Mom, Catholic Mom could spend all day listening to these people without sparing them something to eat. Eventually, whenever she wasn't looking, I sneaked food into the radio. Stale bread, mashed potatoes, dry beans: anything was better than no food at all.

Then it occurred to me that, with all the talking these radio people did, they must be thirsty. So I squirted some water through the front grille and the back holes. I heard something fizzle, once, twice, and from then on things started to go wrong. First, in the middle of *La Ley Contra el Hampa,* a soap about cops and bad guys, the radio overheated. Mom was worried. What could possibly go wrong with an RCA Victor? They were supposed to last a lifetime. She stared at it long and hard. "Don't you die on me," she said, rather begged, and I understood the solemnity of the moment. She caressed the case and shook it lightly. She cleaned the grille with an old brush and a toothpick, erased all traces of dust between its teeth. Still, the radio crackled, threatening to sever her only connection with the outside world.

While Mom did everything she could to keep the radio alive,

I did everything possible to keep the radio people well fed. It was the least I could do to help Mom at this difficult moment, when the radio threatened to leave her with nothing but silence and the buzz of flies. But then the radio started to lose its voice. I worried that the people inside it were also dying and frantically doubled my food rations. Mom tried cooling the radio with a paper fan printed with Spanish ballerinas, but her treatment didn't work. Her face became longer and graver. "What am I going to do without my radio, huh? No music? No news? No nothing?" She stared at it, untied her apron, and threw it on top of the case. "That's all I need," she said and stormed out of the kitchen. Her face was tense and her lips quivered. Her world was about to go mute.

One morning the tuning dial got stuck. The red needle wouldn't move, the static was louder than ever, and a faint coil of smoke rose above the Bakelite buttons. The radio spurted and shook in little convulsions, the voices drowned by a noisy whir. Mom began to sob. "No, not my radio," she cried. "Not my RCA Victor." She disappeared from the kitchen only to reemerge, undeterred and defiant, with a screwdriver in her hand. She picked up the radio and carried it to the patio to examine it under natural light. I followed her.

Not until she had removed the four screws fastening the cardboard back panel to the frame of the radio did I realize that nobody had eaten my food. Mold covered the inside of the panel, and I felt my hands dampen and chill. The fungal cardboard fell onto Mom's lap, followed by green, hairy-looking balls of rice, velvety bread crumbs, wispy maize beans, and a cluster of flies. Only then did it dawn on me that I might have killed Mom's radio with my feeding frenzy.

"Any idea who did this?" she asked. Her face was red, and the vein on her right temple throbbed furiously.

Any attempt at lying would have been futile. Mom could see

right through every living creature. Nobody could fool her. She could smell a lie before our brains could concoct one. I dropped my gaze and stared at the patio floor. My eyes swelled with tears. I braced myself for a slap. I had never seen Mom hit any of us, but I was certain this would be the first time.

She rasped, "What were you thinking? Huh? *Malcriada.*" She shot a hateful look at me, then at the rotten banquet spread over the belly of her beloved radio. "What were you thinking?" she repeated, louder this time. "Huh? Huh?" Her hands gyrated in the air as if she were screwing in light bulbs.

Then, suddenly, she did something with her mouth. I will never know whether she was about to shout or laugh, but I still remember the frozen *O* of her dark lips, followed by a prolonged sigh that made her shoulders slump. She looked at me, at the sky, back at me, at the radio, at the piles of rotten food, back at me, and I knew now that she wouldn't hit me. My fear subsided, and it was entirely replaced by shame.

"Nobody lives here," she said tapping the top of the radio with the screwdriver. "Don't ask me how this radio thing works, but *no one* lives here, see?" Mom said *nobody* and *no one* many times as she cleaned up the mess I had made.

The radio never worked again.

Mom's new best friend was a small portable transistor radio, which she used to lock in the closet when she wasn't using it. She had a special place for it, next to her wallet, underneath her cotton underwear, a dark, dry hiding place that no termites could reach. It came out of the closet only at night, when it became Mom's bedside companion. The radio was a black rectangle with a worn-out dial, chipped paint on the speaker, and a narrow plastic window too scratched to reveal the station numbers. She came to know her transistor well, like a woman knows her husband—his whims, his strengths and weaknesses, and how to get the most out of him.

Every Wednesday at 9:30 P.M., she would turn off her bedroom lights and invite me to join her in bed so that we could be frightened together. My next-youngest sister was fourteen going on fifteen, too old to cuddle under the sheets with Mom. But me? I was only eight going on nine, still lovable, still smitten with Mom, still her most loyal follower. Because I was still easy to be around, she was easy on me. So I gladly jumped into bed with her and waited for whatever Mom, the radio, and the night might deliver.

"Almost time," she said, and the blood began to thump in my ears. She opened the closet, dug out the radio, and cleaned it with a cloth. Then, with a steady hand, she turned the dial, searching for *El Código del Terror,* a Colombian-style version of "Tales from the Crypt."

As she turned the dial, we heard scraps of music, news, static, commercials, more static. Mom closed her eyes, willing the station to come forward. The frown between her eyebrows looked like the letter *H*. Eventually she would pull out the antenna and begin pointing it here, there, and everywhere until finally we could hear macabre laughter. This cackle from the crypt announced the beginning of the program. Gently, so as not to disturb the voice, she carried the transistor into bed, tucking it between our heads with the antenna pointing toward the window, where the reception was best. I could hear heartbeats, some mine, some Mom's. We clasped hands, hers calloused, mine small. I felt her hot breath on my neck and breathed in her scent, a fusion of soap and onions.

Our favorite horror story was about good men trapped in salamanders' bodies and bad men whose rotten deeds were punished with an invasion of these salamanders. One night we heard the story of a trapped salamander-man who had fallen into the hands of a curious young boy. He dismembered the salamander-man little by little: first the tail, then the limbs. Then he performed a vicious dissection in order to see the salamander's heart. He didn't know he was dismembering a human being. The trapped man screamed in pain: "No-o-o-o!" But the boy, pure at heart, could not hear his cry. The shriek pierced our ears, and Mom and I screamed along with the trapped man: first, "No-o-o-o!" and then "*Ay dios mío!*" Mom's hands squeezed my shoulders while my fists beat on the mattress in panic. We wriggled under the sheets, toenails tearing on something, panting, mouths half-open, eyes shut, her legs wrapped around mine, my head buried somewhere in her armpit.

"Are you scared?" she asked.

"Yes, ma'am. You?"

"Of course not."

The salamander story must have been a hit with the audience because we listened to several variations of the original tale. There was one about an evil lawyer who cheated a widow of the mansion she had inherited from her deceased husband. The swindler moved onto the widow's property, thinking that he was set for life. Unfortunately, a horde of salamander-men also moved in. Repulsed, the evil man set out to exterminate them; but every time he tried to kill one, he heard the man inside the salamander pleading for his life. Naturally, he lost his mind, and the salamanders ate him alive.

"That's what you get for taking advantage of women," Mom said from beneath the sheets.

The horror of these stories was real; we felt its furry hand on our napes, heard its bloodcurdling shrieks. There was nothing outside as frightening as this radio program. The terrors of Bogotá at night were nothing compared to what we experienced under the sheets. Outside, people were being robbed, women violated, children abused, pedestrians mugged. Even if there had been a civil war brewing around the corner, nothing could have scared us as much as *El Código del Terror*.

The transistor's successor was a wall-to-wall turntable-radio console complete with two waist-high detached speakers. This handcrafted monster was made of solid wood and veneers and included an AM/FM radio with knobs the size of my hands. The three-speed turntable discreetly hidden under the hinged lid added to our house a dose of sophistication that Mom had never before experienced. Soon the bottom half of the *radiola* was filled with 33-rpm long-play vinyl records; bone, shellac, and Bakelite 78s; and a formidable collection of stackable 45s. Mom never looked back.

In years to come, she would play LPs of instrumental music by renowned orchestra directors such as Frank Purcell, Raymond LeFevre, and Paul Mauriat. Someone introduced us to Richard Clayderman, a French pianist, who made Mom sigh melodramatically whenever she caught sight of his photo on the album cover: deep blue eyes, thin blond hair, a set of wonderful teeth, perfect dimples. Even after we'd played it twenty times, his *Ballade pour Adeline* felt like a divine gift delivered to our Victrola by God himself.

PART III

Opal and Topaz #3

I stroke Mom's face on the glossy photograph, brushing a finger over her perfectly shaped nose. An urge to look at myself in a mirror seizes me. I have my father's nose and my mother's lips. I inherited my father's wavy hair and curly eyelashes, yet in the mirror I see Mom's wounded eyes and grave expression. I ask her photograph, "Did you feel loved, Mom? Did you love my father? Did you really think you could be happy?"

"Yes, yes, and yes!" she screams from the picture. I feel her spirit rising and falling above the frame. I touch her, not with my hands but with my heart, fractured by her departure. We lock gazes, and I hear her voice. She speaks to me from the photograph; she tells me the story once more.

Her husband had a tough man's job. Carmen liked this. A man with calloused hands and smelly feet, rings of dry sweat in the underarms of his shirts, an aching back and torn fingernails was also a man who would appreciate a loving woman at the end of the day. He operated a Caterpillar bulldozer, building roads, wrestling with muck, man and machine flattening the earth. He came home with muddy boots and caked overalls, which she washed by hand, scrubbing and pounding the heavy fabric against the concrete trough until her knuckles bled. Then she ironed his clothes, now smelling of soap, folded them, placed them neatly, lovingly, in the drawers of their secondhand armoire.

He never said thank you. He was a busy man with no time for pleasantries. She understood this. God had made men inexpressive, her own mother had taught her that. It was her job to make sure that everything she did for her husband was an act of love, a leap of faith. Every word she spoke was molded to fit neatly into his life; every smile was timed, every sign of passion welcomed. And when he spoke, she listened because he seemed to know everything. For instance, it was he who taught her that it was the woman who decided the sex of the children.

"The man plants the seed," he said, grabbing his crotch in a way that made her feel uncomfortable, "but the woman decides what to make of it."

"I didn't know that," she said.

Drizzle was beginning to fall on Armenia. The moist air hung above their neighborhood, impregnating the streets with whiffs of coffee as the *cafetales* themselves drowned in their own verdure. Everything was ripe, everything hungry, everything ready.

Eleven months and seven days after their wedding day, Carmen gave birth to a baby boy in the bed where he had been conceived. Twelve months and twenty days after the birth of the boy, she delivered a baby girl with playful dimples under each eye and a nose so perfect that Mr. B. said it looked as if God had chiseled it himself.

There was tenderness when Mr. B. lifted the children. She had seen it. He no longer was the chevalier that she had met in Mariq-

122

uita, this was true, but there was something in him unhealed, a bitter wound masked with machismo that she wanted to expose and mend so that his gallant self could resurface.

"I'm so happy," she told Mr. B. one night as she watched the babies sleep side by side. She expected him to agree, but he didn't say a word. He was looking out the window, scratching his head as he did when he was worried—a quick gallop of his fingers across the scalp. He rolled a cigarette, lit it; his hard face disappeared behind a cloud of smoke. He blew into a cup of black coffee, and the chipped cup billowed steam back at him. Was he looking at the communal yard with its balding grass, plastic nativity sets, and bicycles left to rust in the rain? She couldn't tell. "Aren't you happy?" she asked.

"Happiness is a state of mind," he said. "It's transitory, like being horny."

She wondered what to say next. "This house is nice," she ventured. "Just perfect for the four of us, don't you think?"

"I'll tell you what I think," he said, flicking ashes onto the floor. She moved the ashtray onto the windowsill, closer to him. He didn't touch it. "You need to stop having babies. That's what I think. Four mouths are all I can feed." He stood up, belched, flicked ashes into the air, and wiped the tips of his fingers on the freshly washed curtain. "Let alone more hinges."

"Hinges?" she asked.

"Yes, hinges. Girls, women, they all open and close like this." Mr. B. set his wrists together, then clapped his hands open and closed.

She tried to smile at the obscene comment. "You shouldn't talk like that. You have a little girl now," she said, shaking her head and glancing toward the children.

"I say whatever the hell I want, *carajo!*"

The next morning she fixed breakfast, washed the dishes, and made her rounds into each room, erasing whatever evidence Mr. B. had left behind—cigarette butts and mounds of ashes, dirty socks, muddy boots, cups of unfinished black coffee, an empty bottle of liquor. She was washing diapers when he came into the room to announce that they were leaving Armenia. She paused, sighed, and replied, "Whatever you say." She pretended to be happy.

They were going to where the money was, a small town called Fresno in the state of Tolima. Hundreds of years ago it had been a prosperous Spanish colony with gold mines, access to snow-covered Herveo Peak, and a road that headed straight toward Mariquita. "The gold is gone, and so is the access to the peak, but Mariquita is around the corner, a bus ride away."

She liked the idea of being closer to Mariquita and the fact that Fresno was dwarfed by the thunderous Medina cataracts. She loved being near the water; her mind was constantly wandering its shores, drifting downriver to her beloved Mariquita, her mother's kitchen, the mango trees in their vast backyard, the naughty jokes shared with a sister now married, no longer a little girl.

It was said that Fresno grew avocados year round, that branches of the laden trees snapped under the weight of the fruit, which dropped on the ground but never rotted. She had heard that the upper-class women of Fresno made avocado masks to soften their skin and that their shiny hair owed its luster to a concoction of avocado and olive oil. She wouldn't do either herself. It was a sin to use God's fruits to pretty oneself. Yet it was also said that avocados, whether eaten or rubbed on during pregnancy, would guarantee the delivery of a baby boy. So when, for the third time, she felt life knocking on the walls of her womb, she used avocados to sway God's will. Violation of Mr. B.'s "no more children" edict would only be forgiven if the baby were a boy.

Avocado belly rub: smash avocado with onions and tomatoes.

124

Garnish food with ground avocado peel. Beneath the belly button, arrange a long avocado and two seeds, one on each side, to symbolize the genitals of the desired sex.

Carmen did all she could to appease Mr. B's wrath, which he didn't express through blows but through long periods of apathetic silence (on a good day) or disdain (on a bad day). She got into the habit of pinching her arms when he was around, a way of convincing herself that she still existed. That she had not become what remains after the coals stop burning. Ashes.

But not even the avocados kept her from bringing another baby girl into this world.

"Another hinge?" Mr. B. asked when the midwife presented him with a little baby bundled in white cotton. He paced up and down the corridor outside their tiny apartment as if deciding what to do next. He chain-smoked, extinguishing each cigarette with the tip of his shoe and kicking the butt sideways with his heel. He cursed. He turned the radio on, then off. Then he put his fist through a wall. Carmen heard the thud and immediately, without thinking, pushed her nipple into the baby's mouth. She needed to feel needed.

Fresno had turned out to be a mirage, an unfulfilled promise. There were no jobs for Mr. B., no future, nothing for him to do there. He decided to leave town, and leave along with it his wife, the boy, and the two hinges. He would go to a larger, faraway city to look for a job. And if, in the process, a woman or two, or more, fell under his spell, so be it.

A few minutes later, his suitcase was packed. He dropped a few crumpled pesos onto the wobbly table next to the blue couch and slammed the door shut behind him. And as soon as he left, as if nature alone was teaching Carmen a lesson, a surge of angry afterpains came over her. She knew, from that day forward, she'd have to fend for herself—that he had returned to his nomadic nature, become as transient as autumn clouds, that he'd come back home to her only if he were wounded or his clothes were dirty.

Something within her hardened. She plucked her breast out of the baby's mouth. Her milk curdled. She tightened her lips and clenched her fists, took a deep breath, held it, closed her eyes as if steadying her mind, and when she felt ready she let out a noisy sigh. "Good riddance," she said. *"Lo que no sirve que no estorbe."*

But a couple of years later, Mr. B. moved his family to Bogotá, the country's capital, where it never stopped raining and everybody wore black as if their lives were a perpetual wake. Bogotá was a noisy cement jungle with no rivers and no trees. Mr. B. told Carmen that Bogotá was the third-highest capital city in the world, a fact that was supposed to make her feel as if he had taken her somewhere special. But perched at 8,700 feet above sea level, she had trouble breathing. She was oppressed by the city's constant rain, its tense and crowded streets crammed with people rushing to jobs and appointments. Everyone moved with such urgency that she wondered if she was the only woman in Bogotá with nowhere to go. The days were long and lonely in this city bursting with cars, buildings, things. Terrified, she passed hour upon hour locked inside her room, the door fastened with two security chains and a spring-bolt.

Rain fell in horizontal sheets of cold. Carmen had bundled up the kids as best she could and, one by one, laid them together in the family's only bed. Earlier that week Mr. B had sent her a telegram that read, "Arriving Tuesday evening. Have food ready." Today was Tuesday, and already she'd been waiting for him for hours.

For Carmen, cleaning was an act of love. So she had made the house as cozy as possible, tried to turn it into a place he would want to come back to. She had scrubbed, swept, and waxed the wooden floor, and the pristine kitchen smelled of Ajax. She had sprayed the window with vinegar and rubbed it clean with crumpled newspaper. Now she could clearly see the landfill outside their building and the dozens of vultures that circled it. She looked at the clock again, put on some lipstick, and sat by the window. He was coming back from one of his business ventures, as he liked to call what she already knew were escapades. She understood that a man needs time away from home, away from the domesticity of family life, from the noise of his children's laughter and cries.

When Mr. B. arrived, he tried to kick the door open, his new way of knocking. He was tipsy and playful. She opened the door and moved out of his way.

"How's my *Virgen del Carmen* doing?" he said and bowed as he burst in. He'd brought along her favorite food, *lechona*, but the stuffed roasted pork was not fresh. It was more like a package of leftovers bound in waxed paper that had been already unwrapped and wrapped again too many times. "Like the smell?" He held the package, still warm, under her nose.

"Yes, yes," she said. Even though it wasn't freshly cooked, the *lechona* smelled of Mariquita. Yes, she loved the smell and, yes, she'd love to eat some, even though it was 3 A.M. and in truth she'd rather be asleep after a day of running after the kids, cleaning, and cooking. But Mr. B was very playful that night. He held the package up high where she couldn't reach it and forced her to jump for it with open hands that clasped one inch too low. He moved the package higher. Grains of warm rice spilled through one greasy corner.

"Well, want some or not?" he taunted.

In the broken mirror hanging by the door, she caught a glimpse of herself, as she must have looked to him: a haggard woman jumping up into the air like a dog trying to catch a treat. She was still in her twenties, but she had the hard look of the neglected housewife. She had lost her innocence and had filled its void with bitterness.

Where once was transparency now thick bile flowed. Her face reddened and a wave of heat rose up all the way to her nape. Angry tears began streaming down her face, and her lips quivered in exactly the way he hated.

"To eat or to cry, that's the question." He laughed so hard that he started to cough.

"Please stop," she said, folding her arms across her chest. "I'm too tired for this."

"This," he said wagging his index finger in her face, "is the last time I bring you something nice." And with that, he let the package fall onto the shiny wooden floor. Pulled pork, green beans, and grains of rice splattered all over the manicured surface. Sinking to her knees, Carmen hurried to clean up the mess. But Mr. B. wasn't done; he still wanted to play.

"Let's dance," he commanded.

"Not now," she murmured. "You'll wake up the kids." And as she spoke, she felt a cleaving in her heart. Something split wide open at the seams and she had to remind herself that, if a man wants to dance with his wife and his wife refuses, he'll find himself a dancing partner around the corner. So she tried to mend what was broken and scooped two handfuls of *lechona* under the table to make room. They were going to dance.

Mr. B. found a radio station that played tangos all night long, cranking up the volume as soon as he heard Carlos Gardel's voice. He bowed mockingly. Carmen tried to smile but instead her face pulled downwards at the corners of her mouth. They began to dance. He glided, as always, but her legs felt heavy like lead. He was beyond tipsy, she noticed, now that her face was pressed close to his chest. She also took notice of the smell. His body exuded a mixture of cheap patchouli, *aguardiente,* and nicotine. She caught sight of their reflection in the mirror. He hadn't changed, she thought; only she had aged, only she looked worn out, only she had gained in clumsiness what she had lost in grace.

A chunk of pulled pork stuck to her shoe, but she kept dancing, determined to follow his quick back kicks and fancy steps. They danced a few more tangos. He hummed to all of them with eyes closed. He might as well have been dancing by himself. She was not his partner; she was an instrument he was using to sharpen his tango skills. She, too, closed her eyes, leaning her face gently on his shirt stained with grease, lipstick that wasn't hers, and liquor. For a few minutes she pretended to be happy, to be loved. For a few minutes, she felt alive.

The next day, he was gone again. Eight months, three weeks, and two days later, she gave birth to their fourth child, another hinge. Three years later a fifth child was born—also a hinge. Six years later, at age thirty-four, she gave birth to me—yet another hinge, her afterthought, her sixth and last child. Then Mr. B. left for good. There was money to be made; there were treasures to be found; there were women to be seduced. A wife, a son, and five hinges were nothing but a hindrance. The world was waiting for him, and he threw himself into its arms, carelessly, unflinchingly. Alone.

Requiem Mass

This is Mom's requiem mass. The tenor bell has sung its deepest notes, and Mom's coffin has been placed before the altar, her feet toward the priest as Catholic funeral rituals dictate that a layperson should be positioned before God. I stand in the second row. The first is empty. Maybe nobody wants to sit so close to a dead woman. A choir sings an entrance antiphon as the priest steps behind the pulpit. "In the name of the Father, and of the Son, and of the Holy Spirit."

I make the sign of the cross and reply, "Amen."

"We gather today to pray for our beloved departed—" The priest pauses, hurriedly flips two or three pages of his Bible and reads out my mother's name, which someone has scribbled on a piece of paper. His fill-in-the-blank tactic enrages me. I think back to the legendary boxing match between Muhammad Ali and Ernie Terrell, when Ali mortified his contender by asking him over and over, "What's my name? What's my name, Uncle Tom?" I know this is a shallow thought. I know I shouldn't be thinking it, but I am. I want to lean into the priest's face and do my best Ali impersonation— What's my mother's name, Padre? What's my mother's name?—until he screams it and asks for forgiveness.

This priest, who had never met my mother in person, sprinkles holy water over her coffin. He tells us that she was a great woman. I think, How do you know, Padre? Do you have a cheat sheet that lists her virtues? He calls her an exemplary mother much loved by her children and husband. What? I say to myself. Much loved by her husband? Who told you that? I'm enraged at him for invoking my father when all we should be thinking about is Mom.

An animal exuberance comes over me. I take in preemptive, hungry, greedy lungsful of air, and tell myself, I won't die asphyxiated like Mom. I won't die from respiratory arrest. I focus on my breathing: in, hold, out. I hear my heart drumming, my blood rushing. I'm wholly alert; nothing seems to elude this fantastic radar I feel buzzing under my skin. I am aware of everything: music, sobs, shuffling feet, the knot in a scarf, a handkerchief crumpled inside a pocket, each person's memories and sins. Grief gives me magical powers.

The choir sings a celestial Kyrie, then a Gloria. The congregation joins in. I can feel, almost see, all of our voices resonating inside my rib cage. My brother's baritone slides into bass; my sister's alto descends into contralto. Where do they find the lucidity to sing at a moment like this?

My brother wraps his dark, strong arm around my shoulders. My brother, a man I barely know, whom I have seen only a few times in the past thirty-five years, embraces me. I feel his warmth on the back of my neck. I begin to cry. Maybe it's the pain of standing alive a few feet away from my mother's dead body, or the shame of having a beating heart, or the outpour of love I feel in my brother's touch. But right at this moment it's not my mother I'm crying over. It's this: I have a brother, I tell myself. I have a brother. A brother. My brother. *Mi hermano.* I want the part of my body that he is embracing to fuse into his being. I want to bury my face in his shoulder and experience him in all his immensity. I want my skin to melt, to turn into liquid wax, and slither through his orphan pores all the way to his orphan essence. I have a brother. I'm safe. This void without Mom is bearable now.

I turn to rest my head on his chest. As always, he's buttoned his shirt all the way up. The collar looks too snug around his neck. My impulse is to undo the top button with a motherly "There! That's better." One of my sisters squeezes my left hand. I don't mean to, but I examine every inch of my sister like a piece of art. Brand-name matching shoes and bag, a tailored black suit, manicured hands, perfect makeup, every strand of hair in an appointed spot. How did Mom and Dad create children who grew up to be so different? I return the squeeze. My hand is a lot darker than her porcelain one. I'm the darkest girl in the family. If you were to see our two hands clasped, you wouldn't know we were sisters.

I hear the priest: "The Lord be with you."

My sister replies, "And also with you." Her voice sounds like Mom's. Mine doesn't. I stifle my sobs. I want to hear that voice once more, so I close my eyes and let Mom talk to me, for the last time, through my sister.

"Lift up your hearts."

Mom says, "We lift them up to the Lord."

"Let us give thanks to the Lord, our God."

Mom responds, "It is right to give him thanks and praise."

We kneel for the transubstantiation. The priest asks the Holy Spirit to convert the bread and wine into the body and blood of Christ. The congregation implores the Holy Spirit alongside him. An adolescent irreverence rises within me. Imagine if the Holy Spirit actually did turn the wine into blood and the host into flesh. For a few seconds visions of the priest spitting blood and vomiting chunks of projectile meat take me hostage.

Next comes the rite of peace. "The peace of the Lord be with you always," the priest says and invites us to offer each other the sign of peace. All of Mom's children are sharing the same pew: two of my sisters sit next to my brother on my left; the other two sit on my right. Yet we manage to huddle in a cramped circle like wounded animals, sharing tears and smiles of resignation and love.

"We are still a family," someone says. I think it's my brother. We may be orphans; but by way of that family hug, we father each other. I have adopted my brother and my oldest sister, and I know that they also are adopting me in their hearts. We have made a silent promise.

After the mass, my sisters and friends exchange words of comfort. Everybody agrees that Mom is in a better place, in heaven, right next to God, surrounded by angels and cherubs. Their unwavering certainty—surely born from the blind faith I no longer feel—makes me envious and not having a celestial Father makes me feel doubly orphaned. I want to believe in afterlife, resurrection, miracles, heaven. Blind faith is something I could use at a moment like this. Yet when my sister Amanda tells me that Mom is watching over us, all I can say is "How do you know?"

"How do I know what?" Amanda asks, her nose red from crying.

"That Mom is watching over us."

There is pity in her eyes as she scrutinizes me in silence. Then, instead of answering, she says, "Close your eyes and pray to her in times of need. She'll guide you. I promise. She'll protect you and your daughter."

"How about my husband? Can he also pray to Mom?"

"Of course, you silly girl."

"In English? How will she know how to help him if she doesn't understand his language?"

My sister cradles the back of my head in her hand. I feel her warmth on my skull. She smells of expensive perfume. I don't know if she holds me because she wants to protect me or because she wants to shut me up. Perhaps deep inside herself she, too, questions the miracle of prayer. Still, she insists, "If you're sick, if you're lonely, if you don't know which way to go, Mom is there for you, watching you day and night."

Somehow the idea of Mom watching me day and night doesn't appeal to me. I don't want her around when I curse, when I cheat, when I'm not a good mother, when I'm lazy or drunk. I don't want her to watch over me when I meet my husband's body under the sheets or against the walls of our house, when he takes me over the kitchen counter, when we play forbidden games in space and time that belong to us alone.

"What if I'm sick?" I whisper into my sister's silk blouse, now stained with tears.

"She'll heal you. I promise," Amanda whispers back.

I'm crying. Now I desperately want to believe. I challenge God to reveal himself to me. This is a good time, Mr. God, I think. Burn something, hit me with a lightning strike, bring Mom back to life. Do something. But he, she, does nothing.

I stand alive and godless, listening to my sister and finding her words interesting. Not soothing. Does Mom speak English in this new realm? How about French? Does Mom understand me if I curse in French? Is everyone a polyglot in heaven? My sister says that if I'm sick, Mom will heal me. Does this mean that in the forty-eight hours since her death, Mom has gained the knowledge of a surgeon? Does she have a specialty? Is she a better neurologist than she is a gastroenterologist? Can she operate on more than one body at a time?

"When our day comes," my sister whispers in my ear, her eyelashes fluttering on my forehead, "we'll be reunited with her. All of us will meet again in heaven."

All of us? Does this mean that Mom has been reunited with

Dad? That he is already smoking and drinking in that pristine haven where Mom keeps us under her celestial thumb? Are they up there with all the other women that he seduced with his short-lived promises, those women whom Mom despised in life: the swingers, the ladies of the night, the red-headed whore from Mariquita? Even Mrs. Ruth, the *arpía* next door, who, Mom swore, seduced Dad more than a few times? All of us will meet in heaven? What about the *godos* who killed Grandpa's friends during *La Violencia?* Does my sister understand the gravity of *all of us?*

"Do you really believe that?" I ask.

She pushes me away from her chest, rubs my shoulders as if they are cold, tucks a strand of my disheveled braid behind one ear, and holds my chin in her free hand. "With all my heart," she says. "Don't you? A little bit?"

"No."

"So what do you believe?"

My heart screams: I believe Mom is dead, and I'll never, ever see her, feel her, hear her again. I believe that's it. No spirit, no ghost, nothing. I believe that you are turning Mom into God by giving her all of these supernatural powers. I believe that Catholics call this heresy and therefore you are a heretic. I believe that Mom doesn't understand more English now than she did when she was alive, that she still doesn't know how to take anyone's pulse let alone heal the sick. I believe that all these fantastic faculties make the dead much more useful than the living. I believe that you're lucky for believing as you do and that I'm a damn fool for not. Or vice versa. I believe you look gorgeous when you kneel to pray with your eyes shut and your face relaxed into a communion with something mysterious that eludes me. I believe that yesterday, when your hair came unpinned in the breeze, a strand got caught in a prism of light and you made me think of peacocks and cardinals.

135

But I don't say a word. I shrug my shoulders, and she pulls my head back to her chest. Her hands rub my back, up and down, up and down, as if soothing my lack of faith, placating my demons, knocking on the doors of my godless world.

La Petite Mort at Thirteen

A girl doesn't become a woman overnight. It happens in hiccups of self-awareness, like coming in and out of consciousness. One minute she is playing tea with imaginary friends; the next she has rivulets of blood flowing down her inner thighs. Or she passes out right before her menarche and comes to in the middle of a lingerie department as she tries to discern the difference between a trainer bra and a 32A. Then she falls comatose again only to be awakened by gentle, dexterous fingers exploring her folds and pleats—so accommodating, so moist, so knowing.

Mom takes the lead down Junín Street. Her pace is fast; her fists pump up and down as she races toward the doctor's office at the end of the pedestrian walkway. We rush past the Coltejer building that is supposed to be shaped like a needle, thus symbolizing, somehow, the prosperity of the local textile industry. But it doesn't look at all like a needle. We pass La Coiffeur de Paris, where lucky girls have their hair styled any way they please, pass the *chance* stand where my sister Dalila plays the same stupid numbers every

Friday but never wins anything, pass the Astoria Bakery. This makes me cranky because it smells of fresh pastries: *pandebonos,* steamy *buñuelos,* and out-of-the-oven *roscones.* I'm starving.

I follow Mom, catching glimpses of my skinny body in the store windows that crowd the walkway. I see that I walk exactly as Mom says I do: with a hunched back, shoulders slightly bent forward, chest caved in, chin down. My tiny indecisive steps make me look like I'm walking on broken glass. The air is heavy and its humidity is styling my unruly hair in all the wrong fashions. Soon the heavens over Medellín will crack open, and Mom will blame my sins for the bad weather.

"You must have done something terrible to infuriate God like that."

"Who? Me? What have I done?"

"We'll see."

I walk awkwardly because I feel awkward—not like my friend Maribel, who seems to have an unlimited amount of talents, and walks like she owns the world. She has fair skin, and a blond mane that she can style à la Olivia Newton John or à la Farrah Fawcett, depending on her mood. If she could sing, she could even pass for ABBA's Agnetha Fältskog and you wouldn't notice anything the next time you saw ABBA in concert. That's how gorgeous she is. The other day she drew a picture of both of us. She drew herself the way she is: curvy, sensuous, cool. She is holding hands with me, the way she sees me: a dark stick figure with long, frizzy hair à la Chaka Khan. Uncool. I can't help it.

Lately, I've been feeling like I have been deployed into the wrong body, like this shapeless frame of mine is not a good fit for all of my as-yet untapped coolness. I'm thirteen but I'm as hairless and flat as I was a few years ago. My breasts are mortifyingly small, like pebbles pushing their way out of my chest. To make things worse, Mom has taken to calling them not lemons, but *limoncitos,* little lemons.

"Your *limoncitos* are perfect the way they are," she says. "You don't even need a bra."

Problem is, I don't want lemons; I want melons, huge balancing melons that bounce and sway and scream, "I'm a woman, look at me!" whenever a man passes me by. I long for a big behind: two giant papayas tucked into my jeans. I want long legs like bamboo shoots, eyes that can be seen from the moon, big perky nipples that make men think of caramel ice cream cones, and a diminutive waist the circumference of a cherry tomato.

I also want a short haircut so I don't look like the Bible-thumping women who come knocking at our door handing out brochures with pictures of a Cat-Stevens-look-alike Jesus, or like the curb crawlers I see each night on my way home from school, with their frizzy hair dyed jet black, cheap patent-leather miniskirts, and wallets tucked in between their pushed-up breasts. The hair on my legs also has to go. Mom says that the first time a woman shaves her legs is an important occasion, that I'm not ready yet but that, when the day arrives, we'll do it together and she'll make chicken soup to celebrate. Oh, and I want, I need, a bra for my lemons so older men will stop pinching and grabbing them in the suffocating darkness of packed buses, making me feel dirty and unworthy.

Had I had any of these attributes, things would have gone differently last night when I took Diego behind the stadium. Mom had allowed me to go for a forty-five-minute bike ride, enough time to meet Diego, who is sixteen and has blond greasy hair that falls to his scrawny shoulders and carries a beat-up guitar strapped to his back, which he doesn't know how to play but makes him look bohemian, interesting, irresistible. He rode his bike without handlebars, and we raced each other down the hill by the church and pedaled hard and breathlessly as we climbed that final steep slope that took us behind the stadium.

139

By the time we arrived at our designated spot, the sun graced me with a crepuscular light that I deemed perfect for my amorous tryst. We got off our bikes and sat next to each other on the grass. While Diego fidgeted with his worn guitar strap, I fidgeted with the three top buttons of my plaid shirt until the gap between the holes and the buttons was big enough to reveal my lemons in all their glory, which by the sheer power of my imagination I was sure would look like melons to Diego.

He sat folded into a lotus position, his thighs cradling the guitar, and strummed the chords to what he said was "Angie" by the Rolling Stones but didn't sound anything like it. Eventually he stopped playing, but instead of admitting his musical handicap, Diego said that some songs shouldn't be "contaminated with instruments, man." I immediately put his free hands to good use, gently guiding one of them under my shirt. Instantly he became anxious. He withdrew his hand quickly and explained that he was "a radical artist, man," who needed his hands to convey the emotion of a song. To prove his point, he began singing his own Spanish version of "Angie," interrupting himself only to argue that "English is the language of imperialism, man, and I will never kiss the tyrant's ass, man." His version was off-key, delivered in the falsetto voice of a castrato, and it would have made me laugh out loud had I not been busy trying to be a woman.

Maribel had shared numerous hints about how to make guys buckle at the knees. Borrowing one of her suggestions, I slipped my hand under Diego's hair and, with a finger, drew invisible figure-eights on his nape as he was working on his Spanish rendition of Carol King's "You've Got a Friend." Then I leaned over and licked his earlobe.

With this move, I finally got him to stop singing and look at me. He gave me a grin and a wink—both products of my ravaging sexual prowess, obviously— and slipped his hand under my shirt. I felt him stroking my chest up and down as if he were looking for something that wasn't there. His hands didn't glide over my skin as I had expected. They were hot and sweaty and stuck to my chest. His fingers moved left to right, right to left, clumsily searching for that nameless thing I wished he'd find.

I felt no explosion of light in my head, no shortness of breath, no compulsion to rub my legs together as Maribel had promised. "That's how you know you're a woman," she had told me one day during recess. "All the touching, the massaging, the tongue kissing make you see colorful firecrackers under your eyelids. It comes right at you, bang! Like a guerrilla assault. The French call it *la petite mort.*" Then she walked away, the pleats of her uniform skirt bouncing off her wide hips, sparkles falling off her blond mane like wheat seeds under the sunlight.

Ever since then, I had been wondering exactly what she'd meant by "it." Would I feel like I was dying on the day I became a woman? Was today the day?

Diego didn't find what he was looking for under my shirt. Instead, he clasped his hands under his head and lay back on the grass. He began talking about Kafka, how "far out it would be to wake up transformed into an insect, man." I, blissfully unaware of my lack of sex appeal, thought that he was inviting me to lie down alongside him. I twined a leg around his, pressed my pelvis against his thigh, ran my tongue up and down the languid lines of his neck and around his prominent Adam's apple. I gently nibbled at his chin, which seemed to annoy him because he couldn't talk. He turned his face away and started to talk about Jean Paul Sartre and Simone de Beauvoir and how rad of them it was to have a relationship based on a two-year lease. Then, at some point during a rant about "existentialism, man," he lit a joint. I wasn't prepared to confess that I had never smoked anything, so I was relieved to learn that "joints are sacred, man," and he didn't share them with anybody. He puffed and I improvised some respiratory aerobatics to stifle my cough but ended up inhaling nosefuls of smoke that I held down in my chest until I could breathe again.

My eyelids grew heavy, Diego's discourse grew dull, and before long my eyelids were drooping, and the world went colorful, then black. I fell asleep. The next thing I knew, a night watchman was shining his flashlight in my face and nudging me with the tip of his boot. Diego, who had also fallen asleep, woke up outraged, more at the idea of "being harassed by a pig, man," than because he was startled. He said he was "a pacifist, bro," and needed to leave before this pig could contaminate his peace-loving soul.

As Diego climbed onto his bike and rode off into the night, I buttoned my shirt under the guard's flashlight and a shower of insults. Repeatedly, he called me *putica,* little whore. But neither his insults nor his old boot poking at my ribs was as terrifying as the prospect of going home to face Mom. I didn't know how long I had slept or what time it was when I woke up, but it was dark, way too late to make up a credible excuse. I contemplated the two possible scenarios. *She'll be sick with worry and will have called the police*. I visualized police cars parked around the apartment, search dogs snuffing up my scent from the dirty socks I had hidden under the bed. *She'll be livid with anger*. I pictured the blue vein on her temple throbbing like a migraine, the color disappearing from her face, her broadened nostrils, the blobs of saliva beginning to form in the corners of her mouth.

Telling the truth was out of the question. How could I tell Mom that the youngest of her daughters, a girl who was barely thirteen, had been rolling in the grass behind the stadium with a greasy hippie? That her baby, who just three years ago had received her first communion, had begged a sixteen-year-old existentialist to touch her lemons, which incidentally she wished were melons? That her bony, inconspicuous teenager had fallen asleep in a marijuana-induced stupor only to be awakened by a righteous security guard who had labeled her a *putica?*

As I pedaled away from the stadium, the word *death* rang in my ears. Death was the only available solution, the only possible avenue to absolution. My death was the only thought that made sense. It would cause Mom a great deal of suffering, but the pain she would feel was miniscule compared to the pain she would inflict on me if I told the truth. I slammed on my brakes and looked around for ways to die as soon as possible. All I saw was a stray dog and a flickering streetlight, neither of which could kill me, as my circumstance required, right there and then. Then I heard the sound of a Kawasaki. I waited until the motorcycle was a few feet away from me. Making the sign of the cross—which I punctuated with a noisy kiss on my right thumb, I said, "Amen," closed my eyes, and veered my bicycle directly into the Kawasaki's path with a zigzag maneuver of the handles.

Tires screeched. Someone screamed an expletive. I felt dust on my face; my mouth went dry. The lights went off. I was happily dead.

When I finally ventured to open my eyes, convinced that I would see God himself smiling at me, welcoming me into his kingdom, I saw the Kawasaki speeding away, vanishing into the night, leaving a whiff of burnt fuel in its wake. I was alive, unscathed, and still standing. Some instinctive sense of self-preservation had made me zigzag out of the motorcycle's path.

I began to feel what I thought were the belated effects of Diego's joint hitting me full force. Dizziness, nausea, and knee tremors overtook over me as I walked away toward my fate. By the time I knocked on our door, I looked disheveled and my long frizzy mane looked more hideous than ever before.

Mom rushed to open the door. "What the hell happened to you?" she asked.

I tried to figure whether she was worried or angry, but she gave me no clue. Behind her stood my sisters, waiting to hear what lie I would tell this time. All I could see from the door frame were their ten impassive eyes.

"Something terrible," I replied, wondering what I was about to say. Now I could see her blue vein and the fading color of her face.

She led me to the blue cordovan recliner that no longer reclined. My sisters crowded onto the sofa, while Mom towered over all, arms folded over her generous breasts, vein throbbing. "Well?" she said.

"I was kidnapped," I blurted. I remembered that over the recliner hung a wooden crucifix, and I wondered if my sin had shifted from venial to deadly just because of the position of the chair.

"You were what?" Mom took two long steps and stood in front of me. "You were what?"

I tried to keep my eyes on her slippers, but something forced me to look toward the sofa, where I saw two of my sisters rolling their eyes. Opening my mouth, I began spewing a story about a slow-moving car that had followed me down the street, a driver who had insisted on giving me a ride. That's when the snowball began to roll. A little green devil sat on my shoulder whispering irresistible ideas into my ears. Why not kill two birds with one stone? Maybe I could get her to forgive me for being late while also getting her to pay for a desperately wanted haircut accompanied by a cute new do and a much-needed first bra.

"The man called me names." I searched my brain for details. "He said that girls with long hair like mine are good for only one thing." I didn't dare to name the thing. "He told me to stop playing hard to get, to jump in the car and give him a good time."

Mom stared at me, unmoved but attentive.

"He said that if I was a decent girl, I would cut my hair and wear a bra."

"Really?" Mom asked.

There I sat, on my blue cordovan seat, right elbow resting on my open left hand, fingertips massaging the space between my eyes, innocently unaware of Mom's power over me, how she could take my God-written-and-handed-out fate, twist it, rewrite it, and deliver it to me in a single blow. Yet my story sounded convincing. I was definitely nailing it.

"Did you get in the car?" Her lips quivered.

"He pulled me in," I said, with a whisking motion to add effect.

"Did he touch you? What happened inside that car? You were there, what, two hours? Oh, God." She began pacing around the living room, her hands cupped to her chest as if they were keeping the air in her lungs. She looked at me, through me, massaging her chin, thinking, thinking.

"I think he drugged me," I said. The tension in the room felt like a thundercloud ready to burst. I could hear Mom's breathing. One of my sisters clicked her nails.

"He what?"

And so I said something about a white powder blown in my face. About passing out, about having no recollection of what had happened. This was plausible: last month, we had heard about two girls who had been drugged with *burundanga*, an alkaloid with a powerful depressant effect. They had been walking in downtown Medellín when they had bumped into a man who had pretended to sneeze into a handkerchief. Instead, he had blown a colorless dust at them. The next thing they knew, they were waking up naked in a dingy brothel in Amsterdam, two Dutch johns on top of them, ravaging bodies that were meant to be deflowered by Colombian lovers.

The silence in the room grew cavernous. Finally Mom said, "Go to bed. I need to talk to your sisters." She was convening one of her periodic council sessions, her attempt at running her family like a *democracia*. During the sessions each sister *had to* voice an opinion and make suggestions. But the idea was silly: in practice, Mom never listened to her daughters, and we always did what she had already decided to do. My sisters had invented a name for this regime—a *mamicracia*—but no one dared to say it to her face.

When I woke up, it was midmorning, and my sisters were gone. I was home alone with an angry mother. Mom's coarse voice roused me: "Get up and take a shower. You and I are going somewhere." You and I, *usted y yo,* sounded more like a threat than an invitation.

My shower was shorter than usual, even though Mom had already gotten into the habit of limiting my time in the bathroom: about three minutes for the toilet and six minutes for a shower, eight if I shampooed my hair. Lengthy showers, she claimed, were an invitation to sin. The longer I stayed under hot running water, the more likely I was to explore parts of my body that, for my own sake, must be left alone.

"Don't bother with breakfast," she said as soon as I stepped out of the bathroom. "We have an appointment." Immediately I concluded that it had to be an appointment with the stylist at the Coiffeur de Paris, the hair salon where my sisters went on special occasions. With yesterday's events put in the past and the news of this impending appointment, I started to fantasize about haircuts. The possibilities were endless but I settled for a layered hairstyle with flaky bangs. I readied myself for a killer Gina Lollobrigida look.

146

Mom's voice quickly destroyed that illusion. "Wear a dress," she said.

I went back into my room, cursing her in my head, secretly pumping both middle fingers into the air. A wave of hatred overcame me. "I hate dresses, I hate this family, I hate being Mom's daughter, I hate Mom, I hate Colombia, I hate the whole world, I hate myself," I repeated under my breath, tears streaming down my face, feeling again this lightning strike wreaking havoc through me, filling my head with thoughts that made me orbit Mom's world in silent enmity and unwholesome love. To make matters worse I was beginning to feel menstrual cramps. I put on a sanitary pad and fastened each end with pins, as Mom had showed me two years earlier when I had had my first period.

Now, forty-five minutes later, I'm walking behind Mom, catching glimpses of my skinny, hairy legs, trying to maneuver in these black clunky sandals that she bought me in a discount store. The moist air thickens my hair into frizzy clumps that I try in vain to tuck behind my ears. I have never wanted long hair; but ever since Mom first read that human hair grows a few inches per year, she has treated my hair as a symbol of permanence, a testimony to the immutability of the life she once shared with Dad. She won't allow me to cut it short.

We arrive at the doctor's office, though I still have no idea why we had to come here. I'm only aware of what's happening to the area below my belly button: it is bloated, in pain, and the sanitary pad is soaked. In the waiting room, Mom sits bolt upright, legs crossed at the ankles, both hands resting on her stomach, lips pursed, eyes darting back and forth between the hallway to the doctor's office and the hem of my dress as if there was an imaginary line on my thighs that the dress shouldn't cross. I try not to look at her but steal a few glances anyway, searching for the clue she will not give away.

147

Mom slaps my left knee. "Keep your knees together, for goodness' sake. You're wearing a dress!"

I'm in trouble. I know that much. But it won't be long before the mystery is solved. Soon the doctor will call Mom's name, I'll wait for her here, and a few minutes later she'll come back, prescription in hand, complaining that so many years of backbreaking work are taking their toll on her aging body. We'll go to the pharmacist to buy the prescription, Mom will barter even though she knows the prices are fixed. Then we'll go home, she'll fix me lunch, and I'll go to school and tell Maribel about my odyssey and that I think everything she told me about boys is a big, fat lie.

To my surprise, it isn't Mom's name that comes out of the doctor's mouth. It's mine. Mom nudges me to get up. "I'm not sick," I protest.

"We'll see," she says, standing up. I follow her into the stark office whose sterile white walls are scarred by tape and thumbtacks.

"Is that her?" the doctor asks Mom as if I'm not here. Mom nods and disappears behind a curtain.

The doctor instructs me to sit down beside her desk and takes my blood pressure and my temperature. I want to tell her that I'm not sick; but whenever I open my mouth, she shoves a thermometer into it. I'm tempted to bite the tip, feel the slippery roundness of its poisonous orbs back there where my tongue turns white, and swallow the column of mercury; to convulse and vomit and piss and die right here, right now. I'm riddled with guilt about the lies I told Mom last night, but now she's called my bluff; she's caught me; she's humiliated me again. I hate her.

"Follow me," the doctor orders. I follow her behind the curtain, where Mom stands at the foot of an examination table. It is painfully obvious that whatever examination I'll be subjected to, Mom will witness it.

"Lie down for me, please," says the doctor.

"What for?"

"You don't get to ask questions, miss," Mom says. "Do as *la doctora* says."

My legs are heavy. I bend over to undo my sandal straps, but the doctor taps me on the shoulder and says that won't be necessary. We'll be out in a jiff. I climb onto the table and lie back. Mom stands a few inches away from my feet. I raise my head a couple of times, imploring her with my eyes to leave the room. She doesn't budge.

"Take your panties off for me, please," says the doctor.

Something inside lodges itself in my throat. I stifle a whimper and defensively cross my legs, a feeble attempt at dignity, a quality I haven't been aware of possessing until now. "I have the ruler," I say, on the verge of tears. "The ruler" is one of Mom's euphemisms for menstruation, which she also calls "the visit," "the sickness," and, worst of all, "Mr. Red's call." In her mind, any term is more decent, more lady-like, than *menstruation*. But I have always liked the forbidden ring of the word, the way my voice hushes when I say it, the secrecy shrouding its pronunciation. Menstruation. Menstruation.

I lift my hips to hike up my dress and slip off my panties. The doctor guides my left foot, then my right one, into the stirrups. On the ceiling above the table is a poster of the female reproductive system, all its glands and tubes and compartments and bulbs, and I feel ashamed about being a girl. Meanwhile, Mom doesn't move. She stays right there between the stirrups. I imagine her as half mother, half beast.

I close my eyes and think about Diego. I escape into his uninterested arms and picture him spreading my legs apart on a cushiony round bed inside a red room with velvet curtains that doesn't resemble the white sterility of the doctor's office. Diego imitates Don Henley's voice, sings "Hotel California" into my ear, and passes me a joint. My body relaxes. Oh, the sweetness of this weed, oh, the prickly tickle of his unripe goatee against my face. This is going to be easy. He won't let me remove my shoes, he says I look womanly with my sandals up on the stirrups, and before I know it he slips two gloved fingers into my most private me. I think, That's right, babe. Can I call you "babe"? Make me a woman. Is that how it works? Is this how it's done? Before you make a woman out of me, can I ask you, hon, are you already a man? How did that go for you? Did your father take you to a doctor's office to ensure that your most private you was untouched, a virginal hood still covering the tip of your penis and all?

Diego's fingers emerge from me. They are stained with menstrual blood. He takes his gloves off and throws them into a basket under the gurney. I hear him rub his hands together, I think he claps, once, maybe twice. Then the woman doctor says, "Good as new." Mom bursts into sobs. When I open my eyes, Diego is gone. Wait, babe, am I a woman? I feel a little bit dead, as the French say. Is that so? Is that how a girl becomes a woman?

The doctor hands me a clean sanitary napkin and closes the curtain behind her. The napkin is a thick slate of cotton so white, so pure, that I feel compelled to prick my fingers with the safety pins that fasten it to my underwear. I bleed my finger onto the pad, leaving a crooked message from me to me: SUM, *Soy Una Mujer*. I am a woman.

"Let's give *la niña* some privacy," the now-sympathetic doctor says. Mom nods and follows her. Through the thin curtain I can see that Mom is crying and hugging the doctor, crying and rubbing her own chest as she always does before and after each eruption of her volcanic heart. With the sanitary napkin I wipe my face, now covered in sweat, snot, and tears, and wonder how many more times in my life—a woman's life—tears, sweat, and blood will commune again.

We go straight to the nearest church. We are alone, kneeling on a wooden pew, hands clasped below our chins, heads bowed before a colossal cross with a dark Jesus affixed to it. He is missing a toe; probably he lost it during an Easter procession. Mom doesn't notice this or the donation box sitting at his feet, with a handwritten note that reads, "Let's give our savior his toe back." Mom whispers prayers. She says we need to thank God, her God, that those kidnappers didn't violate me. All I can think about is the missing toe and how disgusted I am at myself. I made Mom sick with worry last night, I lied to her and my sisters, I let Diego touch my lemons, and a policeman called me a *putica*. I got what I deserved. Me, little liar, me. Me, little whore, me. Me, *putica*.

"*Gracias, Dios mio*, that my girl is still a virgin. *Gracias,* Jesus, for keeping her intact."

Mom can't stop hugging me. She can't get enough of me, of this reassured me, this shiny, untouched me that pleases her so. "I knew it. I knew it," she says to herself and to me, and if given the chance, to every passerby. I am still a virgin and that's all that matters.

Virgin, intact, unadulterated.

Mom says big words all meaning the same thing and her words fit me perfectly. My private self has been identified, and I've been branded.

Virgin.

Goods constantly monitored.

Future husband, do not fear. Virgin under close inspection.

I visualize this membrane inside me, this membrane that makes me what I am. I picture it as pink, thin, and translucent, like a bubble of strawberry gum, like a film of cotton candy, like a delicate Murano glass bowl. Does it resonate like a drum if you tap it with your fingernails? Did the woman doctor strum it with her two gloved fingers? And if she did, was it prickly like the skin of a peach, bumpy like the underside of my tongue, slick and bouncy like a trampoline in the rain?

151

I feel as if I have morphed from being an invisible little girl into a woman with an identity, someone whose best quality can finally be described. Virgin. This transformation, this new definition of myself, propels me into an outer world. So this is what being a woman is all about. This is it, I think. No more hiccups of self-awareness; this time the incline toward full womanhood is steady. I will never slip back, will never be free of this new me. I have a hidden trophy inside my crotch, something so valuable that in thirteen years it has been stroked only by two latex fingers and seen, in all its impish splendor, only by Mom.

I've been brooding all day. By the time the sun sets behind the *cordillera,* I have a pixie haircut, wear a training bra (made of cotton because Mom says that silky underwear encourages precocious sexuality), and my silky legs glisten with a hairless glow. Alone in the bathroom, I shaved my legs, cruelly depriving Mom of a special occasion in our lives that she wanted to be a part of. I took that away from her. Maliciously, gladly, with swift razor runs up and down my legs; a simple act full of spite, an impulse born in the blur of the humiliation on the exam table, my private act of resistance; an urgent moment, uncontrollable and explosive like a spasm. Now we're even.

Tonight, as I lean against the doorjamb in the bedroom Mom and I share, I think of packing my clothes and running away. But I know I can get no farther than the closet where my clothes hang. I know I suffer from a hunger that, for now, only my family can quench. I know that, if I have to choose between freedom and family, I'll choose the tyranny of Mom's love and her futile women's councils that have taught me nothing about democracy and everything about tenacity.

I look at Mom from the hallway. She is sitting in the dark, staring at our black-and-white TV set. I wonder if she is looking at her own reflection on the screen. Does she see the woman I see? Late forties, dark half-moons under her sad eyes, short gray hair, a permanent frown, dark unsmiling lips—a haggard woman with nothing to show for a lifetime of diapers, late-night colics, schools, unpaid bills, hunger, lies, loneliness. I walk to the couch and sit beside her. She puts her arm around me. For a while I sit rigidly, but then I close my eyes, ease against her, rest my head on her shoulder. And I feel like crying for her. I wish I knew a story, a secret recipe that I could give to her. I wish I could cradle her hands in mine as I tell her my secret, that she will wake up tomorrow with the same dreary mother duties and uncertainty and loneliness but somehow feeling that her life is something solid she is carving. I wish this unnamed thing, which I do not posses but long to share with her, will fill her with renewed fortitude and get her ready to face the day, to steer the reins of its hours and claw its quotidian drabness and disembowel it until the day gives her the joy she deserves.But I have nothing to tell her, nothing to give but the reaffirmation of my chastity. I sob quietly.

"Why are you crying?" she whispers.

"I'm crying for you, *Mamá*."

"Well, that's silly," she says. Then she rises and says good-night.

A Commie à la Colombiana

When the Sandinistas ousted Nicaraguan dictator Anastasio Somoza, a wave of hope washed over Central and South America. The Left seemed like a plausible option for our derelict democracies and, if you were young and socially conscious, the only acceptable side to be on. So at fourteen, I became a Communist. As a hardcore leftwing radical, I carried around *The Little Red Book*, *The Communist Manifesto*, and *Das Kapital*—not the botched Spanish translation but the German original. Although I didn't speak German, I figured that, since Karl Marx had written it for the masses, everyone must be able to understand it, not just Germans. Of the three, I liked *The Little Red Book* best because it was tiny and shiny, like my diary. On the cover was a picture of Chairman Mao, with a vertical line of golden Mandarin calligraphy on each side of his pudgy face. I used to stare at his oblique eyes, longing for his wisdom. I used to pray to him, as if he were a saint, begging him to transmit his earnest love for China into my being, to fix Colombia through me. I thought of him as a Chinese Holy Spirit of sorts.

The Communist Manifesto was for heavyweight Communists,

or so I was told. That must have been why my comrades had given it to me; no doubt I was the smartest girl they had ever met. Nonetheless, I had a hard time following their arguments, which revolved around the class struggle and the relationships between the bourgeois and the proletarians, the proletarians and the Communists. The subject was so complicated that the mere act of saying *bourgeois, proletarian* and *Communist* gave me a headache. Still, I was convinced that being a Communist was exactly what I wanted.

Needless to say, my conservative family didn't quite share my political views. The first time I took home a poster of Karl Marx, the sister closest to me in age, a psychology student, mistook it for a portrait of Sigmund Freud. Later she corrected herself, admitting that the poster actually depicted Walt Whitman.

My girlfriend Maribel and I stand in line at recess to get our free lunches. We attend this private school thanks to a scholarship program, the dealings of which only our mothers understand. Lots of paperwork, I'm sure, lots of little white lies to get us in, lots of pleading with the priest, the nun, the school principal. Lots of begging, which is, of course, a role that the oligarchy has always ascribed to the poor: beggars. But Maribel doesn't see it that way. She's happy to be attending this school, happy to be the ping-pong champion, happy to be blonde, curvy, and funny. Although she pays attention to politics and worries about the current state of affairs in Colombia, she is not willing to sacrifice herself for the well-being of the masses. She simply doesn't have it in her; she is what *we* call a conformist, but she respects my political views and understands that I may or may not choose to bear arms to defend the motherland.

I did take her to a couple of party meetings at the Pascual Bravo High School for Boys, but that was it. As we sang "The Internationale," she was licking her lips; and as one of the boys read a proposal about a protest march, she was hiking up her skirt, showing off her white thighs to a Pascual Bravo hotshot, who eventually started choking on his bubble gum as he tried to explain the concept of private property. I don't mind her being like this. I have the brains; she has the looks. That's why we get along so well. I read Kafka, de Beauvoir, and Camus and try my best to explain existentialism to her before our philosophy tests. In exchange, she types for me in typing class. I refuse to sit at the typewriter to *chuzografiar* phony memos because I have no plans of being anyone's secretary. If a boss wants something typed, he can type it himself.

Despite our differences, Maribel and I have conversations that make my head spin. We don't have to say much, but I know she gets me. As we stand in the lunch line today, our conversation goes like this:

"So you're a Commie?"

"Yeah, I'm a Communist."

"Are you like a proletarian or something?"

"Of course. Yes. A proletarian."

"What's communism about?"

"It's all about class struggle."

"What struggle?"

"The struggle for resources among ourselves. Get it?"

"I guess."

"Our society is divided into proletarians, bourgeois, and us, the Communists."

"Can you be rich and Communist at the same time?"

"Of course not. You either are a bourgeois or a Communist, but you can't be both."

"What if you are a Communist but fall in love with a bourgeois hunk?"

"You can't fall for the oppressor, no matter how *papito* he might

156

be. That's exactly what they want."

"So what do you do?"

"You fight a revolution, and then when there are no social classes and we are all equal, you can love him. But not before the revolution, while he is rich and you're poor. That's betrayal."

"Is it?"

"Yeah."

"That's not cool!"

"Not cool at all."

While Mom listened to the Sunday bullfight on the radio, I went to the balcony to read and ponder. I wondered how cute I'd look with an army beret tilted to the side, dressed in full camo, sunglasses, and army boots. Like Ché Guevara but girly. Chic Guevara! Somehow I had reconciled existentialism with fashion and had decided that, because everything was temporary and futile, it would be nice to live this transient illusion looking like a goddamned princess warrior, fierce but sexy. Daydreaming, I didn't hear Mom turn off the radio. I'll never know how long she stood behind me, reading the complex words of Sartre and Kierkegaard over my shoulder. And I'll never know which of their words led her to believe that existentialism was a euphemism for homosexuality.

"Had your grandma caught me reading books about communism and bestiality, she would've killed me," Mom declared.

"Would you like me to read Nietzsche's thoughts on eternal return instead?" I asked her. That was a mistake. I should have known she'd ask me what the hell I was talking about. In truth, I had no idea. Nietzsche's eternal return was a reference I had picked up from friends I'd made at the library, and I'd been dying to mention it in conversation.

"And what's that supposed to mean in Christian?" Mom called

plain language Christian, as if Christianity were some sort of universal tongue.

"It means that God loves us all," I said, trying not to laugh. What I really wanted to tell her was that Nietzsche had also said "God is dead," but I chose not to, in case she might decide to make good on her threat to *voltearme el mascadero al revés*. That's what she said: that next time I talked back, she was going to turn my pie hole upside down.

My antics kept Mom in a permanent state of abject terror. In her eyes revolution, communism, and drug addiction were everywhere, and they all meant the same thing to her. I was growing up, my body evolving into womanhood. She was growing old, her body wilting into menopause. At fourteen, I wanted to create an isthmus between us; I wanted to stop being her baby girl. At forty-eight, she needed someone to cling to. I wanted change. She was terrified of the unknown; the slightest hint of uncertainty pushed her back an inch closer to the wall.

I had my first conversation with a Communist at the Comfama Library across the street from my historic high school building. One day, while I was in the library listening for the first-period bell to ring, I wrote yet another lame poem—this one called "Change."

> *It's dark*
> *Goya's monsters breathe in your neck*
> *Death*
> *No lilies*
> *Silence*
> *Where is the light*
> *Heavy chains rattle against the floor*
> *Your own.*

"Good work, *compañera*, good work," a voice said. He was standing behind me, reading over my shoulder as I wrote. He had a skinny body, a nose shaped like a hook, bad breath, and a very attractive paranoia that made him look over his shoulder, left and right, as if he were being chased by the monsters I had been writing about.

"My name is Carlos, but please call me Ciro, *compañera*. For protection, you know." He introduced me to his two friends, a stocky guy with bowed legs and a handsome boy with irresistibly thick, close-knit eyebrows.

"Ricardo, but my *nom de guerre* is Ruso," the bowlegged boy said.

"Are you from the Soviet Union?" I asked, excited at the prospect of meeting a Russian.

"No, I'm from here, Medellín, but people know me as Ruso. Like the philosopher Jean Jacob Rousseau."

"And I'm Nicolás. Machiavello to my comrades," the handsome boy said, fiddling with the set of pan flutes that were sticking out of his *Arhuaco* woven bag.

"If you believe that the end justifies the means," Ruso said, "this is your man," and he gave the handsome boy a slap on the back. "Get it? His name is Nicolás so we call him Machiavello, after Niccolo Machiavelli. Clever, huh?"

"Are you in a band?" I asked Machiavello, who hadn't stopped fiddling with the pipes in his bag.

"Yeah. Well, it's not a band, band. It's more like a musical expression of nationalism. We need to go back to our roots. Go native. I'd fucking die for this country," he said.

We stood by the library window swapping opinions about politics, our eyes fixed on the pompous gate of my private Catholic high school, talking about how it let in the daughters of the bourgeoisie, all silly, all giggly, all indifferent to the pain of the masses. We pointed at the ones with side ponytails à la Olivia Newton John and speculated about their present and future. "I bet she listens to the

music of imperialism." "She looks like one day she'll be some gringo's wife." "That's what a tyrant's ass kisser looks like." We declared
a philosophical war against everything from the United States. So
when they said that Colombia was fucked up, I had to agree, "Yeah,
it's all fucked up," and it felt great to be able to use grown-up language with other intellectuals like myself.

The three of them were all a few years older than I. They were
avid readers of anything left wing, used fantastic words that I didn't
even know existed, and were about to graduate from Pascual Bravo
High School for Boys, where they told me, a free Colombia was
about to be born. "Come to one of our meetings. Join us. We love
smart women with *pelotas*," they said. I didn't know what I liked
most: having been invited to a boys' secret meeting place, being
called a woman, or hearing that they thought I had *cojones*.

Two days after we met, I skipped the first two periods of classes
to attend my first opposition gathering. The leaders of the *consejo
estudiantil* looked too old to be in high school and spoke a dizzying
language, an intoxicating anti-establishment rhetoric that confused
me as much as it excited me. They gave away cheap T-shirts with
Ché Guevara's face imprinted on the front and "*Libertad o Muerte*,
Freedom or Death," on the back. I caressed Ché's face while speakers talked passionately about the empowerment of women, separation of church and state, the sharing of resources, land reform, the
deposition of the current government, and Communist takeover. I
was sold. I wanted it all. Change! *Cambio! Cambio!*

Ciro, Ruso, and Machiavello patiently taught me everything
they believed a *revolucionario* should know: about Lenin, Mao,
Castro, Ché, and even Camilo Torres, a priest who had dedicated his
life to the reconciliation of Marxism and Catholicism because he
believed that, in order to secure justice for the people, Christians
had a duty to use violent action.

"So radical," Ruso said.

"Yeah, yeah, radical," I agreed. I noticed that Ciro said "rad" instead of "radical."

The lesson continued. Back in the sixties, the National Liberation Army, or ELN, had organized itself into a self-governing republic, a sort of utopian society called Marquetalia. I wondered if, maybe in some distant future, Machiavello would like to live with me in one of those utopian villages, have a few dark-skinned kids with bushy eyebrows, and together play native music, plant our own food, and love our land the way he'd said we should.

But in 1964 Marquetalia was bombed by the Colombian army with the help of the CIA, forcing other leftist groups to take up arms. That's when the pro-Soviet Revolutionary Armed Forces of Colombia (FARC) was formed. Unlike the ELN, FARC believed in bullets rather than words. It was led by a man known as *Tirofijo*, Sure Shot, and just the sound of his name made the hairs on my arms stand on end. Whenever we saw his face on the news, Mom shouted, "Assassin, bloodthirsty monster, a cannibal just like that African guy, what's his name? Idi Amin something?" Having lived through *La Violencia,* Mom was suspicious of anyone who carried a weapon. "Do you want peace, murderer?" she would ask Tirofijo on the TV screen. "Put a bullet in your own head. That'll bring peace."

Every lesson with my new comrades included information about a new group, a rad organization, with brilliant ideas about how to destroy the status quo—though none on how to build a better one. There were so many groups, so many leftist organizations: ELN, EPL, FARC, USO, ANAPO. Some were pro-China, some pro-Russia; some were subdued, some combative; some were already defunct, some brand new. Often I walked away from our meetings with the distinct impression that my three comrades had their own creative versions of politics and history.

And what was the point, I wondered, of going by aliases if they had introduced themselves using their real names? Ciro looked over his shoulder before he spoke. "But this is jungle warfare. There are other types, *compañera*. We are waging an all-out war on different fronts." I noticed that his hands trembled. "The other one is urban. Our mission is to educate the masses in the city. That's what the M-19 does."

According to my new friends, the M-19, with its mixture of populism and nationalistic revolutionary socialism, had gained many sympathizers because of its symbolic actions. Members connected with people in the big cities by acting like Robin Hood—for instance, by giving away food and toys in marginalized areas and schools. They interrupted TV programs, sent messages on the radio, and in 1974 had stolen one of Simón Bolívar's swords from the *Quinta de Bolívar.*

Then my friends told me what the M-19 had done on New Year's Eve 1979, just last year, before I had woken to the revolution. On that day, while Mom was sharing a chilled bottle of her precious Manischewitz with neighbors and friends and serving each of us a plate of *lechona,* the M-19 had raided the Cantón Norte, a military garrison in the north of Bogotá. Using a tunnel that linked to a nearby house, members took more than 5,700 weapons from a cache belonging to the Colombian army. I started laughing the moment I heard the words "New Year's Eve." A double-entendre vallenato hit called *"El Polvorete"* was being played on every radio station. Mom loved the upbeat song which she sang along to without realizing that a *polvorete* is a euphemism for a fuck; the song was about a rooster that trembled after mounting a hen. I couldn't get over the hilarity of it all. While Mom had been innocently dancing to *"El Polvorete"* and pouring out a last glass of Manischewitz, a few fearless *guerrilleros* had taken a bunch of weapons stashed at the army depot.

I became an M-19 fan on the spot. Clearly they were not your typical poker-faced thinkers. I saw them exactly as they were presented to me: a bunch of good guys with a great sense of humor.

Maribel and I kneel at the pews in the oratorio, a tiny room in a corner of the school's third floor. We love this space, which contains nothing but a cross, two pews, a Bible, and a few candles. Nobody else comes here. The other girls know that Maribel and I are *uña y mugre*, inseparable, and that this is our meeting place. The nuns say that students are supposed to visit this room when they're confused or feel misunderstood, when they realize that Jesus is the only one willing to hear them out. Or so the nun says. But not us. We come here to talk about politics, philosophy, and sex, although sometimes we also paint each other's fingernails and give one another beauty spots with a Sharpie.

Today I need Maribel's help with my *nom de guerre*.

"How about Tango?" she says.

"Tango? Why?"

"I don't know. It sounds combative."

"It sounds like a hooker, Maribel, *por favor.*"

"You're right. I'm sorry."

"I like Jackie."

"But Jackie is a gringo name."

"Is it?"

"*Sí*. Jackie Onassis. She was with that American guy that got shot."

"Oh. I'd better choose a different one then."

"Can you go by Ché? Like Ché Guevara? It would be *muy bacano* if you were Ché Adriana."

"But it's got my real name in it. Everyone would know it's me."

"Oh, that's too bad. Ché Adriana would have been great."

We take our time. She thinks of names, and I think of names, but we can't come up with anything. Then out of the blue she says, "Got something to tell you. Promise you won't get mad at me." And she does this up and down shoulder thing and covers a giggle with her manicured hands. "Today at the library, before you arrived, I took Ruso to the back row, you know, the one with the reference books, and guess what?"

"What?"

"I gave him a boner."

The first person Mom recruits to bring me back to earth is my homeroom and algebra teacher, Mr. Tavares. He arrives to school on a moped scooter that is too small for his big hairy body. Even though his ass spills over the miniscule seat, he acts like he is riding a mean Harley. Sometimes Mr. Tavares stops at the traffic light at the corner of the school, checks himself in the mirror, and wiggles his tongue side to side at the girls crossing the street. Occasionally, just for chuckles, Maribel accosts him in the lobby, where he parks the scooter, and tells him that he looks very *papito* today. He stares at her cleavage and says, "Oh, yeah, come over here, *monita*," rubbing his hairy chest, which looks like a Bon Bril scouring pad. And Mom thinks this is the man who can straighten me up.

Mr. Tavares asks me to stay after algebra class. He moves his chair from behind his desk so that he can sit close to me. He plants his hand on my knee and slowly licks his lips. I think I just puked a little bit in my mouth. "Let me start by saying you look more delicious today than you did yesterday," he begins. I can feel the warmth of his hand through my skirt. "Your mother is very worried about you. She wants me to be your friend. Your male friend," he says and he's beginning to breathe funny. "You're not a little girl anymore. Look at you." He wriggles in his chair. "I bet lots of exciting things are happening to you, right here," he says, touching my

164

temple with his index finger, "and right here." He reaches toward my chest, but I jerk my head back so he misses me. He smirks like I'm playing hard to get. "Let me help you," he says. And because he wants to help me and be my male friend, he would like to know if I have already let a boy touch me up here or down there.

I think about how misguided Mom can be. How she has guarded my chastity for years only to offer it inadvertently on a silver plate to a man old enough to be my father. Everybody knows he is an *avión*, a dummy trying to pass as a player, yet Mom thinks he is respectable. Please! Anger surges through me. I'm angry at her, not at this idiot whose hand creeps under my skirt, a thumb pressing the inside of my knee.

"So what do you say? Friends?"

I look at him. He looks back at me. I'm not afraid. I can take care of myself; I'm a *revolucionaria*. Like an amulet, the Ché Guevara T-shirt beneath my uniform blouse gives me strength. I know Mr. Tavares's game stops right here. I have learned this much from Mom; men go as far as women let them get—"*el hombre va hasta donde la mujer lo deja llegar*." I stow away my anger at her and instead think of ways to take care of this nuisance. I look at the blackboard as if searching for sources of inspiration. On it, written with chalk, I spot tomorrow's algebra homework. Maribel must have forgotten to erase the board; it's one of her duties in his class.

"I'm going to tell the principal about this conversation," I announce in my most assertive voice.

"And I'll tell your mother that you've been skipping first period for months," he replies. He pulls his hand from under my skirt and combs back his hair back with all his fingers. I still feel the lingering warmth of his sweat on my knee.

I counter, "I'll make an appointment with the school psychologist and tell her about your behavior."

"You might fail algebra and be held back one grade. How'd you like that?"

We lock gazes, each of us considering what's at stake. Silently, we both decide that the situation is not worth pursuing, that neither of us is likely to win a he-says-she-says war. He gets up, slips his left hand into the pocket of the white coat he wears over his street clothes, and holds the door open for me. I grab my backpack, get up, and leave the room.

From then on, we avoid each other during homeroom and try our best not to cross paths outside the classroom or during the school's daily mass. Mr. Tavares acts like I've hurt his feelings, like I have caused him a great deal of suffering and he still can't believe the extent of my cruelty. Yet *achantado* or not, he gets to keep his job, and I earn effortless *As* in algebra. We're even.

Ciro was jittery that afternoon. He looked like he had lost weight, and his army boots gave him a clownish air; they seemed too big for his bony frame. He urged me to be on the lookout for pigs. They were everywhere, these government pigs, disguised as students, attending opposition meetings, taking pictures of attendees, and then making them disappear into the night. "They're out to get me," he said, looking left and right over his shoulders. He laughed, coughed, laughed, coughed. "Soon they'll come for you."

"Why me?" I wanted to know.

"Because girls are easy to spot. You need to stop wearing your uniform to our meetings. The pigs have already earmarked you," he told me.

I couldn't ignore his certainty, yet I didn't understand half of what he was saying. Although Ciro often slurred his words, his tongue seemed heavier than usual that day; and his eyelids were behaving strangely, first fluttering and then closing as if he were about to fall asleep in broad daylight. When I asked him if he was okay, he said yes but that he wasn't sleeping or eating well. He was spending his days and nights studying, training his body and mind, readying himself for the big day.

"What big day?"

"Shh." He placed a finger over his cracked lips. "The day when I'm recruited to bear arms and wage the real war instead of blabbering sophistry." I memorized the word *sophistry* for later. Ciro nibbled on a fingernail. "I'm already a leader of an urban cell," he said and sniffed. He always had a runny nose, which he wiped on his shirtsleeve because, he told me, handkerchiefs were for the bourgeoisie.

"Have you seen your mark?" he asked. I was not sure what my mark was, so I shook my head.

"It's a warning the pigs send before they catch you. Yours is a capital *A* with a circle around it. *A* for Adriana. Have you seen it?"

I had. These circled *As* were everywhere in Medellín. There was one spray-painted on the Comfama wall across the street from our school, but nobody knew what it meant. I didn't know what to make of his claim. Part of me felt, thought, knew that the story was bullshit, that the revolution was making Ciro a bit crazy in the head. I sensed the absurdity of his paranoia and realized that I was not dangerous enough for anyone in power to bother with. I was still a cucaracha trying to crash the hens' party. The same bit of me also suspected that Ciro's brain was full of dope even though he preached that you couldn't be a good *revolucionario* if your mind was polluted.

But another part of me was enamored with the idea of belonging to something larger than family, school, or church. So I clung to Ciro's delusions, hoping that this revolution, imagined or not, would carry me to the other side of adolescence, to a place where my body and my mind would be in perfect adult sync, where the fog would lift, the clouds dissolve, the rain abate.

The deeper I immersed myself in communism, the more concerned Mom grew. She looked at me like I was a terminal patient. Like, if she could, she would trade bodies with me so that I'd not be afflicted by nihilism, existentialism, or communism. All those terrible things. Mom decided that all this talk about revolution, bestiality, and *The Little Red Book* was a threat to my chastity and she was determined to isolate me from any boy on the Communist periphery. She started by taking full control of our rotary telephone, running a padlock through the dial so that no one could use it without her knowledge. If any of my sisters wanted to make a phone call, she needed to ask Mom for the key. I wasn't allowed to use it at all.

In my diary I wrote heart-wrenching denouncements of her actions. I said that my own mother had stripped me of my most basic human rights, that for all intents and purposes she had put me under house arrest. To keep her from reading these entries, I devised what I thought was a very sophisticated numerical code: 1 equaled *A,* 2 equaled *B,* 3 equaled *C,* and so on. I alternated between subscript and superscript letters. No one would ever figure that one out. I considered myself a $16^{15}23$: a POW.

Next, Mom took control of the shower. We had never been allowed to take showers in the nude, but with the bathroom door closed she hadn't been able to enforce this regulation. But one day I came home from school to discover that our bathroom now had an acrylic door.

"Panties on," Mom said before I stepped into the shower. Grabbing the flyswatter, she sat down in front of the bathroom, peering in through the translucent door, making sure that I was not doing anything too leftist like taking my panties off and touching myself as I rubbed Rexona soap between my legs.

"I installed the door myself," she shouted proudly. "Who needs a handyman, right?" To save money, Mom always fixed and installed everything herself. She wasn't skilled, but she had guts. I always gave her that.

"The water is hot," I shouted back, surprised and delighted at the novelty of a hot shower.

"I installed that too," she said.

While I shampooed my hair, I imagined Mom *cacharriando*, opening the water-heater package, studying its components, grabbing a screwdriver, putting the parts together this way and that way, sorting out wires and screws as if she knew what she was doing. "It can't be that difficult," I imagined her saying as she peeled back the green insulation, exposed the copper wiring, and connected wires at random with plumber's tape, which was cheaper than electrician's tape but worked just as well, according to her.

I reached out to turn on the shower tap full blast when I felt a cold throb run through my hand, surge into my forearm, then my shoulder, and slam my back against the wall. I screamed.

"Is that Communist enough for you?" Mom asked.

There was a short circuit somewhere in the wiring of the heater.

"A minor electrical fault," Mom said.

Later my sisters explained to her that any of us might be electrocuted, including her, but to no avail. Mom insisted that God wouldn't forsake his children, especially those who kept their panties on.

A few months after I became a Communist, my school report card landed in Mom's hands. She summoned me to the kitchen, which doubled as her courtroom. According to the report card, I had twenty-two unexcused absences, always for first period. Mom glanced at me sideways, one of her watch-your-mouth-young-lady looks. The kitchen light flickered every time she blinked. Strands of her gray hair stood on end like she was being shocked with static. Mom looked like Medusa, and because of this very reason I didn't look at her. She would've turned me into stone.

"What is this, *señorita?*" She slammed the card onto the table. Her face flushed red, then faded to blue; her chest rose and fell as if she were about to faint. "Where have you been?" she demanded. She moved closer, too close, her nose an inch away from mine. "Where *carajo* have you been?" A blob of her saliva landed on my chin.

My four sisters scurried down the hallway, into the safety of their rooms, where they could ponder their grownup problems. The issue remained, as always, between Mom and me. She spilled her anger all over the kitchen counter; I could feel her disappointment raining on my head, heavy and icy on my shoulders.

"And before you utter a word, let me warn you—" She waved her index finger so close to my face that I could feel its warmth. "You lie to me, and I swear to God, *le volteo el mascadero al revés.*"

I believed her. If I made the wrong move, today really would be the day she'd turn my pie hole upside down.

"I'm sorry, Mom."

"The hell you are," she said, unmoved. "Start talking. Where were you these twenty-two times?"

She fanned herself with the report card. As I opened my mouth to tell her the truth, a sheet of paper flew out of the green plastic jacket protecting the report. It was a list of grievances from the disciplinary committee. Unless I got my act together, the school threatened to put me under disciplinary probation.

Mom held the letter with shaking hands. She read a few lines and then looked up at me. "You did what?" she rubbed her eyes and read the paragraph again. "You pulled the nun's wimple? Why? *Porqué? Porqué?*"

I searched for a good reason, some substantial excuse for having committed what Mom made look like an abomination. I found none. "Because I wanted to see her hair," I said.

"*Un momento, un momentico,*" she said, raising her free hand in the air. "You wrote what in your religion test?" Her lips were so tightly pursed that I could hardly understand the words coming out of her mouth. She wiped her forehead with her wrist. "You think you are more *avizpada* than the rest of us? I'm all ears. Talk."

I tried to explain. On a test, Father Ignacio had asked which people we would send to heaven based on their unwavering commitment, resilience, and faith. Instead of giving him a simple answer, I had smugly listed Pelé, Stalin, Fidel Castro, Mohammad Ali, and Hitler. I think it was the German dictator's name that had ticked off Father Ignacio.

Mom shook her head, incredulous. She was *jarta* of my shenanigans, she told me. I was going to really get it this time; I had no idea what I had gotten myself into. Her scolding went on and on. She never spoke of concrete punishments but favored open-ended, wait-and-see threats, which she delivered in code. Luckily, this sort of cryptogram no longer puzzled me. I was fourteen, incredibly wise, and the old woman's code was obsolete. I had cracked it a long time ago.

She read on. The principal had gotten wind of a certain petition I had taken to school, one that lobbied on behalf of a noble cause that would benefit a group of underprivileged women from the red-light district. The municipality had announced plans to demolish the derelict buildings in the Cisneros barrio where there had been an epidemic of venereal disease. In my mind, no cause could possibly be more virtuous than defending the rights of sex workers, forgotten and objectified by the rest of society. My petition read, "Save the Whores. Bad Girls Are the Best."

Mom asked, "Where did you learn that? Have you ever heard me say those words? Have I not been a good example?" She continued to read, pacing back and forth with the letter in her hand.

The French teacher had caught me writing revolutionary graffiti on the newly painted hallway. Parents had paid for paint and labor with raffle tickets and the sale of *empanadas* and *cocadas* during PTA meetings. As far as I was concerned, I had ruined nothing. Paint wasn't that expensive, I reasoned, although parents had talked about the project as if they were repainting the Sistine Chapel.

The list of grievances went on. The French teacher had also caught me plastering leaflets on the restroom walls. *Wake Up and Fight. Ditch Boys, Date the Revolution. Marriage Is a Symbol of Oppression; Long Live Concubines. Put Down Your Lip Gloss; Take Up a Rifle.*

"Take up a rifle?" Mom asked. This time her eyes turned glossy and before I knew it, a stream of tears ran down her face. *"Un fusil?* What do you mean, a rifle? A rifle for what? *Dios mío, San Gregorio Bendito, Ánimas del purgatorio."*

I stood there, looking at her crying, enraptured by the fluidity of her tears, awed with the same intensity as I was ashamed at the power of my actions. I wanted to melt into her the way Chairman Mao had into me, hold her in my arms, tell her, "Don't worry; it's nothing, a silly, fleeting phase." Instead, I was assaulted by a profound bout of self-doubt. What rifle? I asked myself. What goddamn rifle was I talking about? "A rhetorical one," I blurted, "a symbolic one, one that represents insurgence, an emblem of much-needed change. Not one that fires real bullets and kills people. Of course not. No way. We're not that kind of Communists. Commies are good people, like new-age saints or something."

"Saints?" Mom said. "I want you to take a good look at something." Wiping away tears with her open palms, she disappeared down the hallway. I thought she looked smaller than she used to

172

be. My sisters had told me that women's bodies changed during menopause, and I wondered if shrinkage was one of those changes. But more than shrinking, Mom looked as if she were shriveling, disintegrating, like a withered flower. With each passing year, she left something behind: youth, clarity, dreams, things that I needed another thirty years to name.

Mom returned with a shoebox. She placed it on the counter, and slowly opened it without taking her eyes off me. Inside the box was a collection of old newspaper clippings. Among them I saw pictures of swollen bodies piled in common graves, hostages blindfolded and gagged and chained to walls, a group of amputees under a sign that read, "What the Landmines Took."

The words *guerrilla, revolucionarios, rebeldes* assaulted my eyes, my heart, my revolutionary spirit; they were shards of undeniable truth sparking before my eyes like flashes of blinding neon. On the clippings, I saw the familiar acronyms—FARC, ELN—and my heart quailed. Mom didn't say a word. She didn't have to. She took the pictures out and with her index finger pinned them one by one to the counter, letting out grunts with each clipping: "Huh? Huh?" I didn't know why but tears began to swell inside me. She showed me the picture of a police station raided by guerillas. The bullet holes in its walls made it look like a punch card. In front of the shattered building lay the bodies of three young cops. I thought of Machiavello, Ciro, and Ruso and began to sob.

"One more unexcused absence, just one more, and you can kiss the rest of your education good-bye. You want to be a mule like me?" Mom planted her hands on her hips. "*Una bruta* like me? Suit yourself. I can use some help in the kitchen. You don't want to study? Fine. Be someone's maid." She took a long, deep breath. "Now get out of my sight. I need to talk to your sisters."

Before long Mom found a way to keep me from skipping class:

a yellow cab and with it an unfriendly, no-nonsense driver. As she instructed, he took me to school and didn't leave until I was on the other side of the gate. I tried to talk my way around him, but he was the Iron Curtain in overalls. All he ever said to me were a few words about his son. The moment I started to speak, he would turn on the radio. Mom had warned him that I could be very persuasive. "Before you know, you'll be handing her the keys," I heard her tell him. Every day, at the end of school, he was parked in front of the gate, giving me no chance to catch sight of my comrades. Soon I lost my contacts in the freedom-fighting world.

Maribel brings me the news. She says Machiavello won a scholarship to study avionics in Russia and left a week ago. Maribel gave him a farewell boner and would have given Ciro one too had he kept his hook-like nose clean instead of stuffing it with the *porquerías* that sent him to the emergency room and later to a rehab center in Bogotá. Maribel has heard that the leaders of the *consejo estudiantil* at Pascual Bravo High were not real students but members of the urban cell that the M-19 was harvesting in Medellín. They have gone missing, *desaparecidos*, which, she says, is a pity because she liked the one with the pointy boots. He was a super *papito*.

I ask her about Ruso, and she giggles. I already know they sucked each other's tongues in the library, so I don't know what her fuss is about.

"Ruso?" she says.

"Yes, Ruso."

"Here is the thing. Please don't get mad. You know how much I like dancing, right?"

I nod.

"Okay, get this. There is going to be a dance-off in my barrio, and the winners get new clothes and shoes and shit.

174

"What's that have to do with Ruso?"

"I asked him to be my partner."

That's a funny thought. Thinker Ruso, bowlegged, introvert Ruso on the dance floor? No way. But Maribel tells me he is one hell of a disco dancer. I repeat, disco dancer. They've been practicing the moves and have memorized the English lyrics. They're going to be Danny Zuko and Sandy Olsson.

"What?"

"From the movie *Grease*," she says, her eyes already dreaming of the "clothes and shoes and shit" she might win. "He'll do Travolta, and I'll do Olivia Newton-John. *Muy bacano,* right?"

Mom's clippings, my phony comrades, the dislike in the driver's eyes whenever he looked at me: all of them gave me a sinking feeling that nothing that had happened in the past few months was real. While I imagined Ciro awake at night, trying to decipher the language of opposition, he was actually stuffing his nose with a street mixture of cocaine and talcum powder. While I dreamed of a future with Machiavello somewhere in our beloved Colombia, which will be free by the time we're grown up, he was scheming his way out of the country, applying for scholarships even in oppressive countries like *Gringolandia*. The bastard. He had sworn to defend Colombia with his own life. And Ruso? How the hell was Ruso going to change this fucked-up country by gelling his hair back and donning a leather jacket, high-water pants, and white socks? How was he going to live up to Rousseau's principles, walking like an idiot, rubbing his crotch with a roll of cling paper, "Greased Lightning," doing the chicken dance on some bleachers, "Summer Nights" chasing Maribel and singing "You'd Better Shape Up"?

Mom's strategy to force me out of my delusions into the real world was to keep me incommunicado. At first, I felt violated, under solitary confinement, a victim of extreme and unusual, $3^{18}21^{5}12^{20}25$, cruelty. But often I caught myself thinking of that decimated police station, the amputees, the senseless violence, and along with the images came a feeling of futility, a visceral exhaustion with that left-wing language that I wasn't sure I had ever mastered or understood. Slowly, I began to like the silence and poise that Mom's sanctions had imposed on my life. She had forced me into early retirement just as the revolution was getting muddled up. A section of the library burned after a couple of Molotov cocktails found their way in through a window. A small bomb went off at my school, and the historic building that we had been so proud of was now missing chunks of concrete. One side of the school looked like a chewed-up piece of bread. Colombia was awash with a wave of kidnappings, and M-19, the ELN, and FARC took turns with the EPL, the ANAPO, the USO, and every other acronym under the sun at claiming the kidnappings. They seemed to trip over each other in their anxiety to take responsibility for massacres, *fosas communes*—mass graves—and executions. Whenever there was bloodshed, every leftist organization proclaimed, "Us, us, us. It was us."

Before the end of October 1980, I heard that a few thousand Cubans had started a mass exodus to gringo land. About 125,000 of them had left Mariel Harbor for the United States, an event that confused me immensely. I could understand that ten members of the bourgeoisie might have wanted to leave what my comrades had called "the only free country in the western hemisphere," but 125,000? A mass escape from freedom? My head hurt.

I'm sick of this. This evening, when the taxi driver picks me up from school, I'll ask him about his son, the one he sent to Spain to study robotics and whose education Mom is indirectly funding with the crumpled pesos she puts into his dad's greasy hand every Friday.

"When is your son coming back?" I'll ask him.

"Nothing to come back to," he'll say. "I hope he stays there."

"Do you send him stuff?"

"All the time. LPs, food, and pictures of his family, but mainly music. Why?"

"The next time you make him a package, please send him this," I'll say. And I'll take out my copy of *Das Kapital* in German, tap it on the driver's shoulder, and give it to him without hesitation.

I'm done with communism. $4^{15}14^5$. Done!

PART IV

Opal and Topaz #4

The picture of the six of us by the calabash tree reminds me of what my sisters and I have become: orphans. The calabash tree is a landmark in the geography of our lives and this picture itself an imaginary timeline demarcating the events that took place either side of it. Three years after this picture was taken, after the five hinges had left home and the boy's boys were already in college, Mr. B., my dad, came back to die in Mom's arms. An act that shouldn't be mistaken for proof of love for it was a desperate act of surrender. He didn't come to give, so Mom didn't take. He came back, broke and broken, and Mom found both qualities lovable.

Mr. B. disappeared for two decades. In those twenty years, he worked for oil companies as a welder, earning an oiler's salary. He never sent a penny to us, but we heard rumors about the things he was buying with his money: pretty girls, antique cars, golden cufflinks. He wore expensive colognes, shiny shoes, and designer clothes. He drank expensive whiskey and rubbed elbows with obscure poets and drunken intellectuals. But eventually the money ran out; and when he could no longer afford girls, cars, or clothes, God played a celestial, murderous prank on him in the form of a lethal dose of cancer so angry, so determined to kill him, that when he came back to Mom, she didn't even have time to set out the good china, the one reserved for special occasions.

Mr. B. broke his twenty-year silence with a single knock on Mom's door. She opened it, and instantly her hands began to sweat, her vision to blur. Nonetheless, she invited him in, as if she had been waiting for him all her life, which she had been.

"Want some coffee?" she asked, and at this moment she did not want apologies or explanations.

"Coffee. Yes," he said, although what she heard was "Yes, coffee, please. That'd be nice. Thank you."

"Do you still like coffee like you like your women? Dark and strong?" she asked, reaching into the pantry for a jar of Nescafé. He didn't answer, and she was fine with it.

He coughed up blood into a crumpled hanky. No longer was he ugly-handsome. He was an ordinary old man, eyes blue with cataracts, and a dark mouth enclosed now by a parenthesis of saggy skin. Yet she still found him so attractive that an urge, animal and reckless, came over her. Watching his reflection in the glass of the pantry door, she said, "Whenever you look at me, I feel transported to Mohammed's heaven, lightly engulfed by opal and topaz."

"What the hell was that?" he asked.

"A poem," she replied. "A letter, actually."

"Did you write that?" he asked, looking around, examining the kitchen ceiling, the tiled floor, the washboard, and the refrigerator, all so new, all so unexpected. It was as if he were taken aback by the realization that Mom had created a life without him.

"No. You did." Mom sat down beside him.

"Don't remember. How do you know it was me?"

"Because you gave it to me," she said, laying her hands on his. "You wrote the letter for me."

He asked her to repeat the words, and then again and again, until he had memorized them.

"And you said I wrote that for you?" he asked.

She nodded, and he burst out laughing. He slapped his thigh and stamped his foot, coughing and laughing, coughing and laughing. Laughing.

"That's the most ridiculous thing I've heard in twenty years," he said and picked up his coffee cup.

Mr. B. didn't have much longer to live. The cancer devoured him, blooming in patches up and down his long dark body. After surgeons removed a chunk of his cancer-eaten brain, he also relinquished a few of his faculties. Mom sent me a picture of him after the surgery. It shows him in a wheelchair, head down, chin buried in the concavity of his hollow chest. He sports a steely white crew cut, and an awkward smile pulls down the corners of his mouth. In the photo he doesn't resemble the elusive father of my childhood. As I looked at it, I tried to reconcile the old man in the picture with my memory of him: tall, smug, assertive, well read; a man who could drink anyone under the table, who used words nobody else knew, who recognized poems that nobody else had ever heard of; detached, absent, intriguing, as detestable as he was interesting. To no avail. Only one of the two men was real: the old man in the picture.

I was living in Alaska when my father came back to my mother. Still in my twenties, I had left Colombia because I was sick of the oil industry's trickery, of Bogotá's street violence, of Medellín's drug lords. Exhausted, I was trying to get over a bad relationship with a man who didn't love me and desperately seeking a peaceful place for my daughter to grow up. Over the phone, my sisters filled me in on the details of his return: Dad's broke, he's sick, he's in the hospital, he's in the surgery room, he's in a wheelchair, he's in pain, he's in good hands, he's with us.

Hard as I tried, I could not understand how Mom and my sisters had dredged up the forgiveness he had never asked for. How did they receive him without reproach? How could they run their fingers through his coarse hair and feel love for this man who had never wanted anything to do with us? But they took him in as if nothing had happened. Maybe they still felt a bond with him. Twenty years ago, when he left, my sisters were thirteen, fifteen, nineteen, and twenty, and my brother was twenty-one. All of them had built up some sort of history with Dad, had walked a messy trail with him. Or maybe they accepted him back into their lives because that was the duty of any decent Catholic woman. Or maybe, maybe, they really did love him.

But I was seven years old when he abandoned us and had seen him only a few times. He and I had no history. We had nothing. Not even the time to feel any resemblance of mutual love or lack thereof.

As the youngest member of a household of women, I had seen all of them afflicted with love in its various stages, like malaria. My four sisters had constant bouts of it: fitful love attacks that consumed them, made them delirious and feverish for a while then left them pale, weak, enraged, or dazed, depending on the severity of the bout. Mom herself suffered from a terminal case of it, a chronic type of heartbrokenness, a kind of malaria for which there was no cure.

Mom used to say that every time a woman falls in love she loses a part of herself. She said that love leaves wounds that never heal and that a woman might as well get shot by a bazooka. When my father deserted her, he broke her heart and the wound that came with it never healed. From then on Mom lived infinitely damaged, as if

184

my father's departure had sealed her fate. She may have been Carmen the daughter, Carmen the mother, Carmen the caregiver, Carmen the *abuelita,* Carmen the head of the household, anything but Carmen the lover. She would never be Carmen the beloved wife.

By the time my father was diagnosed with cancer, the eldest of my four sisters was in her early forties, Mom was in her sixties, yet nothing had changed. They were still afflicted with this malarial type of love. Sometimes when we spoke on the phone, I wished I could tell them about Parvati, one of the idols of my youth. During high school, I had begun delving timidly into Hinduism, which made more sense to me than my monotheistic Catholic upbringing did. At sixteen, I wanted a god for the weather and a goddess for matters of the heart, a male deity for prosperity and a female one for sustenance. And as I explored the Hindu pantheon, I came across Parvati, a woman with divine attributes, goddess of the household, marriage, motherhood, and family, married to the god Shiva. I liked that she was depicted with lotus flowers in her delicate hands as she walked on dainty feet when in the presence of Lord Shiva. When she was with her husband, Parvati was a sort of Hindu Stepford wife. But when she was alone, she had two, four, sometimes six arms like tentacles, and she rode bareback on a tiger or a lion. She found her strength when she was alone. She was fierce in her wholeness. How I would have liked to tell my family about Parvati, this divine woman who didn't need a male companion to be complete—just as Mom didn't need Dad and my sisters didn't need the men, including Dad, who broke their hearts.

According to my sisters, he had been living with a younger woman in a little town whose name escapes me. They told me she was white, had eyes that were green like emeralds on some days and blue like a Medellín summer sky on others. They told me that she and Dad had run a dingy little store, that she was educated, that she was nice. *Agradable, amable, buena gente.* When I first heard my sisters describe my father's lover as *nice,* I felt like crying. I thought that they had betrayed Mom by acknowledging the qualities of a woman who had, for all intents and purposes, usurped Mom's place in Dad's life. But of course that was my own foolish sentimentalism. Had he not been with this woman with green-blue eyes, he would have been with another one—a *mulata* with firm hips and generous breasts, a *mestiza* with an indomitable character and an insatiable sexual appetite, a tango dancer with quick feet and crimson mouth, a *negra bembona* who made men weak in the knees. He would have been with anyone, everyone, but his wife.

Even in his final illness, while Mom cooked him chopped liver with copious amounts of cilantro just the way he liked it; while she rubbed his back with baby oil, massaged his feet with Nivea, cleaned his ears with *copitos* Johnson, rubbed his chest with *vicvaporú,* he planned his life without her. "When I get out of here," he told one of my sisters, "I'm going to expand the store. Diversify like the competition. That's what I'll do."

Despite being a shadow of his former self, he never showed any humility, any sign that he was trying to redeem himself. When the cancer reached his bones, when the word *terminal* defined his condition, when opiates gave him no respite and pain contorted his face, he asked Mom for a memory-foam pillow, not a regular one but the ergonomic version he and his lover had seen advertised on TV but couldn't afford. That night he slept with his head nestled into a brand-new memory-foam pillow, the most ergonomic pillow Mom could find in the shops.

In a matter of weeks Dad was bedridden. He alternated between stages of consciousness. He stopped talking. Pain replaced words with grunts and guttural noises varying in length and pitch as each day progressed. Morning short shrills became prolonged agonal rattles by afternoon and furious staccatos by evening. By midnight he snored like a trombone without valves. A perfect musical *portamento*.

It would be fair to say that Mom and my sisters ushered Dad out of this world. They held hands around his bed and gently, lovingly, asked him to go

"It's okay, Dad, you can go now," one sister said.

"*Ya, ya, descansa, papi*, there, rest," another said.

They touched him, kissed him, gave him all the love they had to give, and asked him to die so that he could rest. So that they could live. So that Mom could be the widow who had stuck by her husband for better and for worse, for richer and for poorer, in sickness and in health, until death did them part, as she had promised a lifetime ago in La Ermita Cathedral in Mariquita.

"*Váyase, mi viejo*. Go, my old man," Mom said, wiping away tears with the back of both hands.

As if on cue, he opened his eyes and for a few seconds looked at the five women around his bed. "Thank God they're all here," he said. Then he exhaled for the last time.

One of my sisters told me all of this over the phone. "Take me there," I asked her. "Let me see what you saw, hear what you heard. Tell me everything."

So she told me what he looked like, what she felt, what she heard, what he had been wearing. She described every moment meticulously, but as soon as I heard her repeat Dad's last words, I stopped listening. "Thank God they're all here," he had said. But what about his boy, my brother? And, more to the point, what about *me?*

What about *me?*

I can't remember if I talked to each of my sisters about his last moments or only to one. All I remember is that Mom didn't talk to me until later that day. "*Mi viejo, ay, mi viejo,*" was all she said when I answered the phone. And her pain was so fluid and so swift that it made it out of Colombia, across the Gulf of Mexico; it traversed the expanse of the United States, trekked effortlessly over the Canadian Rocky Mountains, until it reached me in Alaska. I knelt by my bed with the receiver in my hand and wept with her, not because my father had died but because her pain was mine. I felt now as I had felt when I was five years old and she had asked me to be her little girl forever. I cried with her because I knew Mom had loved him dearly, because I, a twenty-eight-year-old single mother with a history of bad relationships, also knew a thing or two about love. I, like Mom, had love shrapnel lodged near my heart.

"Can you be completely honest with me if I ask you something?" I said when she had stopped crying.

"Anything," she said. "I'll give you nothing but the truth."

"Did Dad ask for me?"

"No," she said and immediately hurried to smooth the blow. "He was in a lot of pain, *mija*. He didn't know day from night."

"Did he realize that I wasn't there?" I insisted, hoping that if I pushed hard enough Mom would recant, my sister would reorganize her memories, and magically they would make Dad utter my name as he drew his last breath.

"No, *mijita,*" Mom said. "He didn't."

The Crematorium

We are at the crematorium, a place that resembles my high school oratorio, that room where Maribel and I paved our way into womanhood. It's simple and sterile but, unlike the oratorio, this room has fire in its belly. Below the floor lurk the flames that will char Mom's skin, reduce her to a mound of scorched bones and finally to particles of powder. Ashes to ashes, dust to dust.

There is nothing distracting in the room. Its architecture is one of mechanized laws, well lit and airy, composed of right angles, a place of efficiency, sterility, and perfunctory perfection. Mom's coffin rests on what looks like a sarcophagus made of granite, maybe marble. It's a contraption engineered to swallow the coffin, while giving mourners the illusion that it is solemnly descending into the earth, a futile attempt at minimizing the mystery of death. Two rows of metal chairs are arranged to form a *T* with the coffin, though my guess is that not many people wish to witness a machine swallow their loved ones.

"Our cremation services include a deacon," a funerary representative tells us. "He'll say a brief mass, if you ladies want him to."

My sisters and I shake our heads. We don't want anyone else in the room. Disposing of Mom's body is nobody's business but ours.

My sister Amanda starts a litany of prayers. The other sisters join in, while I think about my mother's body, which is about to be reduced to ashes. I wonder how I'll manage to walk out of this room knowing that all that remains of her is two pounds of dust. I'll have to learn to walk again. First, I'll need a sturdy pair of crutches, then a cane, then I'll venture into the world again, one step at a time, one foot in front of the other, stumbling, staggering, walking the orphan walk. Falling.

Within minutes, my mother's body will be engulfed in flames. I close my eyes. My eyelids are curtains between the coffin and me. I set my mind free, and usher it into the world to wander and creep into the amusement park where, as a child, I experienced my first and most likely only fleeting moments of wondrous courage. I'm there again, about to climb onto the highest, fastest, scariest rollercoaster in the world. My soul gets sucked into this vacuum of infinite solitude and sorrow. Fearless, I feel my car slowly ascend, and now my heart picks up speed as we near the top of the track. I no longer hear the sound of my sisters' prayers. All I can hear is the click-clack of my car dragging its weight to the top. I look down. I feel no vertigo. Everything down below shrinks: the ice-cream cart, the cotton-candy stand, my mother and the children who trail behind her, the fire, and the crematorium itself fade into speckles. A warm breeze tickles the back of my neck. I am filled with inexplicable joy.

My mother's body is about to be lowered into the fire. Amanda squeezes my arm. Reluctantly I open my eyes. "Do you want to say good-bye?" she asks.

It's not a matter of wanting, I think. It's a matter of having the courage.

Amanda tightens her grip. Her pain digs its fingernails into my bicep. Mom has been dead for forty-eight hours, and I haven't yet convinced myself to look at her face.

Now I walk around the coffin, scan its silvery surface in a series of saccades, taking with each a still photograph of whatever I can capture for posterity. Maybe I can steal some courage from my imaginary rollercoaster ride. I take a step toward the casket. This is it, I tell myself. It's now or never. Keep walking, coward. After that first step, I repeat in my head, Easy does it, easy does it. I take another step, then freeze.

"It's okay," says Amanda and helps me back to my seat. Dalila stifles a wail; another sister hugs the coffin; my brother's wife sobs and whispers sweet farewells.

The mechanism underneath the coffin begins to churn, and Mom's body starts its slow, somber descent. I close my eyes again. The pulleys creak. My rollercoaster car screeches. I cover my face with both hands, eclipsing the light, reclaiming my fantasy. Two feet ahead of my car, the track will drop. I can't see the rails. "Are you afraid?" I ask myself. My answer is "No. Not now." I rub my temples with both index fingers, take a deep breath, and let go. I let go of everything, past, present, and future. The rollercoaster car sucks me down toward the ground. My mother's body is halfway through its descent into the ultimate fire. I close the invisible eyelids, the ones I think I have underneath my visible eyelids. I cover my ears and cling to my hallucination. That vision, that figment of my imagination, is all I want. The drop is brutal. My stomach climbs to my throat; my throat stretches toward my brain; my brain hits the top of my skull. I raise my arms into the air as rollercoaster daredevils do and shriek with joy. The quick plunge leaves my lungs empty and feather-light. I'm out of oxygen, but I don't need to breathe. Breathing is for mortals. I transcend everything worldly, everything tangible. My fall is quick, vertiginous, and thunderously liberating. By the time the wagon touches the tracks on the ground, my mother's body is being swallowed by flames. The lights go off. I briefly float above the steel shutters, now closed, and feel, almost see, how exhilaration is replaced by infinite peace and the peace itself by a marvelous type of numbness. I have escaped the swirling vacuum of death, unscathed and joyful. Slowly I return to myself, still suspended in what feels like a bank of benign mist. I'm completely and irrefutably free, freer than I had ever imagined. Free from my fears—fear of Mom, of failure, of being unloved or loved too much, of being alive and but not able to move on.

I wish I had been blessed with a good voice so that I could sing my mother's favorite bolero. Instead, I stand by the space where the coffin had been, feeling alive, giddy with a mixture of bliss and sorrow. I'm not confused, not at all. This crematorium is my bodhi tree, and under its roof, its branches, I have been given a gift of enlightenment of sorts. I take a secret Bodhisattva vow, which I promise to keep for as long as I can, even though I know that won't be for more than a few hours.

I walk out of the crematorium hand in hand with two of my sisters. I don't know which ones, but it doesn't matter. They are my blood, my flesh. These Amazons are my sisters, my favorite women in the world. Before we get into the car, we stop and look back at the crematorium. Smoke is rising from the chimney. We don't say a word. The clean air doesn't smell of burnt flesh. I inhale, hold my breath, and exhale, comforted.

Before our eyes, an orange butterfly flutters and glides. "That's a good sign," the sister on my right says, following the butterfly path with her finger. I look up to the sky and let the sun dry my tears.

Napoleon's White Horse

Her name is Blanca. She is Mom's companion, maid, protégée, and Parcheesi apprentice. Today she hobbles into downtown Itagüí looking for a new Parcheesi board for Mom. The old one is in tatters, and Mom is tired of looking at the pictures on the board: José Bardina and Lupita Ferrer—the hottest Venezuelan soap opera actors of 1970s—a couple of professional wrestlers, and, right in the middle of it, Ana and Jaime—a brother and sister duo of social protest songs. Mom instructed Blanca to look for pictures of soccer players, preferably Pelé, or bolero singers. But nobody seems to make Parcheesi boards nowadays, and she has come home empty-handed.

To get to Mom's apartment complex, Blanca staggers through what's left of the gypsy community. Once the gypsies were the kings of Itagüí, but now they are pariahs, a caste of untouchables with their mattresses lying in the sun, their houses without furniture, and their naked children playing in unkempt yards smelling of human urine and animal manure, yards that allegedly also hide cardboard boxes full of goods that the gypsies have "borrowed" from their white neighbors.

The gypsies move out of her way as Blanca hobbles through. Some of them whisper things in *Caló,* a language she doesn't understand. Words that, she is sure, have something to do with their parts wanting to plunge into her parts. A couple of gypsy women accost her with their street chiromancy rant. She shakes her head, *"No, gracias,"* and for a few seconds dares to look into the copper eyes of one of the women. God, she is gorgeous; all of them are, with their fleshy lips, the braless generous breasts that bounce as they walk, the thick eyeliner that turns their eyes into Rumanian windows, the sexual prowess they carry under their long skirts, which, rumor has it, they share freely with the whole gypsy community. Why didn't God give her the body of a gypsy instead of this uneven shell that limps and makes her wilted foot go *swish, swish* when it touches the ground?

Blanca drags her feet through a labyrinth of fruit vendors and their open coconuts, past an ocean of sliced and paired avocados, bags of green mango sprinkled with salt, and small heaps of *chontaduro*—a fibrous yellow fruit said to restore dead passions as quickly as God brought Lazarus back to life. From a distance, she looks as if she is about to fall over, limping, dragging with the good leg the dead weight of her other. But today there is determination in her unsteady gait. The last thing she wants is to upset Mom, her new employer, so she hurries past the factory that exports boxes of Levi's jeans to Central and North America, complete with little tags that read "Made in the USA." This business is so popular and has added so much finesse to the lives of the factory workers that more than one neighborhood baby has been christened Madeinusa, religiously followed, as customary in this part of the country, by a middle name and two family names: father's and then mother's.

Blanca is reasonably attractive, with two big dimples on each side of her tiny mouth and eyes that squint every time Mom makes her laugh, which is often. She is also a Jehovah's Witness. At first Mom wasn't sure she wanted a woman around who wasn't Catholic; but once it was established that they both believed in the same God, Mom took Blanca under her wing. She is a big-boned woman in her mid-twenties; and if she sits still and doesn't flail her limp arm, the paralysis on the right side of her body is unnoticeable. But when Blanca stands up, the whole world tilts. Her right buttock is rounder, more prominent, and moves higher up in the air than the left as she limps. From her right forearm, fixed and parallel to the floor, her clenched hand hangs lifelessly. A coat of black steely hair covers her extremities. Later, when they get to know each other better, Mom asks her to shave her legs. "She's got pubic hair all over, poor thing."

Blanca is neither an exceptional cook nor a meticulous cleaner. She isn't very smart either and has an intermittent nervous lisp that is half-endearing, half-annoying. But she is a virgin, and that is good enough for Mom. A woman who can keep her legs crossed for so many years is worthy of my mother's trust. By virtue of her chastity (confirmed by Blanca's parents not once but several times before Mom had even met her), she had earned the privilege of watching the four o'clock soap opera from Mom's bed, sharing the same toilet, and eating at the same table.

Rule number 1 for anyone who wants to work for Mom: learn to play Parcheesi. Blanca, who is new to this board game, and to the mean streak it arouses in Mom, loses one game after another. Mom is delighted. This Blanca girl is a keeper.

Rule number 2 for anyone who works for Mom and already knows how to play Parcheesi: never touch the yellow pawns. They are Mom's lucky pieces. The blue ones are not so bad, but the red and the green? Forget it. Mom doesn't touch them unless, of course, one of her yellow pawns lands on an opponent's space. Then, with a boastful smirk, she pinches the red, green, or blue piece between her fingers as she sends her unlucky rival *a la cárcel,* to jail.

Rule number 3 for Mom's Parcheesi opponent: never hand her the dice. She is superstitious about it; the dice might carry a bad-luck wish from her opponent. When someone does make the mistake of giving her the dice, she wards off bad luck by shaking them loosely in her fist and then blowing into it. If she rolls a coveted double, she shakes and blows again, even more vigorously. If luck is on her side, she gets a second double and sometimes even a third, which releases one pawn, leaving her with only three pawns to play. This is when she really starts to laugh.

Blanca's gullibility is a perfect match for Mom's cardsharp nature. Whenever Blanca is ahead, Mom buys herself some time by trying to confuse her. "Blanca, what color was Napoleon Bonaparte's white horse?" she asks, eyes fixed on the board, mind working out her next move.

Blanca looks up. "Black?" she suggests, twirling a strand of hair with her good hand, her eyes off the board.

Mom, straight-faced, repeats the question, and Blanca keeps guessing—"Grey? Brown? Green?"—until Mom has figured out a new strategy.

Or she says to Blanca, "Listen up. Repeat and Rebound went to the ocean. Rebound drowned, who's left?"

"Repeat!" Blanca exclaims.

"Listen up. Repeat and Rebound went to the ocean. Rebound drowned, who's left?"

"I already said it: Repeat!"

"Listen up. Repeat and Rebound went to the ocean. Rebound drowned, who's left?"

I slip into my jeans, throw my college books into a torn backpack, and come out of my room to see Blanca and Mom getting ready to go for their morning walk. Mom wears a pink tracksuit and a pair of white Keds. She grabs her reading glasses and her wallet, though she won't need either, and walks out of the apartment, already two steps ahead of Blanca, as if she is saying, "We are not together."

Away they go, past the preserves factory with its rancid smell of fermented fruit.

Past the house where contraband Marlboros are sold by the carton only to those who know a secret code word, which changes every week. Iron bars protect an arabesque letter box strategically located at chest height to conceal the identities of vendor and buyers. Knock twice, say the password, say the number of cartons desired, hand the exact cash through the iron bars, don't ask questions. Come back soon.

Past the pharmacy that sells conventional medicine without a prescription as well as potions, spells, amulets, and herbal concoctions made from sacred trees found only in the heart of the Amazonian jungle. The pharmacist wanted to be a physician but never made it to college, which is not a problem. The locals know that experience is more important than formal training. He gives penicillin injections with abandon, especially if the patient is in her teens and too feverish to realize that his hands are rubbing her backside. If asked, he says the rubbing helps the penicillin spread out evenly.

Past the pink and yellow two-story house where a widow runs an unlicensed nursery school. For a few extra pesos, a maid washes soiled diapers and vomit-soaked bibs. At the end of the day, which is sometimes late in the evening, the widow sprays each child's hair with water and tidies it with a communal brush, washes his face clean, and wipes his nose. Then she gives him a bear hug, a kiss on the cheek, a smack on his behind: "I'll see you tomorrow, my love." Some parents leave the house holding only a child by the hand. The ones who can't afford the maid also carry a heavy plastic bag of filthy, reeking diapers.

197

By the time they finish their walk through these narrow alleys and busy streets, Mom and Blanca are quite a sight. They are limping. Not just limping, but limping in perfect harmony with each other, as if on cue.

The rainy season has begun, and *El Niño* is sweeping across Colombia, leaving behind a trail of muddy destruction. Mom and Blanca sit by the window to play Parcheesi and exchange beliefs.

Blanca believes that the recent avalanches have nothing to do with *El Niño* but are caused by *La Madre Monte,* a terrifying force in the shape of a woman who floods and devastates swaths of land whenever she washes her vine-like tresses.

Mom laughs. *"La Madre Monte,* huh?"

"Yeth," Blanca says, mildly offended.

Her lisp makes Mom laugh harder. "Really? Let's hear the San Isidro Labrador's prayer." The one *campesinos* pray to ward off *La Madre Monte.*

But Blanca insists that this particular prayer doesn't scare *La Madre Monte.* Not in the city, anyway. The only way to protect house and possessions is to "thmock a thigar."

"Smoke a cigar?" Mom raises her eyebrows and shakes her head, amused. In the meantime, she's sent every one of Blanca's pawns back to jail. *"A la cárcel!"* she shouts, rubbing her hands together, delighted. "My yellow pawns and I are *lo máximo.*" She gets ready for another game, but Blanca is still confused by Mom's last move.

Sometimes I wonder why she gets such a huge kick out of winning. It's as if with every win, she vindicates herself. As if with every win, she gets a little more even with life.

It's a hot summer day. Mom opens the apartment door and the shutter windows in the kitchen while Blanca makes passion-fruit juice in water. They gulp the weak mixture noisily and rub the chilled glasses on their throats and necks. God, it's hot. Mom sits in her plastic chair by the window. Through the shutters they spot a neighbor's daughter and her boyfriend kissing passionately under the calabash tree. They try not to look, but they do. Mom shakes her head and clicks her tongue. "I know how this—" she points at the kissing couple "—is going to end."

She looks over her shoulder at Blanca, who is breathing down her neck, enthralled. "They're in love," Blanca says, hands flat on the left side of her chest. "It's so sweet."

"Sweet? You call that sweet?" Mom stands up and moves away from the window. "He's sticking his tongue down her throat, for goodness' sake. What's sweet about that?"

"They look nice together. Look again."

"No, thank you." Mom walks over to the sink and begins wiping up bits of passion fruit with a rag, rinses out the metal basin, polishes it with a soft sponge, then repeats the process. She's doing more than cleaning the sink; she's cleansing the whole world of every carnal sin.

Blanca kneels on Mom's plastic chair, keeping her eyes at window level. "Maybe he'll propose right there under the tree. Imagine, one knee on the ground, like this." She puts her bad leg on the ground, does something close to a genuflection, and continues. "Then they'll get married, and she'll look so pretty in a white gown. Then, you know, they'll make babies." She covers her mouth with the good hand. The idea of a couple making babies makes her giggle.

Mom is not amused. "She won't be wearing white. I can tell you that much."

"Why not?"

"Because white is for virgins."

Blanca's jaw drops. "She isn't?"

199

"Don't you see? He's rubbing his stuff against her. Of course she's not."

Mom scratches her head, looking for something else to do, but keeps talking. "He's got the shiniest belt buckle in Itagüí. I'm sure you can see it from the moon."

Mom is disgusted, but Blanca wants to know more about the belt. "What does the shiny buckle have to do with her virginity?"

Mom turns to face Blanca but gets distracted by the electric coil stove. "Who knows where his hands have been?" She removes the four drip pans from underneath the burners. "If she lets him do that in public, imagine all the things she lets him do in private." She replaces the tinfoil lining up each pan, slips them back under the coils, and then shoots Blanca a threatening look. "Watch and learn. That's how a woman, should not, I repeat, should not behave."

"But they look happy."

"Happy? Sure he'll be happy when he gets what he wants, if he hasn't gotten it already, but her? She's damaged goods." Mom stands by the door and fans her face with both hands. "He won't stick around. Men never do."

Sure enough, a few months later, the neighbor, who is about my age, is visibly pregnant. The owner of the shiny buckle hasn't been around for weeks.

"I told you," Mom says to Blanca. *"La mujer es paja, el hombre es candela. Llega el diablo y los quema.* Woman is hay, man is fire. Then the devil comes and burns them both."

"How?"

"How what, Blanca?"

"How does the devil burn them?"

Soon after I graduate from college as a petroleum engineer, BP offers me a job in Bogotá as a geophysicist. I am the last of Mom's children to leave home. But by now, Blanca has become an integral part of her life. She is Mom's appendage. In her company, Mom feels smart, in control; she regains relevance because Blanca still has a lot to learn and Mom is there to teach her everything a woman needs to know, as she did with every one of her daughters.

Blanca is also around when Mom starts developing little annoying habits, like waving the flyswatter at invisible flying things. There are no flies in Mom's apartment, but she swings the swatter by its handle and the vented sheet makes a *boing boing* noise as it reverberates in the air. So she takes to sitting by the kitchen window, swatter at the ready, and watching Blanca make *arepas* from scratch with her good hand. Mix water, quicklime, and dry white maize. Boil the mixture for thirty minutes in the pressure cooker. Check the valve regularly; you never know. Drain and rinse the cooked maize with cold water. Fill the hand mill with the cooked maize and spoonfuls of wet lard. Grind. Pat the brown dough into disks and bronze them on a griddle. Spread them with butter. Eat. Lick your fingers. Repeat.

Mom likes food, especially *arepas*. So does Blanca. And when they eat, they eat a lot. Gradually, as Mom puts on weight, the joints of her legs begin to ache. By the time I quit my job with BP and decide to move to Alaska, Mom's daily walks have become shorter and shorter, her breathing difficult, her mind errant. She is only sixty years old, but the word *Alzheimer's* has already been uttered in various doctors' offices. Mom is in a sort of "wellness limbo," my sisters tell me when we talk on the phone. She's not well enough to live alone because she has episodes of depression, panic attacks, and spurts of disorientation, but she's not impaired enough to require assisted living: she takes showers, looks after herself, does household chores.

Other than a feeble mind and minor old-age aches and pains, she's in good health. Nonetheless, she needs to lose weight, her doctor says. And so a food restriction campaign ensues. First, the starches must go: the beloved *arepas*.

My sisters put Mom on *arepa* watch. Blanca is not to feed her more than one *arepa* a day. Mom protests. She isn't a little girl; how dare anyone ration her food? And how is it that the maid is allowed to eat *arepas* while the lady of the house isn't? To avoid conflicts, maize is scratched from the grocery list. That way neither Blanca nor Mom can eat their favorite maize patties.

"If I can't eat *arepas,* I won't eat anything else, thank you very much," Mom says. She is adamant in her refusal to consume anything other than toast and maybe water, and Blanca has joined her out of solidarity. But by midmorning their bellies are rumbling—*arepas* withdrawal symptoms. Blanca sheepishly suggests a fruit salad with two cans of sweetened condensed milk, for everybody knows fruits are not real food. Later they gorge on two cans of Vienna sausages.

By noon, Blanca sighs a nonchalant "Oh well, too bad we're fasting," for in a few minutes the neighborhood baker will put out loaves of French bread still hot from the oven. The seed has been planted; they swear they can smell the bread from the living room even though the bakery is at least a mile away. Yet Mom feigns reluctance, announcing that she really doesn't want to break her fast.

"But Jethus ate French bread. Ith in the Bible," Blanca reasons, "and Moseth did too, remember?"

Jesus and Moses seal the deal. Mom and Blanca spend the rest of the afternoon eating the bread and pastries they've bought at the bakery. Had the baker offered Jesus warm *buñuelos* or hot *empanadas,* they assure each other, he would not have turned the poor man down.

After a few years of companionship, something mysterious begins to happen. Blanca is making trips to the telephone booth in the parking lot of the apartment complex. Each time she returns to Mom's apartment, she is all giggles, as if she's a bit tipsy. Mom doesn't like the looks of this. Over the years she has seen the same coy smile cross each of her daughters' faces. Foreboding sits in Mom's heart. She knows how the story goes: Blanca's hair will shine with drops of Jupiter made to be held in a man's hands, the skin of her face will turn velvety like a ripe peach ready to be savored, her lips will plump up with mysterious nectars begging to be suckled, she'll discover parts of her she didn't know she owned, and that would be the end of it. Blanca will leave, just as Mom's own girls did, one by one. Men do that to women. They get into their heads with silly nonsense, then into their panties. Next thing you know the girls are gone. Forever.

Instead of playing Parcheesi with Mom, Blanca takes to reading magazine articles with titles such as "How to Know If He Is into You," "Ten Tricks to Drive Him Crazy on the First Date," and "Are You a Good Kisser?" The gates to paradise have been opened, and all of its promised gifts are finally within Blanca's reach. So she declines Mom's invitation to a Parcheesi game and instead devours the magazine, engrossed. While Mom takes her afternoon nap, Blanca tries out different hair styles in front of the mirror. She smudges the wrong shade of makeup onto her eyelids. Mascara clots her short, straight eyelashes. Giddy, happy, and dreamy, Blanca is in love. Mom's fort is under attack; her last bastion sits on quicksand.

"You don't know what love is," she hisses. "You're *muy biche,* too green, to know." The vein on her temple throbs with jealousy.

"Why don't you want me to be happy?"

"You don't know what happiness is either."

As Blanca becomes acquainted with love, Mom becomes acquainted with dementia. Blanca needs the money; Mom needs Blanca.

They watch each other sullenly, their minds muddled with confusing thoughts full of thinning compassion and growing rage. Mom switches from mood to mood like a capricious adolescent and expects everyone else to follow her lead. Guerilla-style, she launches sneak attacks on Blanca's reputation, then retreats to her plastic chair by the kitchen window, looking as innocent as the morning star.

Mom can smell it. It's pungent, and if she could touch this smell it would be warm and viscous like sin itself. It comes from Blanca's body. Mom is certain of this. Each morning, as soon as Blanca walks in the apartment, the smell of sex meanders deep into Mom's nostrils, makes its way down her throat and sits below the ribcage, making her gag with disgust.

"Don't touch my food," says Mom. "Don't sit next to me, don't use the restroom, don't make my bed."

"I haven't given it up, I thwear!"

Blanca's lisp used to make Mom smile, but a woman who sleeps around and gives off an abhorrent smell of sex is no longer trustworthy.

"I'm not that kind of woman," Blanca insists. "I'm not thleeping around!"

Like an unhappily married couple, the two constantly quarrel over Blanca's private affairs. As Blanca grows more and more in love with her boyfriend, Mom becomes more and more jealous, her insults more hurtful, more irrational with each passing day, her fear of abandonment knocking against cold, unchanging reality. *"No se deje engatusar por ese socarrón,* Blanca. Don't let that fool play you," she advises. *"No se pordebajié,* don't humiliate yourself."

But all this *cantaleta* about dignity, all these endless sermons about what a good woman should and shouldn't do, eventually take their toll. Like a boy concerned about hurting his sweetheart's feelings if he breaks up face to face, Blanca telephones Mom and says she doesn't want to be a maid all her life. She's taking a job somewhere else. She'll visit once in a while. "You understand, right?" Blanca chokes up a bit.

"Don't. You. Worry. About. A. Thing." Carefully punctuating each word, Mom frantically searches for her statue of Saint Anthony of Padua, the one with the little boy in his arms, the one who locates what is lost—her glasses, her house keys, her wallet, and now maybe Blanca. The process is simple: blindfold the baby and the saint, flip the statue upside down in a little cup of water, make sure both heads are submerged, and say threateningly, "You can breathe again when you give me back my _____." (Fill in the blank with the name of what you want to find.) Either for his own sake or the baby's, the saint never holds out for long. The object is found, the blindfold removed, the faces patted dry and then moistened with grateful kisses.

Two weeks later, Saint Anthony of Padua and the little boy suffer a horrendous death. They lie now at the bottom of Mom's garbage bag under banana peels, stale bread, and moldy leftovers. She turns instead to Saint Jude Thaddeus, patron of lost causes. When all other avenues are closed, Mom calls on him: "Holy Apostle, pray for me. I am so helpless and alone. Make use, I implore you, of that particular privilege given to you, to bring visible and speedy help where help is almost despaired of. Come to my assistance in this great need that I may receive the consolation and help of heaven in all my necessities, tribulations, and *achaques,* particularly _____, and that I may praise God with you and all the elect forever. Amen."

On the day I turn thirty, my sisters call me in Alaska to wish me a happy birthday and to fill me in on the latest details of the Blanca-Mom saga.

"Mom called her and told her to come and collect her things," one sister says. I can see them in my mind, all gathered at Mom's apartment so that they can place a single international call. Mom must be in the bathroom, out of earshot. My sister goes on: "Blanca said she hadn't left anything here, but Mom was adamant that if she didn't come to pick her stuff up, she was going to throw it into the garbage."

I hear laughter in the background. Another sister comes to the phone and continues: "So Blanca is intrigued, right? And comes anyway. And surprise, surprise, there is nothing for her to collect because, according to Mom, she had already thrown it all away. Can you believe these two?"

I am seized with guilt. I should be there with Mom, saving her from loneliness. I should fly back home and rescue her from fate, snatch her away from the uncertainty of old age, from the claws of abandonment.

"Go on," I say.

"Oh, there's nothing more to say. Blanca looked around, like she didn't know what to do, and then went to give Mom a good-bye hug, and Mom stood there stone-cold and didn't even shake hands with her. She looked Blanca square in the eye and said, 'Have a nice life.' It was funny but sad. You know how it is with Mom."

"Yeah," I murmur. What I really want to say is that I don't know anymore how it is with Mom. Every time I talk to her on the phone, there seems to be a sliver less of her. I'm losing her as much as my sisters are; but by virtue of my absence, I can't quantify my loss. I can only speculate. The situation reminds me of Gregor Samsa in Kafka's *Metamorphosis,* who wakes up from strange dreams to find himself transformed into an insect. Despite his terrifying transformation, his family keeps reassuring themselves that things will be fine again "when he comes back to us." I want that hope.

Meanwhile, my sisters are telling me that they need to do something, *pronto;* they are afraid Mom is no longer capable of completely functioning alone. As they speak, I imagine Blanca limping her way out of Mom's apartment, dragging her good foot across the parking lot, slapping her belly with her lifeless hand as she hobbles past the calabash tree. She stops to catch her breath and tries her hardest not to look back, but she can't help herself. She turns and sees Mom standing rigidly by the kitchen window. She staggers, regains her bearings, and hobbles out of the community gate, out of Mom's life.

"I'm looking for a replacement," says a sister, "but it's not easy. Mom doesn't like anyone I send in for an interview."

"She goes out of her way to scare the shit out of them," she adds. I hear laughter.

"At this rate, Mom is going to have to live with a gypsy maid. Wouldn't that be funny?" I volunteer. "Mom living with one of those gypsies she despises so much?"

"Jesus, Adriana. How long have you been away? There are no gypsies in Itagüí anymore. They moved away years and years ago," my sister tells me.

I don't know why this adds another dimension to my guilt. Mom without Blanca; Itagüí without gypsies. A double void. In my mind, I reenact a scene from an old *Twilight Zone* episode. The one about the loneliness that follows a universal cataclysm that leaves nothing behind but debris and shadows. Mom is in this post-apocalyptic world, crawling on the floor, her hands reaching out, tapping, circling. She is looking for her reading glasses; she is calling Blanca's name, but nobody comes to her aid. Itagüí is a memory. It's all rubble and dust, and Mom may be the only survivor.

Various versions of Mom make cameo appearances in this invented episode. One is a woman broken by neglect and self-deprivation who finds strength to surround her sixth child with love and kindness. This woman hardens when her youngest reaches adolescence; she becomes an iron-fisted tyrant. Then she softens with the birth of her first granddaughter. The rough edges of things disappear until she touches sixty. Then she coarsens again, flickering on and off like a faulty light bulb. Nothing can save her now.

That night I cry myself to sleep. Outside, the aurora borealis sweeps across the sky.

Soon after Blanca's departure, Mom wakes up in the middle of the night, agitated and confused. She can't remember where the restroom is, doesn't recognize the apartment she's lived in for twenty years, and is afraid of getting lost. She needs a companion, now.

First comes Emperatriz, a little woman from the Andes. Shy and unassuming, she avoids eye contact and answers, "Yes, *sumercé;* no, *sumercé.* Yes, your mercy; no, your mercy," in a whispered lilt. She walks with hurried little steps, dragging her feet like a geisha might, shoulders hunched, head down, hands tugging at invisible threads inside the pockets of her black apron. Mom launches an effective civil disobedience campaign, engaging in acts of deliberate subversion. Emperatriz lasts for one week.

Next comes Juana Teresa de los Angeles, a middle-aged black woman from the Atlantic coast. There is nothing demure about Tere, as she likes to be called. She is tall and thick; and when she walks, which she does with a stiff spine like a pedestrian coconut palm, her gelatinous flesh trembles under her dress. She wears oversized hoop earrings with matching necklaces and bangles in every color of the rainbow. She gels back her dense hair and pins it with sparkly plastic barrettes. When she's feeling pretty, which is often, she sports white-rimmed sunglasses and matching shiny white pumps. Her thunderous laughter that sounds like the earth is rocking on broken glass fills every corner of Mom's apartment.

Tere loves to laugh and claims to have a list of 777 jokes written out on a notepad; and if Mom won't be offended, she'll gladly share them one of these days. On her day off, of course, over a cold glass of whiskey, maybe.

Tere only cooks coastal food, and *bollos* are her specialty. *Bollo* made with green maize and sugar, plain *bollo* with regular maize, or coconut bollo with sugar and anise. She makes them with cheese or yucca. When we ask her to stop cooking maize-based food for Mom, all she does is to start bringing *bollos* from her home. "Leave your mom alone," she smiles. "The woman needs food." The smile becomes a laugh. "An old woman that doesn't smoke, doesn't drink, and has no man needs something." She starts to choke with laughter. "Every woman needs at least one vice. Let Tere's *bollos* be your mom's." She lets out a raucous chortle that exposes a mouth full of perfect teeth without fillings, a baby-pink tongue, followed by a dark cave guarded by two tonsils and a playful uvula that bounces like a Slinky.

Today Tere is feeling pretty. Instead of slicking back her hair, she is wearing it *au naturel*. It's an out-of-shape Afro that she's let puff into a halo. She looks like a black cherub. Problem is, Mom doesn't like Afros. "How do I know you're not growing potatoes in there?" she asks, pointing at Tere's head. Mom is in one of her combative moods today. She is critical of Tere's green polka-dotted dress. "You look like a broken traffic light."

Ignoring her, Tere focuses on swaying what she calls Mom's "bile juices." She offers her best coastal dishes—*carimañolas, mote de queso, butifarra, arepa'e huevo, sancocho de rabo y costilla*—but to no avail. Mom won't take the bait.

Bile juices begin to dictate their days. They no longer take afternoon walks because Mom refuses to go outside with Tere and her afro and Tere refuses to slick back her hair. Mom listens to boleros

209

on the radio, but Tere insists that they are making Mom depressed. She keeps changing the station to one that plays *vallenatos* and *cumbias*. When all else fails, Tere shows Mom the 777 jokes. This seals her doom. She lasts seventeen weeks, three days, and eleven hours.

Next comes Azucena, a frail woman in her early twenties who accepts the job on the condition she be allowed to bring along her sick premature baby. At some point between a Parcheesi game and a diaper change, or between a bout of infant projectile vomiting and Mom's lessons on childrearing, Azucena has a nervous breakdown. Her stay is shorter than Tere's was.

When Mom's money starts disappearing, my sisters take over her finances, do her grocery shopping themselves, and put her on a limited allowance. They never stop searching for a companion. Women of all colors, sizes, and creeds come and go. Some stay for a long time; some quit after a few weeks; some don't show up after the first day. Some do the work out of financial need, some out of compassion, some out of loyalty to their Christian tenets. All are thrust against Mom's steely will. She is determined to remain independent, self-sufficient. Every tantrum she throws, every cruel comment she makes is a cry for help. She can see her dignity slithering out of her existence. She is unable to see my sisters' efforts as noble acts of love. Instead, she believes that they are giving strangers authority over her life. She feels infantilized, cornered, reduced. She wants her money back, right now. And no, she will not accept a companion.

"*Todavía no estoy muerta*. I'm not dead yet," she tells me on the phone.

But in ten years my mother will be dead, and her death will teach me a new definition of grief: one that surpasses just the heart being hurt because the pain is hugely widespread. I will feel her void in my cells, in the follicles of my hair, in the cuticles of my nails, in unsuspected places and at unexpected times. At Mom's funeral I will run into Blanca's arms. I'll tell her that she hasn't changed, that she looks exactly the way she did when I left Colombia. She'll sob and say that I look exactly like Mom. I'll feel her limp arm on my back, I'll hobble in sync with her to the back of the funeral parlor, and after realizing that her dimples still give her a childish look and that she still has a lisp, later, without thinking, I'll blurt, "Hey, Blanca, did you ever find out the color of Napoleon's white horse?"

PART V

Home One Last Time

My mother's house. This is where I grew up. I know the worn magic of every sound from every room in every season. This is the house I never expected would change. This is the house where, in my daughter's mind, everything remains transfixed, like the Taj Mahal; everything is exactly as it was when I left it, when I took my daughter north to a country full of glittery promises.

This is the same barrio, Itagüí, only louder. The two-lane Guayabal Road has become a four-lane avenue. The alleyways where the gypsies used to beat their mattresses and tout their phony psychic powers have been invaded by hoards of hawkers. Everybody has something to sell—something cheap, something indispensable. The hawkers from the clothing factories are the worst. They clap in the faces of passersby, grab them by the hands, and pull them inside their stores. "What do you want, *mi amor?* What size are you looking for, *bizcocho?* We have the perfect top for those trousers, *mi vida!* Miniskirts, bustiers, *levantacolas* jeans? Got them all, *mami.*"

All six siblings are riding in our sister's car. Playing the role of man of the house, my brother takes the wheel. He signals a right turn as we approach the Guayabal Avenue exit to Mom's apartment. As we wait at the traffic light, one sister asks, "Look, is that Don Elías?" Her finger taps the car window.

"How could a dirty old bastard like him outlive Mom?"

Yet there he was, Don Elías, sitting on Coca-Cola crates inside his grocery store. Twenty years ago before the big supermarket was built, his was the nearest place to buy fresh vegetables. He was known for shortchanging his patrons; and whenever Mom and I went shopping there, she would make me count and recount the change.

"Damn cataracts," he would say if caught. "Can't see a thing with only one eye." This was true, although the blue cloud that fogged his sight always seemed to work in his favor.

When business was slow, Don Elías sat trimming his dirty nails with a pocket knife. But when business was good, he'd get busy. He'd capitalize on rush hour—usually midmorning—when house-wives and maids dashed through his dimly lit store hurriedly sniff-ing fruits, scratching yuccas and potatoes, poking eggplants, trying to decide which items were best for the dishes they intended to cook for lunch. Don Elías would walk around officiously, the steely hairs on his sweaty arms rubbing against any female part within their reach. Every item in his store was strategically positioned: staple foods lay low on burlap bags so that women had to squat or bend over them. This gave Don Elías the opportunity to peek between their knees or rub himself against their behinds. He hung the scales a couple of inches too high, even for the tallest woman, forcing them to expose precious inches of midriff as they strained to reach the bottom of the deep tray. But what he really loved were women in tight jeans. The sight of those two crescent moons that taut jeans form under a woman's buttocks seemed to catapult him into pure ecstasy; and if he had a frontal view of where the den-

216

im inseam splits a woman's parts into halves like sweet tangerine wedges, he would begin dancing from one corner of the store to another, touching, rubbing, fondling every female in his path as he shouted his fake litany: "Sorry, excuse me, pardon me, passing through."

"He ever touches me or you," Mom would say, her voice loud enough for Don Elías to hear, "I'll give him my own kind of cataracts in his good eye."

He knew all too well that Mom meant every word.

Mom wore scarcity like a badge of honor and remained impervious to the steady improvements in our quality of life. She was thrifty, saved items that she deemed reusable, and never threw food away. If she ever wanted anything, she never told us about it. She bought only what was needed. Yet by the 1980s, when I was in high school, we had really become a middle-class family, not just middle-class wannabes. Gone were the times when we had chicken only for special occasions, mostly birthdays. Mom used to honor the birthday girl by giving her the best part of the chicken, the legs. The meatiest parts of the *pollo* were distributed according to seniority, meaning that I, the youngest, almost always got the wings. I grew up thinking that a chicken was mostly made of wings. But now, instead of cooking our own chicken at home, we could afford go out to Kokoriko and buy a basketful of fried chicken legs with *criolla* potatoes and honey or mild *ají picante*.

Gone, too, was the telegram era. Once this had been the cheapest, fastest, most reliable means of communication. It had finesse. There was a kind of creative elegance to the way Mom wrote her telegrams. She scribbled her message on a piece of paper, and then we went to the nearest Telecom. At the counter, pencil in hand, she modified the wording, scratched her head, read a few words aloud, adjusted her reading glasses on her perfect nose, and waited for the muses to descend. "Should I say, 'Dear Sister,' or 'My Always Remembered and Loved Sister'?" she might ask. Then she would count the words and decide that the second option was too long, too expensive.

When it came to writing telegrams, Mom had her own short-hand code, a succinct way of getting the message across. Her standard wording for a birthday greeting included some variation of "*Que el Señor la colme de bendiciones hoy y siempre*, may the Lord bless you today and always," signed "Carmen and daughters." But when she was strapped for money, she would join her name to the word *hijas* so that, instead of being charged for three words for "Carmen and daughters," she was charged for only one. Carmen and hijas became *Carijas*.

Dad's telegrams were even more succinct, not because he was strapped for money but because he was running out of words to say to Mom. I remember the telegrams that arrived when I was five years old. All were variations of "Expect wire coming week." Four words with no signature told us that he was about to wire some money and that he was not fond of pleasantries. He never specified the amount, so it always came as a surprise, keeping Mom in a state of panic and unable to plan further than a week or two ahead. So she held tight to every penny. She never knew if there would be enough for rent, food, medicine, uniforms, school supplies, buses, lunches.

Miraculously, and thanks to my three eldest sisters, who sold ice cream at The Salitre Amusement Park, made polypropylene purses for sale, and took to school trays of homemade food to sell at recess, Mom made do with what she had. When my father eventually deserted us and stopped wiring money, she put my sisters in charge of earning. She continued to cook, clean, and impart discipline—*sin disciplina no hay ejército*, no discipline, no army.

Our financial situation started to improve when we moved to Medellín, and Dalila, Amanda, and Ligia got secretarial jobs that required them to wear nylons, high heels, and modest suits. Eventually they began going back to school at night, but they never stopped working, never stopped rescuing Mom and their two younger sisters from the constant panic of uncertainty. I owe everything I am to the women in my family—to my sisters and Mom. Nobody else.

The leap forward that Mom took by moving us from Bogotá to Medellín didn't change who she was. She continued to trust no one, never accepted freebies from anyone, although she didn't stop asking for the customary lagniappe, *la ñapa*, kept her wallet locked in her closet, and carried her purse close to her chest, one hand clutching the strap, as if staving off an impending mugging. Only her face changed; her frown got deeper with time and the corners of her mouth looked as if they were pulled down by invisible threads.

Yet she never allowed us to forget we were still a working-class family. My sister and I had our dresses custom-made because this was cheaper than buying clothes off the rack and allowed Mom to control our clothes. When I was eleven and my sister seventeen, we were still wearing matching tailored dresses made by our neighbor Atala, a terrible self-taught seamstress with a sartorial fashion sense inspired in the fifties, a little woman with killer Parcheesi moves that made Mom reconsider her own techniques. Atala, like Mom, was constantly adding new skills to her list of talents. Unfortunately for us she decided to delve into ear piercing, and Mom volunteered her two youngest daughters as Atala's guinea pigs. So on a perfect Medellín afternoon, my sister and I found ourselves sitting on a bench at Atala's place, waiting for the water in her ice-cube tray to freeze. Because her refrigerator's malfunctioning freezer didn't cool its contents evenly, she had been rotating the tray every hour since morning "so all the *cubitos* are ready at the same time."

Atala lived in a typical *paisa* house with a central courtyard and the main rooms spread around it, a Mediterranean architectural style left behind by the Spaniards. From the wooden beams framing her courtyard, she hung fragrant orchids that were always in bloom, an assortment of nectar-rich flowers that attracted dozens of hummingbirds, and a splendid horn fern that was the envy of every housewife on the block. As we waited there for the ice to freeze, my sister and I taunted each other. I called her chicken for not wanting to go first; she called me mommy's baby, and got her way: I went first. I sat in the shady courtyard imagining the fabulous hoops I would sport in my ears—the colors, the shapes, the materials.

Finally, the ice was ready. Atala wrapped her apron around her hand before pressing an ice cube on each side of my right earlobe. "Your ear is the one that needs to go to sleep, not my fingers," she explained. Then she started pinching my earlobes. "Can you feel this? How about now? Ready?" I said yes, yes, yes until I could no longer feel anything. As I waited for my ear to grow numb, I couldn't take my eyes off her needle—too thick for sewing clothes, too thin for mending upholstery, but something in between—or the double strand of black thread she had painstakingly forced through the elongated eye of the needle.

When she pierced my earlobe, I bit my tongue. If I flinch, I thought, my sister will call me mommy's baby. The needle hurt so much that I contemplated telling Atala that girls these days were wearing just one earring, but my sister would have called my bluff. So I endured the same procedure on the other ear, later rejoicing in the thought that my big sister was also in pain and also too proud to flinch.

We left Atala's house with unsightly loops of black thread hanging from our sore ears. She'd instructed us to move the thread around to keep it from attaching itself to our skin, but the exercise was too painful so we decided not to follow her advice. Our school-mates teased us about the string, and two weeks later our ears were swollen with infection and the lobes heavy with pus. We went back to Atala, who proceeded to yank out the thread. I had to wait a couple of years before I could wear my first pair of earrings.

In the 1980s, Mom devised a precarious bookkeeping strategy to keep track of the family finances. Account "Carmen" was an emergency fund to be tapped only when account "Carmencita," the everyday source of money for groceries and bills, had run dry. If the funds in account "Carmen" were to run out, there was a third account, "Cari-jas," to back it up. But if all went well, account "Carijas" would be the money my daughter was supposed to inherit after Mom's death. These were Mom's three main accounts; there were also some other smaller ones. And once Mom's mind started its downward spiral, keeping them up to date and intelligible was daunting.

Now that all my sisters were working and supporting her, the family's financial situation was no longer desperate. Nonetheless, Mom insisted that poverty was a virtue and that Saint Peter opens the doors of paradise only to the poor.

"So, where do the rich go?" I asked her one day on our weekly trip to Don Elías's store.

"Don't know. Don't care," she said as, pinching our noses shut, we walked past the foul-smelling chemical plant. "It's in the Bible: 'blessed are the poor, for theirs is the kingdom of heaven.'"

"How about the 'poor in spirit' bit?" I asked. "Being poor and being poor in *spirit* are two different things."

Mom and I were holding hands, dodging cars, scooters, and other pedestrians as we tried to cross Guayabal Road. "Same thing," she said. A speeding Renault made us retreat to the curb. "You know, the Bible has already been written," Mom added as we looked right, left, and attempted to cross the street for a second time. The traffic was relentless. A stream of scooters zoomed by. We retreated once more to the curb. "So write your own book and leave the word of God alone."

As soon as the traffic slowed, we began sprinting, determined to make it across the road, but a mule-drawn buggy carrying heaps of aluminum cans and cardboard boxes to the recycling center, stopped us cold in the middle of the busy street. We watched as, in slow motion, the emaciated mule collapsed. Her brittle bones made a crackling noise as they shattered onto each other, followed by the din of cans and worthless knick-knacks as they fell off the sides of the wooden carriage. Passersby on the side of the road stopped to look at the dead mule and the disconcerted driver, a thin, sooty-faced boy in his late teens draped in layers of oversized clothing. His grimy hair hadn't seen water in months. Then the gawkers moved on. There was nothing they could do for the mule, the boy, or the two women trapped in the middle of the road like mice on a sticky pad.

Paisa wisdom dictates that misery is a hand we're dealt sooner rather than later and whining doesn't improve our fortunes. Back then, the local panacea was five shots of *aguardiente*, someone to beat the dance floor with, and a trip down blackout lane. That was before we imported depression and insomnia, expensive psychoanalysis sessions and antidepressants. Our communal motto was "*deje de quejarse,* stop whining"; and during the drug-fueled violence that gripped Medellín in the 1980s, these signs became popular in grocery stores and homes, a collective effort to keep our spirits up.

Now we could hear Don Elías's uncouth voice above the screeching cars as he came running out of his grocery store, flailing his sweaty arms in the air like a Sicilian peddler. "Get your *hijueputa* garbage together! You're going to get someone killed with all this shit," he said to the young man who still hadn't moved. The boy was frozen, bewildered, staring at the dead mule, the cans, the sheets of flattened cardboard boxes.

With vigor we didn't know he possessed, Don Elías came to our aid. He darted across the road, shouting all the way, cursing the speeding drivers for not slowing down for "the ladies." When he finally reached us, he apologized to Mom for using foul language in her "fine" presence. In the sunlight his blue cataract-affected eye shone with a formidable bluish sparkle and his gold tooth flickered beneath his unkempt mustache.

Then Don Elías made a mistake. How misguided he was in assuming that he could take advantage of the situation and catch Mom off guard. He gave her a smirk that said, "Well, it looks like I finally get to lay my hands on you," and then reached out to take her elbow, offering to escort her to his "humble" store. But the words *off guard* and *Mom* did not belong in the same sentence. Still standing in the middle of the busy road, she let go of my hand and turned on her heels to face him. Then she put both hands on her hips and gave Don Elías the coldest and meanest stare I had ever seen. Twitching her right eyebrow, she opened her eyes wide and then slowly narrowed them into a mean squint.

"Get your hands off me, you dirty old man," she hissed. *"Viejo verde. Descarado!"*

"Forgive me for being *pobre y viejo,* poor and ugly," he said in the voice of an insincere little boy. He retrieved his hand, cast his eyes down, and crossed back to his grocery store without looking both ways.

I burst out laughing, and Mom gave my hand a cautionary little jerk. "You think it's funny?" She tried to keep a straight face but I knew she wanted to laugh too. *"Viejo desgraciado"* was all she said rubbing her elbow clean.

223

We crossed the street and turned left. That day we walked the mile and a half to the open-air market.

The calabash tree still stands in the middle of the apartment complex. Every year on December 8, the neighbors who lived in the five buildings of our gated community used to light candles at its foot to mark the beginning of the Christmas season. From that *dia de los alumbrados,* night of lights, until the December 24, we met every night to sing *villancicos* with the neighbors' children and pray to baby Jesus for a bountiful Christmas day.

On New Year's Eve, we used to gather by the calabash tree to fly *globos,* hot-air balloons, at midnight. The ritual is timeless, simple, and has a powerful effect. First, acquire several balloons—the bigger, the better. Unfold them gently so as not to tear the thin paper, hold them by their ring, and then run around the parking lot to fill them with air. Next, soak the wick with kerosene, make sure you don't get fuel on the paper; otherwise, the whole thing goes up in flames before taking off. Then light the wick and hold the ring until the hot air fills the balloon, which will begin tugging at your hands. When it feels like it is about to take off, pull it back down. Show it who's boss. Finally, though, let it win, let it go, for with it will also go your sorrows and those of everyone around you. Feel the lightness as your vicissitudes leave your life. As you release the balloon chant, "Go away, sadness, poverty! Injustice, be gone! Away, disease, rancor, troubles! Go away, away!" Stare teary-eyed at the flame propelling the balloon aloft into the sky. Chug an *aguardiente,* if you're a man, or rum with Coke, if you're a woman, and fervently hope that the balloons have indeed whisked away your collective sorrows.

"What happens when the balloon falls?" a neighbor's little boy asked on one of those festive evenings. "Will it burn a house if it falls on top of it?"

224

At first, no one answered. It seemed unfathomable that this object that was alleviating our pain could create suffering for another.

Eventually, after giving the question careful consideration, his father said, "Yes, but if you don't know the house or the people that live in it, it doesn't count."

We all agreed. Case closed.

We held raffles, collected money, *hacíamos vacas,* and had community barbeques. If we raised enough money, we splurged and bought a live pig, which we tied to the calabash tree. The kids chased and mortified the animal all day long; and in the cool valley evening when the warm wind bounced from mountain to mountain enveloping the valley in a dry, cool bubble of joy, the men would flip coins to decide who would kill the *marrano.* Usually the winner would stab it through the heart with a butcher's knife, but if it was a particularly fat pig, he would use a screwdriver. Mocking children squealed along with the moribund pig, while the sweating man, on all fours, wiggled the screwdriver into its chest, drops of human sweat and drool falling onto the animal's belly.

Neighbors helped in different ways. Some would take part in buying the pig, some in chasing it, some in mocking it, one or two in killing it, all the adults in cooking it, and everyone in eating it. We helped ourselves to generous portions of roasted pig with *papas saladas,* boiled potatoes covered in salt, along with fried sweet plantains, crates of cool beer, Viejo de Caldas rum with Coke for the ladies, straight *aguardiente antioqueño* for the men who slapped each others' backs in anis-fueled camaraderie. Those were the good times.

When money was tight and no funds could be raised to buy a live pig, we'd buy free-roaming hens from a nearby ranch "out in the country," which for us meant traveling three blocks past the church, turning right and then left at the traffic light, and following the signs that read *Venta de gallinas criollas*. These hens, raised in someone's backyard, scratched around as they pleased, snapping up grass and bugs, eating maize, leftovers, and even their own shit. No chemicals, pesticides, genetic modification, or antibiotics: they were organically raised before the term *organic* had been invented.

A neighbor would bring the live chickens in the trunk of his car, most likely a Renault 4—deemed for decades the Colombian family car—tied together by their legs, doing their rooster's crow imitation the way they do when in danger, flapping their wings against the walls of the trunk left ajar for ventilation, littering the road with a trail of golden feathers that could be traced back to their coops.

A good *gallina criolla* has got to have thick feet that are a shade of deep yellow, almost orange. The fatter their feet, the more succulent the soup will be. Killing chickens was usually an older woman's job, and Mom was known as an effective hen executioner who made the operation seem effortless. She would grab a hen's head in her left hand and place her right hand at the base of its neck, where the breast begins. Slightly twisting her left wrist clockwise, she would twist the rest of the animal counterclockwise, close her eyes, and yank her hands apart with a single sharp jerk, karate-style. Neck broken, the hen's head sagged in Mom's grip. Severing the neck, Mom soaked the body in scalding water to soften the skin. Then the tedious task of plucking the feathers began.

Once, as Mom was about to execute a hen, a woman who had recently moved into apartment 214 suggested a variation that she claimed was more humane. "You grab the *gallina* by her throat, lay it on the ground, and whack it on the head with a rock," she said, delivering a blow with her right hand in the air. "One good *tiestazo*, and the thing is done."

Among the women, a quick consensus was reached. No, the strike to the head wasn't such a good idea. What if the *guarapazo* didn't kill the chicken straight away? The thing would start flapping its wings trying to free itself, and it would most likely end up shitting on Mom's shoes because that's what chickens do under stress. They shit.

To make enough *sancocho de gallina* for everyone in the community, we needed big pots. Every family would offer its largest, each pot more gigantic than the next, all made of thin aluminum that stained everything black when scrubbed clean with a scouring pad. Chunks of peeled green plantain, *arracacha*, yucca, and three kinds of potatoes—yellow, black, and red—along with smashed green onions, cloves of garlic, and Knorr bouillon cubes were thrown into boiling water along with the hen's breasts, legs, feet, and neck.

On such nights small miracles would unfold. Teenage boys mustered the courage to invite the girls under the calabash tree where they licked each other's lips and savored each other's tongues, which tasted of chicken soup and felt like hens' feet, all gelatinous and salty. Couples stopped their daily bickering and made everyone laugh with old, familiar, off-color jokes. In the bowls of *sancocho de gallina criolla,* chicken feet stuck out like candles on a birthday cake. To the sounds of tango music, one by one said good night under the flickering street lamp, under haloes of light, under starry scraps of heaven.

Now no one knows me around here. It's been almost twenty years since I left this place, and nearly everyone I knew is gone. The few who stayed remember the girl I once was; they don't recognize the woman I have become. This is a place where I now get lost, where I have been forgotten. This is a place that will never be home again.

As my siblings and I get out of the car, an urge seizes me. Inside

Mom's apartment are things that only I am entitled to have. I don't know what they are. All I know, as one of my sisters looks for the keys inside her purse, is that I have to make it through that door before anybody else gets there. I envision a bloody battle of sharp elbows and tripping feet.

Either by coincidence or because we all have devised similar plans, three of us try to squeeze through the door at the same time. One sister gives me a playful push; but playful or not, a push is a push, so I push her back.

"What's the matter with you?" she says, moving back, letting me enter first.

I don't care if I've been rude. If she thinks she is going to get to my stuff before me, she's wrong. I walk past the kitchen and begin making a mental list of the things I'll take with me. I'll need this plastic chair, the one Mom spent so many hours in making sense of the world outside the window. From that chair she kept tabs on the flamboyant neighbor who lived on the top floor. He drove a flashy truck, wore silk shirts, came and left at odd hours, and had a clique of young boys who ran errands for him.

"Either he is a drug dealer or a pedophile," Mom speculated. Later, we found out that he was both.

Sitting in that chair by the kitchen window, she predicted not only that our neighbor's teenage daughter would get pregnant but also the sex of her baby. "It's a boy," she told me, looking at the girl through the glass shutters. "Look at her belly, perfectly round and up here." Mom held an imaginary ball above her own stomach. Three months later, the girl gave birth to a baby boy.

From that plastic chair Mom scanned the parking lot, keeping track of when I missed my 10 P.M. curfew or brought home a new boyfriend. She took great pleasure in assigning these boys nicknames based on their least appealing characteristics: *un zancón* if he was tall, *un espartillo* if he was thin, *un enano* if he was short, *un hippie grasoso* if he had long hair, *un juanlanes* if he was too gentle, *un zarrapastroso* if he was poor, *un baboso* if he was shy, *un ñurido* if he wasn't well dressed.

Sitting in that chair, Mom concluded that Tita, a middle-aged neighbor who lived across the hall, and her cousin Beatriz were not cousins but lovers. *"Areperas,"* she said, making a patty-cake, patty-cake hand gesture to indicate lesbians. The pair fooled everyone in the community, everyone except Mom. And when Beatriz left Tita for a younger woman, heartbroken Tita came to cry on Mom's shoulder, to confide in her that she was a lesbian. "I know," Mom told her.

Yes, I'm claiming that chair. That hideous white plastic chair is coming with me.

I'm also taking the flyswatter, the black river stone that for years Mom used to pound garlic and tenderize meat, her plastic apron stamped with sunflowers. I'm taking the broom with magical powers. To get rid of unwanted guests, place the broom behind a door, bristles up, handle to the floor. Your guests will leave within minutes. Or sweep the feet of a woman with a broom's bristles, and she'll never get married.

I'll pack all of this later, for the real prize is in Mom's bedroom, under her bed, inside her locked closet, or in one of the vanity drawers. I don't know what I'm looking for. I don't know which items I need to focus on finding. All I know is that my sisters and brother are ahead of me down the corridor; and if I don't hurry up, they'll make it to the coveted closet and distribute what's mine among themselves.

I continue with my mental list. I'll need the fern that died several times throughout the years and that Mom managed to bring back to life with a mixture of crushed eggshells and black coffee *cuncho*.

I'll need the Japanese tea set that Mom reserved for a very special occasion that never came. Geishas are carved in the bottom of the cups, intricate three-dimensional dragons on the plates.

I'll also take this picture of José Gregorio Hernandez, a Venezuelan physician whom the Vatican has been trying to canonize for more than twenty years. Back in the seventies, Mom had heard doctors and patients attesting to his intercessory powers among poor people seeking diagnosis and healing. So Saint Gregorio, the most fashionable "saint" in Colombia, became our family physician. Whenever we fell sick, Mom prayed a novena to him:

> *O, my all-powerful Lord!*
> *You have brought your beloved servant*
> *José Gregorio to your heart,*
> *to whom, with your great mercy,*
> *you gave the power*
> *to heal the sick of this world. . . .*

On one occasion, I caught Mom tenderly looking at his picture. In it the doctor-saint stands in a field against a backdrop of high mountains, while behind him a surgical operation is underway in the open air. He wears a black suit and hat and stands with his hands clasped behind his back.

"You know, he isn't a saint yet," I blurted. I was an adolescent, and I was bored, and it was Tuesday, and it had been more than twenty-four hours since I'd last said something mean to anyone.

"Don't mess with my saints." She fogged the picture glass with her breath and wiped it clean with the sleeve of her sweater. "Do I stick my nose in your books and mess with your numbers?"

I explained that his beatification was still underway and that the Vatican hadn't pronounced him a saint yet.

"I don't care what the pope says." She shook her head lightly, eyes shut, right palm up as if taking an oath. "And anyway, how dare you say anything bad about the very same man that saved *you* from blindness?"

At age ten, I had been diagnosed with hypermetropic astigmatism. We walked out of the ophthalmologist's office with a prescription for glasses.

"Nice little business these doctors have." Mom put the prescription into her purse without looking at it. "You don't need glasses. What you need is exercises like this," and she proceeded to show me how to fix my problem by looking at the tip of a pencil—first up close, then far away.

When my eyesight took a turn for the worse and the headaches became migraines, Mom decided it was time for divine intervention, time for Saint Gregorio to lay his healing hands on me.

Tucked into bed, dozing off as she always did, Mom prayed the novena for nine nights in a row, at the end of which she announced that Saint Gregorio had agreed to intervene on my behalf. "He'll be operating on you soon. Maybe tonight." There was no hint of uncertainty in her voice. "I can't tell how many operations he has scheduled ahead of yours. We'll have to wait."

On my night table Mom left what the saint would need for surgery: a shot glass filled with rubbing alcohol, two cotton balls, her picture of Saint Gregorio, and some coins as tokens of gratitude. Every morning she stared at the night table, looking for clues, trying to ascertain if the saint had paid me a visit. She examined the cotton balls, looked in and around the shot glass, counted the coins. "Not yet" was her verdict for seven consecutive days. But on the ninth night, he operated on me. Mom knew this because the rubbing alcohol in the glass was almost gone.

"It's called evaporation, Mom," I said, a little unnerved. "I learned that in school."

231

She wasn't listening. "Look, he didn't even charge us," she said, counting the coins. She threw away the prescription for glasses, lit a candle by the saint's picture, covered my eyelids with kisses, and cried out, "*Gracias, San Gregorio, gracias, San Gregorio!* She's cured. She's healed!"

This is the room where Mom took her last breath, the place where I expect to feel her presence, where her soul and mine will meet in a farewell embrace. So I wander around it like a lost child, my eyes trailing my heart as if searching for clues, unearthing rubies, floating in my memories of her hair, gray like liquid silver. But I feel nothing. This room that for more than twenty years smelled of Mom and palpitated along with her heart today is nothing more than a sterile box, cold like a sheet of slate.

Each of her children is on a quest to capture a figment of what is believed to linger in the air after a person's passing: the shuffle of her feet, a ghostly cough, an ethereal utterance, a rainbow without rain, something fantastic that we can experience together. But better yet, I think, I want my own, private, cosmic rendezvous with Mom. I sit on the edge of the bed holding the pajamas she was wearing when she died. I sniff at the soft cotton, with inhalations that gradually grow in intensity and desperation. I move from chest to neck to armpits. Nothing. Mom must have taken away her scent with her.

"This smells like Mom," my sisters say as they pass around her sweater. I snatch it from their hands and bury my face in the wool. I turn the pockets inside out and take a long lungful of cardigan. But whatever they smelled a moment ago is forever gone. My sisters must have breathed in the last traces. I curse them in my head for stealing Mom from me.

My sisters claim that the dress she wore on her last day on earth

232

carries her essence within its seams, that her warmth lingers on her pillowcase, that she is still unmistakably with us. They feel her presence, and I am consumed by jealousy. I have always assumed that Mom and I loved each other best. I don't know how to cope with the discovery that my sisters have infringed on this assumption. I don't know how to tell them that in those afternoons of my childhood while they were at work or school, Mom and I created a private life together. And because none of them listened to "*Aqui Resolvemos su Caso*" or "*Boleros en su Ruta*" with her, they can't understand what we created. Because they were too old to jump under the sheets with her to listen to "*El Código del Terror*" they don't know what she looked like when she was terrified, how she dug her fingernails into the mattress until the sheet was crumpled up and wet with her sweat. They don't know the Mom that I know.

A silent auction of sorts takes place. "Can I have this?" one sister asks, holding Mom's wooden crucifix.

"I'll keep this," another sister says, her eyes fixed on the framed painting of the *Virgen del Carmen*.

"This is mine."

"This is for me."

"Do you girls mind?"

These are the last slivers of the previous forty years of our lives. When marriages went sour and we were heartbroken, this was home. This was the anchor in our lives, a place that, unlike us, didn't change. I realize that my attachment to Mom's apartment is umbilical, and I don't want to be expulsed from a womb again. Yet in a few minutes, La Hortensia Gated Community on Eighty-first Street will be a part of my past. I'll turn on my heels and will never come back to apartment 113 with its kitchen overlooking the *totumo* tree; its living room facing west; its two contiguous bedrooms, the girls' rooms that went dark every evening

233

as the sun sank behind the tree line along the community fence. I'll never come back to the shower stall with translucent doors and low acrylic ceiling, its outdated neon lights constantly flickering, the miswired water heater that was never completely repaired. I'll leave behind the built-in bookcase at the end of the hall where for years Mom kept twelve volumes of the *Encyclopedia Britannica,* a weighty ashtray made out of yellow Murano glass, a battery-operated antique automobile with a driver whose head bobbed when it was turned on, the gold-leaf wine dispenser set with matching shot glasses that Mom used every Christmas to treat us to Manischewitz, a copy of Cela's *La Familia de Pascual Duarte* and one of *The Interview with History* and *Letter to a Child Never Born,* both by Oriana Fallaci, the one writer we all loved. Mom's room will be someone else's room, and whatever of her that still lingers in the air will be extinguished forever.

A part of me is dying today.

"*Dios Santo*, look at this!" my brother says, his voice faint, as if he is drowning.

In a far corner of Mom's closet lies an old letter folded into quarters. It appears to have been composed on a portable Deluxe Model 5 Remington typewriter, and it opens with *Estimada señorita.* The first paragraph tells the story of a young man's sleepless nights, the fortitude of his unwavering heart, and how he longs for permission to look into the eyes of a woman more perfect than he deserves.

Magic spills over us. My brother reads the second paragraph aloud, and the moment he says, "Whenever you look at me—" we complete the sentence in unison. We know these words by heart. Mom told us countless times about this very letter, the first love letter Dad wrote for her. "*Cuando usted me mira me siento transportado al cielo de Mahoma enardecido levemente en ópalo y*

234

topacio. Whenever you look at me, I feel transported to Moham-med's heaven, lightly engulfed by opal and topaz." Our voices move through me like the vibration of a tuning fork. Soon the awesome feeling will be gone, I know. The world will return to what it was and I'll belatedly graduate into womanhood. So I hold onto the words *opal* and *topaz* for as long as I can.

Secretly we had all doubted the existence of this letter, had chalked it up to Mom's overactive imagination, but here it lay, im-pudent and defiant, irrevocable proof that our father had once been a young prince with a pure heart. The hellish fifty years that had fol-lowed the letter's composition couldn't destroy its truth: Mom had experienced love, and Dad had once loved her. All of us, including my brother, aloft in a fizz of lost memories, begin to cry.

My mind hums the opening of a *vallenato.* When I was about six, my parents slow-danced to this song in our apartment. Dad was tipsy enough to look like he cared. Eyes closed, Mom lay her smooth cheek against his shirt. Her quiet smile was a signpost: "Do not disturb; woman in love." I remember Alfredo Gutierrez's na-sal voice submerged beneath the frantic, melancholic sound of his devil-possessed accordion. *"Anhelos tengo de verte vida mia. . . . "* While Mom dreamed against his chest, Dad sang along, dragging out each word, enunciating every syllable, finishing each verse with his head upright, his mouth making a dark *O* as he held the final note. *"Anhelos de besarte noche y dia. . . . "*

Mom was not as good a dancer as Dad was; but that night, in front of my little girl's eyes, Mom seemed to levitate with him. I didn't spend too much time looking at Dad for everything a little girl needs to know is written in her mother's face. So I engraved her face in my memory, paid attention, and learned from Mom my first definition of love: a magnificent force that transforms a small woman into a giant as tall as the man she loves; a force that makes her weightless and uncatchable, like a dust mote tumbling in lazy light.

My brother holds the letter in his hand and then, without looking at any of us, starts to fold it back up. Before he puts it into his pocket, one of my sisters and I reach to touch it. Perhaps the paper holds some magic, some essence of what my parents had shared a lifetime ago, in those days when Dad cared and Mom dreamed. My brother concedes and lets us touch a corner or two. I want to tell him that he doesn't deserve to keep the letter, that one of the girls should have it, preferably me, that he doesn't have the foggiest idea about how many times Mom had mentioned the damn letter with its opal and topaz, but mostly I resist the need to cry. That letter is my only evidence that Mom had been more than a mother. She had also been a woman.

It takes us a few hours to dissect the house, to distribute among ourselves the things that took Mom a lifetime to amass. Most of the furniture will be donated to the local church; the sisters who live in Medellín will take Mom's plants and some kitchen appliances; my brother will keep what's left of her once robust record collection, including an LP with the intermezzo from the opera *Cavalleria rusticana,* which Mom adored, and an old recording of a Japanese violinist playing a version of the Hungarian dance tune known as *czardas,* which made Mom's chest heave with emotion.

I imagine landing in Miami, trying to make it through customs with a fern, a plastic chair, a flyswatter, a river stone, and a broom, and have to laugh at my childishness. I discard my mental list. Instead, I take a pair of earrings that belonged to my grandmother, jewelry that Mom never wore but treasured all her life; a photo of the six women—my four sisters, Mom, and me—that my brother took the day I left Colombia; the locket with a photo of my daughter that Mom wore around her neck like an amulet. I also seize the printout of Mom's last EKG, taken two days ago. "She has the heart of a fifteen-year-old," the doctor had told my sisters.

I don't know this yet but in six years I will look at this EKG and realize that the ink is fading away and with it the only existing traces of Mom's heartbeat. I'll have it tattooed around my left bicep, much to my family's dismay, so that her heartbeat and mine will always be together.

Before we leave home forever, I lie on Mom's bed and face her ransacked closet. A few minutes later, one of my sisters joins me, curling in tight against my body. I visualize the knobs of my spine pushing into her chest. My heart quietly thuds against her hand, so close in sound to her own heart, that after a while she can't tell the two apart. As I lie there on the bed, I spot a pair of shoes in a corner of the closet. We must have overlooked them during our cleanup.

"Are those Mom's tennis shoes?" I ask my sister.

She lifts her head to look. "They sure are."

"I think I'll take them with me," I say. "Maybe I'll finally know what it's like to walk in Mom's shoes."

"You do that," she whispers into my neck and hugs me tightly against her chest.

Leech

My mother used to say that death smelled of sulfur. That there was not such a thing as a sudden death because there were always telltale signs that someone was about to die: a black fly hovering over a deathbed was a sure sign that the sick would never recover; a dark butterfly affixed to a window looking in on the living was a clear death sentence. Even vultures sometimes could foretell death by wheeling overhead. To accept the concept of sudden death was to admit that God possessed a mean streak; and the benevolent creator in whom she so fervently believed could not possibly possess such a mortal flaw. Surely, neither God nor her army of saints, virgins, and the countless souls that dwell in purgatory would possibly allow humans to depart this world without saying their goodbyes. Death was a process, something that the creator customized for each individual. Death was a tunnel, a passageway into hell, heaven, or purgatory (or limbo if the dead hadn't been baptized), one final hurdle before entering a vast universe of nothingness.

Yet she died unexpectedly, proving herself wrong.

I like to think that the night she died, she thought of me, her youngest; that on her way to bed, she stopped, looked at herself in the mirror, and wondered if, in thirty years, I would look like her reflection. And that she nodded and smiled. That she remembered the conversation we'd had fifteen years earlier. I like to think she said to herself, I've got to talk to Adriana and tell her to ignore what I said. To blame it all on the feeble mind of an Alzheimer's patient who sometimes confuses reality with fiction, whose tongue sometimes gallops away. I like to think she was lucid enough to want to call me and recant—which is to say, to lie. I know I would have believed her.

Alaska. That was as far away from home as I could get when I first left Colombia. Two years later, when I had begun to grow roots there and believed that I would be buried under the permafrost, I asked Mom to spend a summer with me. This was the first time she'd ever been out of Colombia, and for her everything in Alaska possessed a glittery splendor: fast highways, big cars, bears and moose wandering in backyards, all-you-can-eat restaurants, the enormity of the mountains, the physical appearance of the Inuit and the Athabaskan, our proximity to the North Pole. Everything was so new, so exciting, so vast.

Still, she seemed to have short periods of confusion. Jetlag, I thought. But as the days passed, I realized that her mind was taking involuntary trips to a dark island where nothing happened and nothing existed, a faraway place where silence was king. For minutes at a time, she would fall into a trance, never blinking or twitching, staring into space—impassive, mute, pitiful. Her mind seemed to have a mind of its own.

On the summer solstice, we woke up to a perfect day in Alaska. Daylight hours: twenty. Temperature: mid-seventies. Chance of rain: negligible. Humidity: low. Flowers were in riotous bloom: wild iris, lupines, monkshood, forget-me-nots, fireweed, bunchberries, jewelweed, salmonberries. It was the kind of day that makes a person take stock of her life. Here I was in Alaska, married to an American. I had a daughter, a house, a car. I ate unfamiliar food, spoke a foreign language. I had discovered a passion for anthropology, found loving friends, and, for the first time, seemed to have made a life of my own that didn't involve family, country, and church. Still, there was something I had always wanted to know, something I needed to hear from Mom, foolishly thinking that this would close the chapter of my life as a child and start a brand-new one as an adult woman. I wanted to know the history of my making.

By midday, Mom, my six-year-old daughter, and I were on Parks Highway en route to Eklutna Glacier. We drove with our windows down, humming to old songs. Occasionally my daughter would tell a knock-knock joke that Mom didn't get or sing a Barney song that Mom had never heard before. I looked at us as I drove. There we were, three women, three generations, right there, confined together in a truck, slowly moving north toward the end of the earth.

Twenty-six miles later, we were in the village of Eklutna. I wanted to show Mom the tiny, colorful buildings called spirit houses that the Dena'ina Athabaskan people built over graves. "What are the houses for?" she asked.

"To house the spirit of the dead," I said.

"You don't need a house after you die."

"Don't they look pretty, though?"

"What's the point if the dead can't see them?"

"Well, some people bring flowers to their dead. The Athabaskan build tiny houses."

"Don't you even think about it. You hear me? I don't want a house on my grave."

"Why not?"

"You think I'd like yet another landlord knocking on my grave-stone? I had enough of those in my lifetime, thank you very much."

She laughed; I laughed; even my daughter seemed to get the joke and laughed.

"Will it get dark today?" Mom asked.

"No. Same as yesterday and the day before. You'll be asleep by the time it gets dark."

"I've never heard of a place like this," she said looking up to the clear sky. "Daylight all day long. I could've used days like this when you were little kids." Before we got into the truck, she added, "There was always so much to do. So many chores. Jesus Christ."

We drove past the blue, frozen valley of the glacier, past the roaring waters of Thunderbird Falls, past a throng of Japanese tourists clicking cameras at a grazing moose, past the vast and empty spaces of Alaska, until we arrived at Mirror Lake, one of the best places in the state for trout fishing. We sat on the shore and had a picnic. Then we lay down on a blanket and held hands, Mom to my right, my daughter to the left. Mom was particularly lucid that day. She was her old self, witty and sardonic, and we gossiped about my sisters and relatives. No one was spared, no topic off limits. It was a mother-daughter moment, the woman-to-woman moment I had been longing for all my life. We were equals now. I was a wife, a mother; the mysteries of womanhood had already been revealed to me. So I asked my question.

"Do you remember when you were pregnant with me?" We were sitting up now, watching my daughter, who was trying in vain to turn cartwheels on the sand. Moving closer to Mom, I put my arm around her.

"Oh yes, I remember each of my five pregnancies."

"Six." I whispered in her ear. Her earlobe was fuzzier and lon-ger than I remembered.

"Yes, six."

I should have stopped talking, stopped pressing for details about her last pregnancy. I should have realized that forcing her to remember details from 1965 would be too much for her.

As it turned out, it was too much for me.

"You ought to understand that you weren't planned. I already had five children," she said, patting my hands, rubbing my forearm, tapping her fingers on mine.

"Your father was never around, but I can tell you this: he, for sure, came to visit me five times." She smiled. A naughty joke from mother to daughter. "Five visits, five children. Get it?"

"Six."

"Yes, six. Anyway, your brother, your four sisters, your dad when he was around, and I were living in a one-bedroom apartment in the projects. Can you imagine that?" she asked, taking her eyes off the water. Our gazes locked. I noticed that her once dark brown eyes were turning grey. "The last thing I wanted was another baby. So you can imagine when I found out I was pregnant. Oh, Jesus, that was terrible." She broke our gaze and looked back out at the water.

The trout were restless. We could see their silvery scales dipping in and out of the water, mouths and gills gaping, dragon eyes shining. A park ranger was leading a group of fishing aficionados down to the lake. I could hear his instructions: "Even the most inexperienced angler knows this: if you decide to kill a trout, kill it quickly, as soon as you land it. A solid whack above the eyes will do this job well. Leaving a trout to gasp to death on the bank will ruin the meat. If you decide not to kill a fish after catching it, try not to handle it at all. Remove the hook while the fish is still in the water so that it doesn't damage itself as it struggles. Lifting a trout out of the water reduces its chances of survival."

Mom said, "And so I did what I had to do to stop you from

being born. I mean, we were struggling. Food, rent, uniforms, everything." She shook her head and then cocked it, as if the motion refreshed her memory. "I went to a *bruja* I knew. She gave me the drink. It was thick, slimy, green stuff that would take twenty-four hours to make the baby, you know, go away. Only it didn't. So I went back to the old witch. She said she had given me her most potent potion. There was nothing else she could do to help me. It was up to me if I wanted to stop this. You." Mom tapped her belly.

"It's all right, Mom. Really," I said, and I kissed her on her temple, not because it really was all right but because I wanted her to stop. I took a beer out of the cooler and gulped it down in a few swigs, until I had yeasty bubbles running down my chin. I burped a loud belch that tasted of hops and sounded like a whimper.

Mom kept going. She described a litany of workout routines that no fetus should have survived: jumping, squatting, running, lying flat on her back with a stack of hardcover encyclopedias on her stomach, pushing, vomiting, chain smoking, praying. When none of these approaches worked, she doubled her intensity: fast sprints, pushups, bicycle crunches, rope jumping. She was desperate to abort me.

My daughter wandered up to us. "Grandma, can I take a picture of you and Mom together?"

I shook my head. "Not now, I'm talking to Grandma."

But Mom said, "I'm ready," and pulled a lipstick from her purse, delighted. "How do I look?" she asked, after applying it a little beyond the corners of her mouth.

"Gorgeous," I said. We put our heads together like a teepee, and I faked a smile, staring into the yellow Kodak box.

After my daughter snapped the photo, I kicked some pebbles with my hiking boots. My eyes welled with tears, and I felt a feral urge to jump into the lake and sink slowly into its frigid waters.

"But you, my girl," Mom continued, "you clung to my womb for dear life. Like a *sanguijuela*."

"Like a leech?" This was more than I could take.

"Yes. Attached. You know what I mean," she said, raising her fists as if she were describing a war hero. "So determined to live. So, how can I put it, stubborn? Do you understand me?"

I nodded. But I couldn't bear another word from her. "We'd better get going," I said. "It's getting cold." I kissed her once on each cheek, wrapped a shawl around her shoulders, collected the blanket, the chairs, the cooler. We started walking back to the truck, and I readied myself to drive past the mountains and the rivers that I could barely imagine existing without her.

The park ranger was still talking: "If the fish must be lifted from the water, a net is best. Try to remove the hook without touching the fish, and tip it back into the water from the net. And never, ever, not even once touch a trout's gills. Trout often go into a kind of catatonic state after being landed but seem to be able to swim away quite rapidly after what looks like a near-death experience."

By the time I got behind the wheel, I was drained, broken. But Mom was hungry. "Can we go to one of those restaurants where you can have seconds?"

"Sure," I said. What I didn't say was, How can you be so cruel and so oblivious at the same time?

"So tell me again. Why doesn't it get dark at night?" Mom asked for the tenth time.

"Because we are very close to the North Pole," I said, trying not to show my irritation. I had been answering the same questions since she arrived. I needed her to be quiet.

"And why did it take me almost two days to get here from Colombia?"

"Because you had to fly across the whole of the United States,"

244

I said, but I was thinking, How many times do I have to tell you?

"Did I fly over the ocean?"

"Yes."

"Did I fly over countries?"

"Yes."

"Which ones?" she asked, breathing on her bifocals and wiping them clean.

"I already told you."

"Well. Obviously. I. For-got." Mom took a notebook out of her purse. "Have you seen my reading glasses?"

"They're on your nose."

"Oh," she said, readjusting them. "Where were we? Oh, the countries. Which ones did I fly over?"

"I'm not sure, Mom."

"Well, *sorry*. Didn't mean to bother you," she said, half-disappointed, half-indignant.

Instead of a list of countries, I gave her what I thought would be a simple geography lesson, something easy to remember so that she would stop asking. "What happens, Mom," I said as if I were about to reveal a big secret, "is that Alaska used to be a part of Russia."

"Russia," she repeated as she took notes. "I thought we were in the United States."

"We are," I said, realizing that Mom was even more confused now. "The United States bought it."

"So we are in Russia."

"No, Mom. We are in the United States. America bought Alaska from Russia. So Alaska is no longer Russian. It's American."

"Nonsense. If the Chinese buy Mariquita, would you say that Mariquita is no longer in Colombia?"

I didn't have the energy to argue with her reasoning. I sighed and watched her write in her notebook. "I didn't know you kept a diary."

"I don't. Diaries are for teenagers."

"So what's that?" I asked, pointing at her notebook.

"What? This? My impressions about Russia. That's all. Beautiful, beautiful land. The Russians too. Good-looking people. Love their little houses at the cemetery. So quaint."

I smiled. I couldn't help it.

"What?" she asked.

"Nothing," I said, shaking my head. "I think you're losing your marbles."

"So will you, eventually. You'll see," she whispered as she leaned over my shoulder. "Quiet now, *la niña* is asleep." Mom held a finger to her lips. I looked in the rear-view mirror, then over my shoulder. There she was, the youngest of this chain of women, mouth half-open, slivers of drool trickling from her tiny mouth, a collection of freshwater shells slipping through her fingers—empty shells, shells that once had life squirming inside them, shells that no longer were oysters or pearls or mussels. Disemboweled shells.

I picture her last night. I think she went to bed early. She was tired, and the real world had lost its luster a long time ago. From her apartment, in diapasons, she could hear the life outside percolate into her room, the cacophony of Medellín: children playing, cars crunching gravel, sirens blaring in the distance. So much noise. People and their whims were also beginning to bother her. She often said, "The more I get to know people, the more I love my dog." But she had no dog.

I think she pulled the covers over her head and breathed in the lavender fragrance of the sheets. As for herself, she no longer smelled of anything. She recalled the various aromas her body had given off over the years: guava jelly when she was a little girl, blood when she became a woman, the patchouli scent one of her children had given her for Mothers' Day, the potpourri of her menopause.

246

After that, nothing. Her body had become a dry riverbed, devoid of milk, blood, or sweat. Her body had become uninhabitable, a condemned house about to implode on its foundations.

She began her nightly prayers, dozing off as she always did. When she woke a few minutes later, she tried to finish them but could not remember which one she had been saying. Was it an "Our Father" or a "Glory Be"?

"One of these days," she used to say, "I'm going to unscrew my head and give it a good wash inside."

She was finding it more and more difficult to keep tabs on life. The days of the week had become indistinguishable. Church on Sundays, or was it Tuesdays? Grocery shopping on Wednesdays, or was it Saturdays? Her life was complicated by misplaced objects. Hairbrushes, reading glasses, house keys all seemed to have mischievous minds of their own. She meant to water her plants every other day, but that night she wasn't sure if she was keeping that schedule. Without water, the exuberant fern that had taken her years to grow might die. Then again, maybe she had already watered it.

She fell asleep wishing for a better tomorrow. Tomorrow, she hoped, she would emerge from this chrysalis of gloom; she would wake up lighter, less clumsy, more nimble, less lost, more assertive, less tight-chested, freer. A noise woke her up. An ominous black witch moth made its way into Mom's room; it fluttered its wings against the walls; it hovered over her bed, the black eyes on its forewings watching Mom. Watching and waiting. Mom gasped for air, making snorts that she didn't recognize as her own. Something had locked beneath her sternum obstructing her breathing. A surge of panic settled in her eyes.

"God, I can't breathe," she said between gasps. Swaths of colors flashed in glittery snapshots of rain under her eyelids. She massaged her throat with one hand, then the other, then both. She pressed at her breastbone. My God. And whatever was lodged in her chest began to expand and sharpen, climbing up her windpipe like a millipede.

"San Gregorio Bendito, Virgen del Carmen, ánimas del purgatorio, don't abandon me," she repeated in her head like a mantra, invoking every one of her divine saviors. Her muscles hardened like cardboard left out to dry in the sun and, in a convulsive burst of speech, she called the live-in nurse. "Don't let me die," were the only words she managed to whisper. She threw a couple of slow-motion punches at the nurse as though she was drowning in quick-sand, then clutched the nurse's skirt. For a few seconds, the nurse wrestled with Mom's grip.

"Don't let me die," she pleaded once more. Her whisper was almost inaudible. My mother's mouth made silent *O*s in moribund exhalations of moist air. Her head lunged up with an involuntary jerk; her body contorted with pain. She felt the nurse's hands on her chest, pressing on her sternum with little pushups that burnt my mother's skin. She heard the nurse fumble with the telephone. Words filled the room: *mom, dying, come, soon.* "You are not alone," the nurse said. "I'm right here with you." She put her arms around my mother.

Mom began to snore in the agonal respiration, a ragged, gurgling pattern of breathing typical of those who are near death. Then her chest jolted as if she had been hit by lightning. A few seconds later came a weaker strike, followed by something similar to a quiet belch. Her jaw shifted south, then east, changing the geography of her face in quick succession. In her face was tension, then pain, then agony, then resignation.

That was what the nurse saw from the outside. But inside Mom felt something similar to drunkenness. Her head swelled and the crown relaxed and quivered, then melted into a blue sky. She was floating; her thoughts were like fireworks exploding into each other; and in a flash of sparks, she found herself in the place she loved most in the world,

248

Mariquita. Here, in this place that smelled of avocado and earth after rain, she was no longer my mother. She was Carmen. Just Carmen.

Childhood. Innocence. Trees. The beats of a slow *cumbia* meander from the house and into the backyard where the little girls chase each other. Carmen and her younger sister Gilma climb an avocado tree, its branches heavy with oily fruit. They are carrying a *guanábana* they found on the ground. A crack opens the soursop's spiky skin, and its white pulp oozes milky juice. The girls chew on wads of the creamy, fibrous flesh, gargle it in the back of their throats, and then cough it out, pretending it's phlegm. They'll get a good whipping if their mother catches them perched up in a tree, acting like men. So they decide to pretend to be grown-up women. They sit cross-legged on the tree branch, smoke imaginary cigarettes, and drink from invisible teacups, pinkies in the air. When this game gets old, they shine up four black soursop seeds and make earrings, which they stick onto each other's earlobes. With the rest of the seeds, they make spitball bullets that they shoot out of the tree like crazed cannoneers.

Food. Family. Home. Carmen's mother is teaching her and her two sisters how to make tamales. They found themselves gravitating toward the kitchen so often that they declared it the only place of the house where they truly felt at home. Her mother cooks pork skin and ribs. She uses the gelatinous fat removed from the pork to make the *guiso* and fries onions, garlic, and saffron in it. When the *guiso* is ready, she mixes it with the rice, peas, and corn dough. On the table Carmen and her sisters lay out plantain leaves for wrapping the tamales. The two of the sisters tie them with twine. But Carmen ties hers with red and blue ribbons sprinkled with glittery dust.

Women. Water. Blood. Carmen stands by the river with her two sisters and her five daughters. They bend their naked bodies over the rocks and wash their wombs and their hearts.

"Who has the bloodiest of all?" one of them asks.

"Carmen!" they shout in unison. The women embrace her, and one of her girls begins to sing. But mid-note her sweet contralto becomes an angry howl. The other women join the howling, and so does Carmen, who seems to be the angriest of all. Soon they hear voices of other women crossing, naked, the *cordillera*. By the time the sun sinks into the horizon, the water is thick and scarlet, and there is not a single silent woman. Or one who isn't angry. Or one with her womb and heart intact.

Earth. Love. Tears. Carmen wraps the letter in a plastic bag and puts it into a small lacquered box. He told her it was from China, but she knows it's a cheap knickknack he probably bought at a bar, either before or after passing out. On the day he leaves her for a younger, prettier woman, she takes the box outside and sets it on the ground. It's Wednesday and rain is beginning to fall. All day she looks out the kitchen window, watching raindrops bounce off the box. From her bedroom at night she imagines the box in the rain. The weight of the life contained inside the box is beginning to bury it in the ground. On Sunday after church, she buys a hand trowel and digs a hole at the center of the earth. She places the box at the bottom and covers it with wet soil that smells of magnolias. She doesn't tell anyone, but whenever he looked at her, she felt transported to Mohammed's heaven, lightly engulfed by opal and topaz.

I think that Mom's memories began to fade. A vacuum sucked her upward with a violent jerk as if an invisible parachute had opened above her head. Then everything was quiet; everything was white; everything stopped. She no longer gasped for air. Her jaw loosened.

Beads of saliva foamed in the corners of her mouth. Her neck yellowed like a withered daffodil, and her eyes fluttered and closed ever so slowly. There was no smell of sulfur; there were no marauding vultures. An unfathomable chasm of nothingness swallowed her whole.

Love. She is in his arms. She is safe. Every concavity of his dark body fits nicely into the corresponding convexities of hers. Perfection. Her cheek fits into his chest like a puzzle piece. His heart plays a tango, hers a *bolero,* and together they hum and dance to all the songs ever written. Husband and wife; man and woman. He is fire; she is the earth. Whatever he destroys, she'll replenish with opal and topaz. Gladly. Lovingly.

Epilogue (Ossuary)

Among Tibetan Buddhists there is a burial custom known as *jhator* in which mourners give alms to birds of prey and offer the body of the deceased to the four great elements: earth, water, fire and air. The vultures are seen as sky dancers, angels that take the soul into heaven. Allowing the birds to eat the flesh of the dead guarantees a safe passage to that great windy place where souls are reincarnated. *Jhator* is an act of love, a last gesture of compassion and generosity. A dead body is an empty vessel; therefore, preventing other creatures from feasting on it is considered the ultimate display of selfishness. Bad karma.

When a person dies, the body is cleaned, wrapped chin to knees in a seamless white cloth, and left untouched for three days. During this time the soul starts its slow migration out of our realm. On the third day, at dawn, body breakers called *rogyapas* lay the body on a flat rock atop a hill, unwrap it, and dismember it. The flesh is offered first to the vultures. After most of the flesh is gone, the *rogyapas*, armed with mallets, break the bones. They grind them with yak butter, flour, and tea and offer the pulp to the waiting smaller

252

birds: crows and hawks. Everything is consumed. Everything is offered. Everything is taken.

I first learned about *jhator* when I was studying to become an anthropologist. Immediately I loved the idea. I imagined my own *jhator,* my body spread wide like a banquet, birds of all sizes landing on my chest, feeding off my thighs, my face; feathery creatures taking off from my navel and landing on the runway of my belly and later coming back for more. My remains would be delicious, transcendent, ripped into submission, and garnished with the savory chemicals the body secretes after rigor mortis.

For years, images of my own *jhator* passed before my eyes in snapshots of morsels of me being whisked up into a vast Sargasso of nothingness. Sharp beaks dredging residual chunks of me from the Mariana depths of my dry arteries. How beautiful. This is how I want to go, how everyone should go, I thought. Everyone. Yet my fixation with sky burials disappeared when Mom died. I came out of her body, and it was only after her death that I secretly claimed proprietorship over her flesh and bones. I didn't want her to be cremated, or buried, or embalmed. I didn't want her to be seen or touched. I didn't want anyone to utter her name. I didn't want her to be dead.

There is beauty in imagined *jhators,* in the funeral pyres I saw along the Ganges, in the Fado songs at funerals in Portugal, in the recitation of the Kaddish, in faraway death rituals where the dead are strangers. But this was Mom's death, followed by a real wake, a real funeral, a real cremation. My sisters and I authorized the reduction of her body to a heap of ashes. None of it was imagined and none of it was beautiful. Three days after her death, the only traces of her lay in a tiny wooden box, and we were about to leave the box behind.

I volunteered to deposit the urn in the crypt.

My sisters had chosen an ossuary in the basement of a church. At the center, hanging low, was a wooden crucifix. I laid the box under the bloody feet of Jesus. Someone had painted his toenails red. With both hands on the box I recited a Buddhist prayer I had learned long ago: "She is taking a great leap. The light of this world has faded for her. She has entered solitude with her karmic forces. She has gone into a vast silence."

As I said the word *silence,* I started to cry and felt as though I was about to break into bits that would never be reunited. Mom and I had been a unified whole. Without her, there was no me. A long time ago I had heard a rabbi on the radio explain why Jews don't cremate their dead. He had said that a grave is a place where the soul of the deceased connects with ours; we honor their memory by returning to the grave. Oh God, we cremated Mom; we have no grave. He said that ashes are the destruction of a memory, a complete divorce of the soul from this world, an act that causes pain to the soul. I choked and began to cough, and the echoes bounced off the cavernous walls of the basement.

Sobbing quietly, my sisters kept their distance.

It was a Sunday, and a chill came over the basement like a shroud. I wanted to put Mom under my sweater, sit with her in a corner of the ossuary, blow hot air onto the box, and cover it with my hair. I wanted to shield her from the cold.

"Let her go," one of my sisters said.

I stood up and pressed the box against my belly, rubbed it on my chest as close to my heart as possible. Then I carried what was left of Mom to her new home: door number 071632. Holding my breath, I slipped the box into the crypt. I pushed her away from this world and into her new realm with a steady hand. The box made a *shhh* sound as it slid out of my life. I locked the ossuary, put the key into my sweater pocket, and let out a sigh.

My sisters and I locked arms, and together we climbed the stairs.

We surrendered the ashes, and together we crossed that terrible threshold.

We stood openly to the four elements, and together we faced the rest of our lives with the invisible scar.

It was dark outside, and it was beginning to rain.

Acknowledgments

I'd like to thank the editors of the following publications in which these excerpts first appeared, often under different titles and form.

"Prologue" in *Thumbnail Magazine*

"Rigor Mortis" in *The Los Angeles Review*

"Radios" in *Alaska Quarterly Journal*

"The Wake" in *Fourteen Hills*

"La Petite Mort at Thirteen" in *F-Magazine*

"A Commie à la Colombiana" in *Lake Effect*

"Skeletons" in *Alaska Quarterly Journal*

"The Cage" in *Line Zero*

"Like a Leech" in *Waccamaw Journal*

"The Yellow Taxi" in *Welter Journal*

A sincere thank you to Ira Sukrungruang for turning the very first draft of this book into a bloody mess of comments, suggestions and cold-blooded, execution-style edits. Without this initial blood-shed this book would have died as a rough draft somewhere on my hard disk.

My deep thanks to my creative nonfiction workshop peers at the University of South Florida for their feedback on sections of this manuscript.

I'm profoundly thankful to the first group of readers who took the time to read and comment on my umpteenth final draft; a beautiful group of daughters with their own memories of mother and motherland: Jennifer Aitken (my big white sister), Jaquira Díaz (my reading series-cofounder and partner in crime), Tony Laas (Toñita, my confidant), and Geannette Roldán (who never failed to make me smile when I was about to shoot myself in a tiny cubicle).

CavanKerry's Mission

CavanKerry Press is a not-for-profit literary press dedicated to art and community. From its inception in 2000, its vision has been to present, through poetry and prose, *Lives Brought to Life* and to create programs that bring CavanKerry books and writers to diverse audiences.

Other Books in the
Memoir Series